The Origins of Radical Criminology, Volume III

"In this important contribution, Stratos Georgoulas offers a comprehensive and in-depth exploration of the origins of critical criminology. Rarely do traditional textbooks cover this material in enough depth for readers to truly understand the historical developments of criminology. Georgoulas conveys his innovative review in a fascinating way that takes the reader into new realms rarely visited in criminology. Students and scholars alike will gain invaluable insights and engage with the rich history presented here."

—Chad Posick, *Associate Professor of Criminal Justice & Criminology, Georgia Southern University, USA* (109 Fletcher Drive, Statesboro, GA 30458)

"*The Origins of Radical Criminology* is a major work. In its three volumes published so far, Stratos Georgoulas conducts a genealogical tour de force against the criminological hegemony that shapes our worldview; a truly critical exercise that, by definition, can only achieve its goal from a radical approach. And so it does, to remind us that the history of resistance is as long and diverse as the history of the powers they must confront, and that the fight goes on.

Los orígenes de la criminología radical es una obra mayúscula. En sus tres volúmenes publicados hasta el momento, el profesor Georgoulas lleva a cabo un *tour de force* genealógico contra la hegemonía criminológica que da forma a nuestra visión del mundo; un ejercicio *verdaderamente crítico* que, por definición, solo puede lograr su objetivo desde un enfoque radical. Y lo consigue, para recordarnos que la historia de las resistencias es tan larga y rica como la de los poderes que estas enfrentan, y que la lucha continúa."

—Daniel Jiménez-Franco, *Coordinator of the European Group for the Study of Deviance & Social Control, Universidad de Zaragoza, Spain*

Stratos Georgoulas

The Origins of Radical Criminology, Volume III

From Middle Ages to Renaissance

Stratos Georgoulas
Department of Sociology
University of the Aegean
Mytilene, Greece

ISBN 978-3-031-05924-7   ISBN 978-3-031-05925-4   (eBook)
https://doi.org/10.1007/978-3-031-05925-4

This Palgrave Macmillan imprint is published by the registered company Springer Nature Switzerland AG
The registered company address is: Gewerbestrasse 11, 6330 Cham, Switzerland

Foreword

On 21 April 1981 Bobby Sands entered the fifty-second day of what would be a fatal hunger strike in Long Kesh Prison, Northern Ireland. His objective, and that of nine others who died, was to have political status ascribed to Irish Republican prisoners. It was the ultimate act of self-sacrifice in the pursuit of a political objective. The UK Prime Minister, Margaret Thatcher, stated: "Crime is crime is crime: it is not political, it is crime, and there can be no question of granting political status."[1]

Over a decade later, Prime Minister and Leader of the Labour Party Tony Blair appealed to the UK electorate by returning to the trope of young people's "anti-social behavior." It proved popular with voters: "Sweep away the dogma—tough on crime, tough on the causes of crime … a crackdown on those who make life hell in their local neighborhoods through noise or disturbance."[2]

Two political soundbites, unrelated in circumstance or substance, each playing to the public gallery. It was a contemporary persistent,

---

[1] https://www.margaretthatcher.org/document/104501.

[2] http://www.britishpoliticalspeech.org/speech-archive.htm?speech=201.

harsh rhetoric derived in, and perpetuating, what Stuart Hall identified as authoritarian populism (Hall 1980). In both cases the objective was to eliminate the specificity of circumstance and complexity of context from the "crime" debate, affirming the politics of criminalization at precisely the moment that demanded carefully considered judgement.

In an astute, provocative intervention Nils Christie (1998: 121) took aim at the naïveté underpinning the politics of criminalization: "Acts are not, they *become*. So also with crime. Crime does not exist. Crime is created. First there are acts. There follows a long process of giving meaning to these acts." Therefore, a crime, in definition, commission, policing and punishment, is the consequence of a process through which meaning becomes ascribed to an act. Even in the most extreme case of killing, legitimacy is conferred by the circumstances of the act—self-defense, threatening behavior, war.

Within critical criminology and socio-legal studies, an analysis of the relationships between *context*, *circumstances* and *consequences* in defining crime, formulating laws and prosecuting acts is central. This emphasizes the significance of social construction, political ideology and material circumstances. Yet, within the positivist framework of administrative criminology, the complexity of motive, meaning and mitigation is compromised by hard-and-fast definitions of "crime" and "deviance" and the simplicity of cause-effect determinism.

Within this framework, "crime" is defined simply as an act or acts in contravention of properly constituted laws within a state or federated jurisdiction, subject to prosecution as an offense/offenses through due process of the courts. While particular circumstances can be introduced to contextualize the "act," this is done in mitigation. "Deviance" is less clearly prescribed. It is as an act, behavior or way of life that disrupts or challenges socially and culturally accepted conventions within a group, class, religion and/or society, often resulting in exclusion, exiling, or ostracism.

However, the seemingly objective application of the "law" or "convention" in regulating acts classified in place, time and culture as criminal or ascribed a negative label is challenged by the subjectivity of their occurrence. The political and ideological construction of criminal or deviant acts, and the differential "meaning" attributed to them, extends beyond personal and social interaction. It is deeply institution-alized, providing the justification for social marginalization, differential policing and harsh punishments. Researching "crime" and "deviance" therefore requires a profound understanding of how labels are socially constructed and applied, how they are subject to continual modifica-tion, and how they play out within societal and community contexts.

In 1959, C. Wright Mills wrote *The Sociological Imagination*, in which he rejected the discipline's association with those wielding polit-ical and economic power: "we become technicians accepting their problems and aims, or ideologists promoting their prestige and author-ity" (Wright Mills 1959: 193). Several years later, in his presidential address to the Society for the Study of Social Problems, Howard Becker reflected on the profound civil unrest in the US Deep South, the ten-sions of the Cold War and the ferocity of the Vietnam War.

Sociologists, he argued, researching the issues of the time, were "caught in the crossfire" of polarized politics—"to have values or not to have values" (Becker 1967: 240). The dilemma was "painful" and rooted in the discipline's myth of value neutrality. To an increasingly polar-ized audience, he affirmed that it was impossible to conduct research "uncontaminated by personal and political sympathies." The central question to be addressed was not "whether we should take sides"—that was unavoidable—but "whose side are we on?"

Becker exposed the naïveté of the proposition that academic social sciences could be free of values central to the administration of dom-inant political, economic, social and cultural priorities. The prevailing "hierarchy of credibility," privileging the powerful while marginalizing the powerless, had to be recognized "for what it is." While, in its focus and methodologies, social science research proclaimed independence, its priorities were predicated on securing and protecting the interests of the powerful while denying credibility to the interests of the powerless.

Hall and Scraton (1981: 465) considered Becker's challenge a "clar-ion call to a more overt radical political commitment, with sociologists and criminologists adopting and pursuing a clear, 'partisan' stance." It was "directed against the State's hidden agenda of control" under-pinning "the liberal front of welfare policies." In demonstrating the incorporation of academic social sciences into mainstream state and corporate interests, the claims to value-freedom and political neutrality were exposed.

Central to the international critique of mainstream social sciences, most notably by critical theorists and community-based practitioners in the US (radical criminology), the UK (critical criminology) and across Europe (the European Group for the Study of Deviance and Social Control), was the proposition that academic research was inextricably bonded to dominant historical, material and political agendas. As Sim, Scraton, and Gordon (1987: 5) asserted in *Law, Order and the Authoritarian State*, "the emphases and methodologies of applied work" were derived in the state's commitment to resolving "the economic, political and social conflicts of the time."

The radical or critical alternative therefore focused on the experiences and tensions of everyday life on the street, within communities and societies—the personal and social contexts of daily interaction and personal conflict—while contextualizing the harsh realities imposed by political, economic and ideological constraints. While liberal theorists asserted the significance of understanding personal agency, critical theorists focused on inhibitions imposed on personal agency by structural determinants.

Living and researching through that period, it was clear that relationships between government departments, grant-awarding bodies, established university departments and mainstream academic journals favored administrative criminology, including its "liberal" or "progressive" wing. There could be no reconciliation of the polar opposite analyses adopted by administrative criminologists as technicians of the state and those of critical analysts who exposed systemically the out-workings of power, authority, and legitimacy.

While critical criminology was criticized as being a contradiction in terms and reductionist in its macro-analysis, neither portrayal was appropriate. For the objective of critical analysis *within* criminology was to expose systemic flaws in the conceptualization of crime and deviance, while critiquing the derivation and due process of the law, the regulation and policing of individuals and communities, the imposition of social order, the discriminatory incarceration of prisoners and the political-ideological roots of punishment. Its analysis focused on manifest structural inequalities derived in and sustained by the "determining contexts" of class, patriarchy, neo-colonialism, ageism (see Scraton 2007).

In taking Nils Christie's critique of "crime" further, critical theorists have argued for refocusing the agenda on "harm" rather than "crime." Derived in the Greek noun ζημιά or *zēmía*, meaning harm, zemiologists affirm the critical criminological assertion that crime is a social construct focusing only on actions classified as crimes located in time and place. Its net-widening, they argue convincingly, leads to increased outlawing, often prioritizing the control of minor infractions while ignoring actions and activities that perpetrate serious societal harm.

While forms of crime control, policing, incarceration and community-based regulation impose an expanding net of criminalization, particularly on politically and economically marginalized communities, social and societal harms as a consequence of corporate or state interests remain unregulated. This returns to one of central propositions of critical analysis of criminalization—the focus on actions of the powerless rather than those of the powerful.

The three volumes tracing the origins of radical criminology demonstrate convincingly that critical analysis of crime and deviance did not originate through the emergence of political interventionist work in the 1960s and 1970s. As the above discussion illustrates, this has been its most recent and persistent phase—from radical/critical/"new" criminology through to zemiology.

In examining the long historical roots of what became the discipline of criminology, Professor Georgoulas demonstrates, in impressive detail and on a broad canvas, the "covert and overt procedures of criminalization, penalization and depenalization, problematization and de-problematization" in the maintenance of power and authority. This is, down the centuries and across all societies, the creation of the insider/outsider, law-abiding/lawless, compliant/deviant as binaries embedded in regimes of control and subservience.

These categories are not static entities; they evolve and mutate to meet the requirements of each developing phase of power, with its attendant rule of law, hegemonic imposition and discourse of control. Within the often ruthless imposition of authority, social scientists become implicit as "interpreters and apologists of the status quo." That authority, derived in autocratic or so-called democratic governance, commands the ownership of truth.

It is in this process, across a wide expanse of time and distinctive regimes, that the analysis is rooted: "the socially accepted definition of order and disorder, the legitimacy of structures and the means employed to maintain order, the capacity of society to take in new groups, or what precisely people expect of the justice system." To address these profound issues, the historical evolution of law, regulation, justice, penalty and punishment is essential.

This Foreword opened with quotes from two British Prime Ministers affirming a shared dogma regarding "crime" and its consequences. Such dogma might appeal to the populist vote at elections, but it masks the reality of criminalization derived in structural inequality, political oppression and socio-economic marginalization. That can only be addressed through critical analysis.

In its journey through time, this unprecedented historiographical work exposes, explores and reclaims the roots of radical/critical criminology as an oppositional presence to the dominant relations of political power, exposing the legitimacy afforded to mainstream academic knowledge.

Phil Scraton
Professor Emeritus
Queen's University Belfast
Belfast, UK

References

Becker, H. (1967). Whose side are we on? *Social Problems*. Winter.

Christie, N. (1998). Between Civility and the State. In V. Ruggiero, N. South & I. Taylor (Eds.), *The new European criminology: Crime and social order in Europe*. Routledge.

Hall, S. (1980). *Drifting into a law and order society*. The Cobden Trust.

Hall, S. & Scraton, P. (1981). Law, class and control. In M. Fitzgerald, G. McLennan & J. Pawson (Eds.), *Crime and Society*. Routledge & Kegan Paul.

Scraton, P. (2007). *Power, conflict and criminalization*. Routledge.

Sim, J., Scraton, P. & Gordon, P. (1987). Crime, the state and critical analysis: An introduction. In P. Scraton (Ed.), *Law, order and the authoritarian state: Readings in critical criminology*. Open University Press.

Wright Mills, C. (1959). *The sociological imagination*. Oxford University Press.

Contents

1

Introduction

1. This book is a sequel to two preceding volumes (Georgoulas, 2018, 2021), and a part of a whole, of a common goal and from a common motivation. All three volumes are entitled "origins of radical criminology." With the word "origins," we would denote the "principle," which precedes the process of creating the object of radical criminology, but at the same time is part of it, as it constitutes all the necessary and capable historical conditions for the primary appearance of this object. This (pre-)history of radical criminology is the past, the present and the prospects of development that constitute a single process of social causality, which must be linked with the critical attitude towards the existing status quo of things and its forms of awareness. So, the "principle" itself ought to be—and is under certain conditions—part of the process of radical criminology. We have to bear in mind that radical criminology does not please the political and administrative elite. And for that there is a cost. It does not reproduce the established knowledge, the hegemonic, the ephemeral, the present. Radical criminology is scientifically consistent and honest when it challenges the dominant scientific examples, conceptual categories, and methods of research, and does not follow that they are "fashionable." When it recognizes the great "enemies"

S. Georgoulas, *The Origins of Radical Criminology, Volume III*,
https://doi.org/10.1007/978-3-031-05925-4_2

and attacks them for deconstruction. Such is the extreme positivism, the determinism, the reification, the supposed "neutrality" of science, and the refusal of politics in science. When it claims a new social structure that can be characterized by opponents as romantic, utopian, and politically irresponsible, but history has shown that it is not only desirable but also a conclusive necessity. It is a science with theory and research that ought to become the driving force of history, to be clear in redrafting the scientific and political agenda for the benefit of the popular needs, a guide for the revolutionary act.

2. We must learn the story in every detail so that our truth and joy are equal, as Shakespeare tells us in *All's Well That Ends Well*. The subject of this third volume on the origins of radical criminology has been worked on in a specific historical canvas, which is presented in more detail in Chapter 3. It is the social history of the common medieval European space that reaches back to the Renaissance, because it is very important for a history of ideas to see transformations and social developments to appreciate politics and ideology, with any differences but also similarities. The common West–East worldview allows us to better see the transformation of the slave-owning society of Late Antiquity into a feudal one and then into structures that facilitated the transition to modern industrial society; it allows us to better understand the social changes that occurred and that, in turn, influenced the transformation of the sovereign discourse and its radical counter-paradigms, and that of the criminal phenomenon.

This history begins with the Roman Empire and later its final division, Christianity becoming the dominant religion and with it the religious policy becoming more intransigent. The creation of bureaucratic organizations with centralized-hierarchical structure. The two languages of the administration that were dominant, Latin in the West and Greek in the East. The common social context, poverty, misery, disasters, and the vast majority of people had to struggle daily to survive. An economy that does not exceed the limits of survival, an economy where land may not be the only one, but it is the most frequent means of payment for services and the source of the economic power of the "strong." The church became an important feudal lord, competing with other feudal lords for profit; however, they had common interests and a complete social representation that wanted and managed to impose, but without ceasing to have opposing patterns of thought. For example, such were the thinking patterns of the Gnostics, the so-called religious inhabitants of the Roman universe, mostly Christian, who argued that redemption was a matter of *knowledge* (*gnosis* → *Gnostics*). They considered *faith* as a preparatory stage for achieving real knowledge. According to the Gnostics, the source of human suffering was ignorance, not sin, and fundamental ignorance took three forms: it was ignorance of the self, ignorance of the world, and ignorance of God.

From a political point of view, the Middle Ages were fragmented and invaded, but this did not change the character of the feudal culture which was the creation of multiple ethno-racial economic mixes, successive struggles, and common beliefs in a society based on the interpersonal relations of people in a whole nexus of dependences. It was also a time when a discipline was established that sought to exclude, to punish all those whom the church regime considered dissidents—a purely repressive society, which developed a persecution mentality and criminal exclusion practices. After all, repression and discipline always had a class sign, the legal rights of the poorer classes were gradually curtailed and reduced to the point of extinction, a witness was valued according to his wealth, and justice was redeemable for those who had the money. And all this while the rural population of medieval Europe was largely dependent on natural forces and luck, with a great inability to change their material conditions. And yet in that society, there had never been a lack of challenges, uprisings, and revolutions. Revolts of nobles against the power of the king which led to the development of an alternative reception of the legal phenomenon (Magna Carta, charter of freedoms, appeal to law), but also revolts of the popular strata. Throughout the Middle Ages, in both the West and the East, rural family collectives revolted and engaged in social banditry, but also in more serious forms of collective action that evolved into something structurally different. In the East the most famous uprising was that of Thessaloniki, which led to the creation of a short-lived popular democracy in the city. The uprising came because of intense class conflicts and against the law and the judicial system that helped the great feudal power in the oppression of rural and bourgeois populations. The People's Republic abolished the privileges and introduced major reforms that concerned all manifesta-tions of economic and social life. It was established by law that all citi-zens were equal before the law and had the same rights. All people aged 18 and over could be appointed to government positions and could have an opinion in popular assemblies. Judges would be elected by the people. The people's power abolished all the old laws and institutions that protected and secured the privileged position of the nobles and the clergy. It equated with the locals equated with the foreign inhabitants who until then belonged to the lower strata of the population. It con-fiscated large fortunes. In essence, a new state was established based on equality and justice. Within the same context, in Central Europe, radi-calism found mass support among the peasants and through uprisings that led to short-lived popular democracies, such as that in Bohemia (the Taborites), the German peasant uprising, Thomas Müntzer and the "League of the Elect," the Anabaptist movement, and similar examples in the Ottoman Empire.

At the same time at the economic level, from the material recovery that took place from the 11th to the 13th centuries, a lively renaissance of the cities began. Towards the end of the 12th century, the culture of the West underwent a fundamental change. The old, rural west-ern civilization has been dominated by the urban phenomenon. In the late Middle Ages, Europe was rocked by calamities that decimated peoples, political unrest intensified, and the foundations of the eccle-siastical edifice creaked as never before. The crisis of medieval feudal-ism, the development of cities, the weakening of papal power, and the creation of strong monarchies transformed the old feudal and peasant society of the Middle Ages into a society with a strong economic and commercial oligarchy, and led to the development of social and polit-ical institutions. The individual's political and economic freedom, the self-determination of the states, the indirect representative democracy as an ideological whole, even the nation state, were neither born in the era of the European Enlightenment nor were privileged conquests of the 19th century. They were ideologically fermented and expressed radically during that period and in that transition to a new bright era, two cul-tural movements, the Renaissance and Humanism, which brought man to the center, put the emphasis on respect for human greatness, while at the same time it was also against absolute submission to God, against any theory that may neglect or seem to neglect man, against any system that may weaken man's responsibility. It was a constant claim. It was a momentum, a militant attitude that aimed at man's gradual emancipation, a constant search for the possibilities that man had to improve and change his destiny.

3. The philosophical contemplation of the Middle Ages is examined in Chapter 4 of this book within a context where, on the one hand, we know that there was continuity between ancient, medieval, Renaissance, modern and modern philosophy, but, on the other hand, we understand that the autonomy of philosophical contemplation in the Middle Ages was extremely limited, as philosophical questions arose within a context that was often of a theological nature. However, especially in the late Middle Ages, several comprehensive epistemological views were recorded (often at the personal cost of those who recorded them) that did not hesitate to question the dominant philosophical paradigm and highlight aspects of an early radical view and issues related to the consideration of the criminal phenomenon. Issues such as the critique of authority that defined the view of "evil" as a transcendental phenomenon, while recognizing conflicting interests that expressed different perspectives and boundaries on the "criminal" phenomenon that were in conflict with authority, but also the impact of a changing socio-historical context that it should define by changing the dominant discourses on crime, were some of these elements that, in turn, if studied in more detail in the development of the same argument, will enrich the arsenal of modern critical thinking about crime.

Augustine's views in the West and those of Pseudo-Dionysius of Areopagite in the East had the greatest influence in the Middle Ages and determined the mainstream view of criminological analysis to this day. And yet even at that time, there were some who said Edgar's words to Shakespeare's King Lear: "The weight of this sad time we must obey. / Speak what we feel, not what we ought to say. / The oldest hath borne most." And this testimony of the soul begins with the conversation (in opposition and under the influence) with philosophical forms of Islamic-Arabic thought such as Averroes (or Ibn Sina) and the Jewish thought (of Moses Maimonides and his work *Guide of the Perplexed*) developed in Europe, and reaches as far as Thomas Aquinas and John Duns Scotus. The former reminds us that there are four kinds of law, and if a human law is contrary to the divine law or the natural law, then it is perverted, and the citizen can (or must if it is disobedience to the divine law) not follow it. The latter emphasizes that obedience to political power is not related to natural, moral, or divine law, but it is simply the result of citizens' agreement and their desire to live in relative peace and without the worries of political power.

The views of Thomas Aquinas and John Dans Scotus would seem, for their time, to be the closest to a radical epistemological paradigm (with the proposal to put limits on power and authority and the rule of law), if there were not two other currents developed between the 12th and 14th centuries: the School of Chartres, and especially John of Salisbury and much more emphatically the Occamism (or Ockhamism) movement which, at least in the field of medieval universities, would be a strong epistemological counter-paradigm, shortly before (and during) the advent of the Renaissance. The School of Chartres was developed at the beginning of the 12th century when special socio-political developments facilitated the development of that different epistemological paradigm. The main proponent of the School, John of Salisbury, and especially the political theory and the theory of law that he developed in his work *Polycraticus*, noted that the social and political problems of the time should be seen more as political and institutional and less as metaphysical, while arguing that the leader's power has moral, political, and legal barriers, which he must respect if he wants to function as a leader and not as a tyrant. These barriers have their origins in the Stoic theory of natural law, thus laying the foundations for the establishment of barriers with intercultural and timeless force. Within the same context, Manegold of Leutenbach had written that the leader had entered a contract with his subjects, the contempt of which gave them the right to revolt and replace him.

However, the dawn of the 14th century saw the most brilliant epistemological paradigm of critical thinking in philosophy and in the discussion of evil and crime. It was the intellectual Occamism (or Ockhamism) movement that marked the development of medieval skepticism. William of Ockham (or Venerabilis Inceptor), the late medieval empiricist and agnostic known for his "Ockham's razor" (i.e., the minimization of the ontological requirements of a scientific or philosophical theory), tried to bring about an overthrow of essentialism and was not afraid to break with the authorities of his time. Universal concepts do not exist and cannot exist, he noted, adding that their existence is conventional and depends on the cultural context to which they belong. Moreover, Nicholas of Autrecourt called into question all things which are not directly perceived and do not depend on or are not related to the principle of contradiction. In this way, the extreme questioning included all the philosophical, theological, and scientific knowledge of his time.

Two other important radical figures of that time were Bartolus de Saxoferrato (Italian: Bartolo da Sassoferrato) and Marsilius of Padua. For the former (Bartolus) the real legislator, and the primary and foremost competent legislative authority is the whole of the social body, citizens' aggregation (Universitas) considered as a whole, and thus leads to the overthrow of the dominant augmentation that every form of law begins imposed by divine command as a simple antidote to the cure of human sin. For Marcilius of Padua, each form of government consolidates its own claims of validity only when it is harmonized with the popular will, while clearly articulating a radical dimension of a "criminal" phenomenon based on a legal status quo: the coupling of the criteria of public good the need to articulate the popular will, the lack of which leads to the pathological functioning of the state.

4. The prevailing view by Enlightenment historians and later has been that, on the one hand, Byzantine society remained stagnant and unchanged over the centuries, and, on the other hand, that the Byzantine intellect, due to its religious orientation, was a philosophy of minor value, or even a negative moment in the history of intellect. Nevertheless, the intellect in Byzantium was nurtured and perfomed in socio-historical terms that, at least in relation to the medieval West, seem familiar to modern reality, and that had an impact on the context in which it was developed and imprinted, and in relation to the dominant paradigm of conceptualization of the criminal phenomenon and the development of its radical counter-paradigm, as we examine in Chapter 5.

It is true that in the specific case of the Byzantine Empire, the concepts of state and justice were closely related both to each other and to the concept of religion. It is also a fact that one of the greatest cultural achievements of Byzantium concerns the field of legal science and the codification of Roman law, while at the same time historical examples of the creation of laws of compromise between secular and ecclesiastical power have been recorded, something that is indicative of the relevance of "values" and the impact of specific interests.

But at the same time in Byzantium, conflicting anti-paradigms were created that clashed with the sovereign until the fall of the Empire. The beginning of this was the great religious dispute between iconoclasts and iconophiles of the 8th century. The importance of this conflict is crucial not only for its political context but for its philosophical and especially in the field of the analysis of the criminal phenomenon, as we can, in this conflict, recognize the basic structure of the Platonic theory of the two worlds. For the iconophiles, who finally prevailed, the world order of phenomena is a tangible representation of the highest order of ideas, where the things of the visible world participate only imperfectly. By analogy, the image is not a metaphor, a sign, or a symbol, but an ontological metaphor in the essence of the represented thing. Thus, we have the legitimation and objectification of determinism and essentialism as the prevailing explanation for the phenomena that take place in both the human and the social body. The opponents, lost iconoclasts, and opponents of this determinism after the iconoclasm of the 8th century took the form of social movements which violently clashed with the power of the Byzantine Empire, were suppressed with blood and in the end, official history record them as heresies. According to these "heretics," Byzantine theologians, and philosophers of the dominant paradigm, while philosophically elaborating the Christian principles, forged the primordial message of Christianity and formed a concept for the expression of Christian teaching beyond the limits of the first, genuine Christian form. Therefore, it is said, we need to return to the primordial purity of Christianity.

Two such examples are the "heresies" of the Paulicians and the Bogomils, two "religious heresies" which were not limited to theological disputes, but put forward a comprehensive questioning of the earthly and celestial order, as it was perceived from the official Church. The social and historical conditions that caused the questioning of the two powers (secular and ecclesiastical) but also the consequences of the widespread spread of "heresies" show that they were a more serious threat to the existing order of things and, therefore, one of the most complex social problems. These two social movements juxtaposed with the official worldview an alternative worldview and ethics that was in complete opposition to it, so it acted as a rejection and subversive of the status quo. They rejected the Byzantine state and the Church as corruptors of society. They taught their followers not to obey the authorities, they discredited the rich, they hated the emperors, they maligned the superiors, they insulted the lords, they believed that the material world was ruled by Satan, and they considered the churches to be demons' abodes. The important thing in the point of view of both "heretical" social movements was that within the context of seeking a convincing explanation for daily sufferings, they considered that they should hold to account the evil and criminal forces that ruled the Earth, to the organs that represented the devil, that is, the emperor and the Church. The disobedience of the slave (cultivator, worker, servant, etc.) to the master (feudal lord, emperor, Church) was a legal and imposed act.

However, apart from the above social movements that tried to express and co-shape the radical counter-paradigm, there were also specific individuals—philosophers. John Italos (or Italus) (1025–1090), a student of Michael Psellos, writes that Christian doctrines did not satisfy him and characterized them as degenerate, while his teaching made ecclesiastical authority unnecessary for matters of good and evil. Christopher of Mytilene, in a poetic satire he wrote about monks, referred to them as the mire of religion and greed. Among the verses of this satire, he mentions that the monks and the church in general (which was the measure of good and evil, legal and illegal) are "bone merchants" and that they will receive a fair and worthy punishment for their illegalities. In 14th and 15th-century Byzantium, a new trend in science, philosophy, and literature emerged that had much in common with humanism. This current is more clearly represented by Barlaam, Manuel Chrysoloras, but much more strongly by Georgios Gemistus Plitho, who formulated a series of pioneering proposals (land reclamation, improvement of working conditions, stimulation of agricultural production and elimination of torture) and co-authored *Nómōn syngraphḗ* (*Νόμων συγγραφή*) or *Nómoi* (*Νόμοι*, *Book of Laws*), in which aspects of a radical approach to the dominant authority and his reflections on the omnipotence of determinism were outlined.

5. The crisis of medieval feudalism, the development of cities due to the abandonment of the countryside, the weakening of papal power, and the creation of powerful monarchies composed a new social canvas marked by the action of two cultural movements, the Renaissance and Humanism, which brought man to the forefront. Within this context, humanist scholars clearly challenged the dominant doctrines of the Middle Ages and criticized the erroneous texts of political and religious life, as we examine in detail in Chapter 6. The Renaissance man became independent from the authority of the Pope and began to think more liberally.

In these cities and especially in the independent states of northern Italy, important philosophers and historians appeared, the first and most famous being Petrarch, who tried to disconnect human life from the theocracy and determinism of other medieval historians by introducing other extrinsic factors that exerted an influence on human life, such as fortune or luck (*fortuna*), and by opposing to the absolute power the freedom of the will of the cultured and educated man. The concept of *fortuna* was of particular importance at that time and opposed the corresponding medieval and scholastic signification, strongly reminiscent of the radical moments of Stoicism in the Hellenistic era.

Within this context, humanists argued that our world and our rational or moral laws are not necessary in the absolute sense, but rather express *contingentia* of Creation as a product of the uncontrollable and unexplored, and therefore potentially infinite divine will, by pointing out the limits of human intellect, which, being forced to rely on the illusory data of the senses, cannot acquire absolute certainties. Returning to Cicero's relevant positions, humanists overturned the Platonic and Aristotelian priority of philosophy over rhetoric, that is, the priority of the philosophical ideal of the one and only truth, which is conquered by logic vis-à-vis the rhetorical ideal of persuasion, which can also be achieved in a way that is only possible or even sophisticated.

Reality, which rhetoric wants to present and at the same time influence, is fluid, fluctuating, and open. The turn to rhetoric implies that things are seen in their dynamic form, in the endless process of dialogue or contradiction, of friendly or hostile communication between people. Language, as an expression of the infinite richness of human attitudes and situations, is thus a component of things themselves in their dynamic formation and view. Rhetoric undermined the causal and metaphysical view since it reinforced relativism and skepticism, in the sense that the orator's ability to support (often equally well) two opposing views embodied the dependence of each "truth" on a particular point of view, specific interests, and different types of argumentations. After all, the world is as it is, constantly changing and constantly complete. Agnosticism, that is, the teaching of the limits of the human intellect and its inability to reasonably know the ultimate essence and cause of things, returned strong many centuries after its last dynamic appearance in Hellenistic times.

Giordano Bruno argued for a general secularism and stressed the unique cosmological and moral value of the heroically fighting and free-thinking man against all authorities and powers. Gianfrancesco reminds us that proof is dependent on ghosts, so on the senses, which are uncertain, as they differ from person to person and from moment to moment. Thus, universal concepts (both for good and evil, illegal and legal) are impossible. With Vives, and Telesio, agnosticism evolved into moral relativism, and that influenced both humanists' analyses of law and crime, and the mainstream issue of opposition to authority, while Melanchthon and de Molina tell us that rigid moral truths and their supposedly final knowledge do not help. Cardano added that knowledge of the outside world can only stop at probabilities or analogous conclusions, and Zabarella went on to connect conceptual relativism with the war against causation. Bellarmine wrote that rulers' political power depends directly on the political community, which has the right to replace them, and, within the same context, Bodin and Althusius promoted political and moral theories which show a strong correlation of political power, law, and ethics.

At the end of the era, Galilei emphasized the relativity and subjectivity of human cognitive perspective. Thus, he writes that, for example, concepts such as "big-small," "near-far," etc. are relevant and are associated with language habits depending on the perspective of some subjects. However, the end of the era of Humanism brought the dawn of a new era. In the first half of the 17th century, a new dominant paradigm began to emerge, science and positivism, that caused changes in the possibilities of shaping the radical and critical counter-paradigm. It was a time when any radical thought about the criminal phenomenon was between "a hard and a rock place"—the old (the theocratic conception) that had not died yet, and the new (positivism) which is a mirror of the transcendental old. But radical thought on crime will not cease to exist: on the one hand, it will just find new, innovative paths to walk on, such as utopias, myths, and literature (as it has always done); on the other hand, it will wait a few years, at the end of the century and beginning of the following to find its place in philosophy in an intellectual current, the Enlightenment, that came to change everything, and to bring in the new era, an era of revolutions.

6. The concept of utopia is timeless, a diachronic type of human social vision that can take different depictions corresponding to different historical moments. It has elements that transcend the historical boundaries of a discourse and can be a seed for overturning dominant scientific discourse at the time. Those elements had the publications on the utopias of the late Middle Ages and the beginning of the Renaissance, which we examine in detail in Chapter 7; they also had elements of criticism and elements of vision for something better in the future that are contained in those works and are ruptures with the mainstream theories of legitimacy in the way of delimitation and dealing with the criminal phenomenon.

In Thomas More's utopia, which was a written presumption for the emergence of an alternative totalitarian view of social reality by influencing theoretical and socio-political currents of an early socialist transformation of society, the author does not hesitate to criticize the evils of the European feudalism and to dare to envision a social change reality, a better tomorrow. He describes a society of equality in the productive process, with equal ownership and six hours of work for all, and relative secularism with laws enacted by social consensus to ensure an equal distribution of goods. "Bad" is to deprive the other for your own benefit, while the system does not need many and complex laws, and the administration of justice is not based on lawyers and judges who— the only thing they do is to- distort things. After all, in utopian society, complex legislation is not only a way of excluding many from knowledge but also the basis for state decline and social decline, and is therefore criticized when it exists in neighboring states. Punishments should be proportionate to the crime because, in the end, if they are too severe, then they are not only ineffective, but they also lead to more serious crimes. We must have alternative punishments and not repressive ones, while free choice can not be the main cause for the criminal phenomenon. Poverty and unemployment are the result of objective conditions. The way of life of those who deviate and those who do not deviate does not differ according to More's *Utopia*, and therefore there is no constitutive differentiation of the deviant and, by extension, no corresponding positivist search for the causes of crime. But the most important thing is that for the first time, an attempt was made to reverse the edifice of the positivist approach to the criminal phenomenon. First, you make them thieves and then you punish them, More tells us, and in this way, he puts more emphasis from the passage in practice on the operation of the mechanisms of official social control and on the stigma attached to the criminal. Within this context, the justice system is inhumane, laws only serve the king's income, and the establishment of exceptions only applies to people in power.

The root of the problem is specific and is called property. No society will be fair and happy as long as it exists, and if everything is judged by money, people will not be happy because a lot belongs to the few. As long as there is property, there can be no equal and fair distribution of wealth. And no reform will work unless you tackle this very root of the problem with the only cure, which is community property.

Community property is also the medicine in the city of Sun, of Campanella, as property and its laws are the cause of all evil and crime. Reminiscent of the Hellenistic utopia of the Pergamon revolution, Campanella dreams of a society without slaves, without trade, without money, with four hours of work every day, a society of equality and a society without crime. A society with judges who do not have a specialization, but a connection to the mode of production, with few laws accessible to all, with penalties with elements of compromise and the greatest crime is to be against this freedom, democracy, and its symbols.

In the paradise of the new Atlantis of Francis Bacon, natural law prevails. Crime and the criminal are not mentioned anywhere because it is such a society, such is its structure and function, that they do not exist. In contrast to the above works, Henry Neville in his book *The Isle of Pines* describes a dystopian society where crime is rife and only an external force and violence can prevent the eventual destruction of that society. Written shortly after the failure of Harrington and Neville's political democratic plan to control large landowners and draw lots as the primary mechanism for administration and justice, the author expressed his fears for the evolution of the society in which he lived.

7. In medieval Europe, peasants and urban dwellers learned through folk poetry, myths about people or groups of people who challenged the socio-economic and political order of things, by questioning those who held or claimed to hold power, law, and control over resources. The respective historical figures either might not have existed or their real-life counterparts might have been completely different from their myth. The oral history recordings may be a very slippery source as these may be distorted from the way they are passed down from generation to generation; however, it is worth making special reference (as we do in Chapter 8) to these symbols because similar stories and myths about people challenging elements of the established order, doing justice, and redistributing social wealth with heroism, violence, or humor were persistently repeated throughout Europe, West Europe-East Europe and Asia Minor and Middle East and around the world, in an era of exploitation and extreme poverty, in severe repression, in a routine life where nothing changed and nothing should change.

The heroes of these myths portrayed in songs and oral narratives initially deny obedience, are beyond the reach of power, are themselves potential agents of power, and therefore are potentially rebellious. They are considered illegal by the authorities, but, at the same time, they remain in the rural society and the people consider them heroes, protectors, avengers, justice fighters, even liberators, and people who deserve admiration, help, and support. They correct wrongdoings, punish, and avenge injustices, especially between the rich and the poor, and between the strong and the weak. They clash with the sovereign (albeit locally), codes of values, and, especially, representatives of law, supporting, even at an ideal level, another world with equality, fraternity, freedom, and above all justice. Many of them are "illegal" knights (or dames) who start their careers as victims of injustice or had being wrongfully prosecuted by authorities for an act. They start from personal injustice and go to collective injustice because their main feature is that these people are inherent in the rural society; they are respectable members of their community which they defend from the rulers who oppress it. They create or belong to collectives with relations of complete solidarity, equality, and identification, and adopt an alternative code of values based on these principles. Robin Hood wants to fight the unjust as a victim of injustice too—the noble bandit who deals with the representative of law, the Sheriff of Nottingham, who pursues him on the orders of the King. The Sheriff committed widespread abuse of power, appropriating land, unjustly hunting the poor and imposing exorbitant taxes on his subjects. Corresponding stories are those of William Wallace, Rob Roy, and El Cid in Spain. Nevertheless, medieval Europe also had myths and didactic stories about women who claimed and succeeded in correcting injustices (to the detriment of themselves or the people at large) or even claimed roles that did not suit their social status. Genevieve (also Genoveva or Genovefa) of Brabant, Lady Godiva, Bluebeard's wife, and Pope Joan (*Ioannes Anglicus*) are similar myths.

In Eastern medieval Europe, the tradition of disobedience and rebellion of the popular strata in rural and urban areas took on the cultural dimension of folk and Akritic songs, and myths that would later lead in the 9th and 10th centuries to the first sample of literature in the vernacular, the *Epic of Digenes Akritas*, a heroic knight of Byzantium who traces his family lineage to the leader of the Paulician movement. It has all the characteristics of illegal knights of the Western Middle Ages. He wages war against injustice, with the emblem that power creates law, while treating the emperor as an equal. Later, in the Ottoman Empire, the hero of folk songs is replaced by the "thief" of folk songs. The hero of these songs is a hero who has a special code of honor targeting the rich and powerful and defending the weak against local authorities. On the occasion of often speculation around the system of rent and collection of taxes, a practice that is often denounced as unfair.

However, myths about heroes, knights, outlaws, and avengers are not the only ones that contradict the value system and produce representations that are in conflict with the established knowledge of right and wrong, of legality and illegality. Equally important for the same purpose are the myths with satirical heroes that demonstrate corresponding issues and they, in turn, clash with the dominant representations of the criminal phenomenon. In Byzantium, the donkey who is accused of crimes it did not commit is threatened with being convicted and eaten by the wolf and the fox, but in the end the donkey, with its cunning, manages to throw the wolf and the fox into the sea. Reynard in the medieval West, the cunning anthropomorphic red fox, engages in stories that usually involve satirizing the aristocracy and the clergy, making Reynard a peasant villain who cleverly challenges the established authority. In the Ottoman reality of medieval times, another manifestation of the popular culture developed, which evolved over the years and has persisted to the present day in modern Greece and Turkey. It is the shadow puppet theater and its hero, Karagiozis (or Karaghiozis, or Karagöz in Turkish), who stars in thousands of short comic stories by unknown authors. Karagiozis is the social type who most successfully embodies the uncorrected agitation with the sparkling sarcastic spirit, the eternal cheerful, the relentless mocker who betrays everyone and everything, even himself. One of his features is the minimal dedication he shows to current ethics. He challenges the system, as well as its fundamental principles, its social cultural and moral order, and its seemingly unshakable rationality. This disobedient, irreconcilable, and catalytic spirit of Karagiozis is activated thanks to the comic finding (mainly through parody) exaggeration or diversion of words, objects, and situations, and is exercised against any element of behavior, mentality, language, lifestyles, and values of superiors. Mocking the sophisticated language of the select members of good society, their knowledge, refined taste, and artistic sensitivity. A mockery of the paternalistic and condescending attitude of the privileged who have invented the poor but honest man. Mocking the good manners that hide hypocrisy and cruelty of the rich boss toward the poor man who is at work. Karagiozis is a hero, who in every short story commits violations and crimes based on the established code of values, but also the hero who has raised many generations of children for many centuries.

8. The great works of literature of each era (which we examine in detail in Chapter 9, and which also address a significant quantitative part of the literate population) play an important role in the mainstream representations of the era. Through the printed words and phrases, the heroes depicted on paper and in the imagination have elements that contribute to the construction of an opposite—counter-paradigm of the prevailing point of view on the criminal phenomenon and law.

Chaucer, the father of English literature with *The Canterbury Tales*, outlines the Christian England of the time, which was going through a deep crisis. These stories act as character projections. While the narrative is linear (one story following another), Chaucer creates levels that relate the stories to each other and the narrators' personalities. Chaucer's characters each express different views of reality, creating an atmosphere of testing, empathy, and relativism; for example, the Pardoner and the Summoner are both portrayed as deeply corrupt, greedy, and to be working on the side of the devil. Equally corrupt is the Judge who appears as one who plots with a low fellow to abduct a beautiful young woman. The Knight is not so noble and ends up using violence. In the story of the Man of Law, a described is given of the unjust incrimination and punishment of a woman.

Shakespeare remains the greatest of all contributors to the English language and his works remain a valuable resource for criminology. He exposes the corrupting influence of money, rejects the aristocratic manner of life, and presents powerful feudal nobles as arrogant and refractories. Kings first commit murder to fulfill their quest for power, and even after they become king, their criminal ploys worsen as they engage in a series of senseless killings or are ambitious egoists who attained power through clever political maneuvering. In his plays we are witnessing the real dangers involved in mocking and demonizing the criminal, the real dangers if we just let a criminal justice system run its course. We can all clearly see the abuses of power that can occur when individual law enforcement agents receive both a mandate to crack down on social disorder and the authority to decide for themselves what counts as disorder and how to combat it. The law enforcement of the time, entrusted with public trust and power, proved to be unethical.

Shakespeare also described in his plays how the forces of change are slowly but surely preparing to sweep all elites aside, the struggle of the new man of the Renaissance against the feudal order. The old world and its law and order must die, because is rotten. Struggle was to him the whole meaning and content of life. A struggle against the authority of divine right and in favor of the authority of responsibility, expressing the collective will of the people and their collective welfare; against the degenerate nobility and the narrow-minded legal system and dominant interpretations of the criminal phenomenon of the time, whose severity in the extermination of vice engendered new vices.

In Italy, Dante Alighieri was involved in the political events of his day, with movements in favor for giving privileges to the common people, at the cost of exile from the city of Florence until the end of his life. In his work *Commedia*—which was renamed *Divine Comedy* (*La Divina Comedia*) when Boccaccio gave it that name—he deals with issues of crime and punishment, good and bad. It is especially important to see that even *Hell (Inferno)* has ranks, and in the highest rank before the traitors in the 8th cycle and under the general name "swindlers" are included types of people who in medieval times exercised power and co-defined the dominant definition of law and practices of dealing with the unjust. In Canto 21, Dante mentions the Barrators, the corrupt politicians, who made money by trafficking in public offices. These are immersed in a lake of boiling pitch, which represents the sticky fingers and dark secrets of their corrupt deals. *Paradise (Paradiso)* has degrees again in the higher realms, above the wise and the defenders of religion are the righteous and the visionaries. In *The Decameron*, Boccaccio writes stories which include mocking the lust and greed of clergymen who are immoral, and feudalists who are violent and vicious.

In Spain, Miguel de Cervantes Saavedra, with *Don Quixote*, issues the death certificate of feudal society, writing one of the finest specimens in world literature. The astonishing irony of aristocratic values, the genesis of vulgar capitalist materialism (indicative of Sancho's surname), the references to religious fundamentalism (which was strong at the time), and the dream of another society ("the golden age doesn't have mine and yours") make it a work of unsurpassed social criticism, centuries before philosophers and politicians realized it. Already in his early stories, a code of values and symbols, which he uses, is recorded, something that makes him different from the dominant model of the time. Don Quixote calls the prostitutes he meets "ladies," he "frees" a slave, he knocks a friar from his horse, his companion, Sancho is just a poor and simple farmer. Later he becomes a criminal himself and is locked in a cage. He tells Sancho and the goat herders about the Golden Age of man, in which property does not exist and men live in peace, describing in essence an anti-hegemonic model of social organization and justice.

In the East, in Byzantium and in the Ottoman Empire, a plethora of literary works of the time were published, which did not hesitate to question the dominant value system, to question law and the mainstream definitions of the criminal phenomenon. Belisarius, Justinian's legendary general, falls victim to the envy of the aristocracy because of his brilliant achievements, and common people's love is shown in *The History of Belissarius*. In the work *Opsarologos* (lit. *Fish Book*), a fish trial is described, and the court process as well as the words and language of the Byzantine court with its stereotypical expressions are parodied. At the final conclusion of the trial, the King-judge Kitos (a whale), unjustly condemns the poor and small fish Tziro (a mackerel), who curses him. In Chortatsis or Chortatzis' *Erofili*, the King's greed for wealth and glory is condemned as coming from Hades, the world of evil. The tragedy ends with an important scene of justice being done by the common people (the Chorus), who kill the King. In Kornaros' *Erotokritos*, it is understood how justice is administered by the King: with absolute arbitrariness.

9. All three volumes with the present attempt to present a logic of history for criminological thinking and to open a dialogue. It is unfortunately understandable that the objective appearance of modern production relations has led many modern criminologists to think that they are captive to managerial criminology as an eternal, unchanging, and only possible scientific truth. Consequently, the scientists of the criminal phenomenon operate almost exclusively only as interpreters and apologists of the status quo of things. This market scientific

consciousness leads them to present the interpretations of the criminal phenomenon using tools such as incoherence, fragmentation, and disintegration of a system. But the written evidence presented in all three books shows another way of analysis. Even in a socio-economic system seemingly as absolute and strict, material conditions have been created for the society's transition to another way of production, carrying away in turn forms of social consciousness. Our history has shown that no empire has survived forever. Perspective is change, and critical thinking about the criminal phenomenon is one of the "apostles" of this change. If we truly want to discuss (modern and future) radical criminological thinking, we could gain from the journey to the genealogy of it, to discuss unity within difference, unity through multiplicity and internal interconnectedness of contradictory processes, sources such as the Homeric work, Hesiod's works, militant lyric poetry and rhetoric, ancient Greek theater, ancient philosophy, the principles of utopias, literature, the New Testament, medieval and Byzantine philosophy, myths and fairytales, More, Shakespeare, and Cervantes in relation to modern radical criminological thought—and all this in a functional unity with the present that is related to the awe-inspiring rival of modern managerial criminology and the future. How could the above specific logic of history communicate with the logic of similar published papers and books in the field of historical criminology? This communication is presented in Chapter 10. E.P. Thompson (1978) has argued that the immediate object of historical knowledge is composed of facts or evidence which certainly have a real existence. Historical knowledge is in its nature provisional and incomplete, selective, and limited, but not therefore untrue and defined by the question is proposed to be evidence. Historical evidence has the determinate properties. Concepts can only acquire a meaning from a particular position in the present, a position of value in search of its own genealogy. Such genealogies exist within the evidence. We present these evidences in these books.

But we also, as Churchill (2017) states, need a clearer recognition of historical criminology as a discrete intellectual enterprise. "Historical criminology" speaks immediately to engagement between two established disciplines or fields—history and criminology—which may range from cross-disciplinary dialogue to interdisciplinary fusion. However, its primary scholarly domain would appear to be criminology, the work of criminology done in an historical mode. Historical criminology should exhibit how "the historical" is central to the core categories, concepts, and theories of criminology at large. He adds that we need to elaborate ways in which scholars might engage further with concepts of historical time, and thus exhibit the historical character of matters of criminological concern.

And if we really want to talk about the future of radical criminology, let's do what Malcolm says in the Epilogue of Shakespeare's *Macbeth*. Things have to be done because circumstances dictate: our self-exiled friends (the past and origins of radical criminology we have forgotten) our self-exiled friends who had gone to escape the rains of the tyrant, the ruthless collaborators of the dead butcher and his underworld queen (modern administrative criminology which wants to erase any criticism and controversy in its empire) must be punished.

References

Churchill, D. (2017). Towards historical criminology. *Crime, History & Societies, 21*(2), 379–386.

Georgoulas, S. (2018). *The origins of radical criminology: From Homer to Pre-Socratic philosophy*. Palgrave Macmillan.

Georgoulas, S. (2021). *The origins of radical criminology, vol II: From classical Greece to early Christianity*. Palgrave Macmillan.

Thompson, E. P. (1978). *The poverty of theory and other essays*. Merlin Press.

2

A Social History of the Common Medieval European Area

1. It is common to view that the history of medieval Europe emphasizes mainly the feudal West and to either silence or downplay the social history of the East in the role of the opposite pair (progress-stagnation). When history of the East is finally mentioned, it is usually based on the analysis of the personality and work of Byzantine emperors, and the history is presented autonomously in relation to social developments that took place on the same continent (in the West), and often in the same geographical area which, in today's terms, is a modern state. For a history of ideas, however, fragmentary social history is problematic—both because it is not true, as ideas and implementations in relation to the criminal phenomenon, they traveled and left their mark, between the Byzantine Empire, the Western Kingdoms and the Arab-Islamic regions in Spain and the Middle East, as well as why it is very important for a history of ideas to see transformations and social developments to appreciate politics and ideology, with any differences and similarities. The common West-East view allows us to better see the transformation of the slave-owning society of Late Antiquity into a feudal one and then into structures that facilitated the transition to modern industrial society; it allows us to better understand the social changes that occurred

© The Author(s), under exclusive license to Springer Nature Switzerland AG 2022
S. Georgoulas, *The Origins of Radical Criminology, Volume III*,
https://doi.org/10.1007/978-3-031-05925-4_3

and which in turn influenced the transformation of the sovereign discourse and its radical counter-examples about the criminal phenomenon as well.

The Roman Empire was a Mediterranean empire. With its center in Rome, it stretched from the Atlantic Ocean in the west to the Black Sea and the Euphrates River in the east, and from the Rhine and Danube Rivers in the north (for some time it included southern England) to the Sahara in the south. Any attempt to exceed these limits was fruitless or short-lived. At the time of Augustus, after decades of wars, its total population should not have exceeded 45,000,000 (which may have represented 15% of the earth's population). Of the inhabitants of the empire, fewer than 5,000,000 people (if women citizens are included) had Roman citizenship, most of whom lived in Italy. One-and-a-half centuries later, the total population of the empire increased and may have exceeded 60,000,000.

The large mass of the population consisted of farmers, scattered in many villages. Less than 20% of the total population was concentrated in approximately 1000 cities, and of that a large part was also engaged in the cultivation of the land. Like all other societies of Antiquity, the Roman Empire was purely rural. The wealth of the upper classes, the administration, and the army were based on the productive work of the peasants, both free and slaves.

Most cities were relatively small, with populations of 2000–20,000 inhabitants. Really big cities existed only in the East. Pergamum may have had 50,000–100,000 inhabitants, Alexandria and Antioch hundreds of thousands. The population of Rome alone may have reached 1,000,000. About 15% of the empire's population, or close to 7,000,000 people, must have been slaves; many of them were concentrated in Italy, where their percentage may have exceeded 30%.

According to the Augustus regulations, 600 men participated in the Senate, while the class of rich cavalry, which staffed many government services and many senior positions in the army, included more than 20,000 people. In most cities the issues of self-government and tax collection were assigned to local parliaments, which usually consisted of the 100 most prominent and affluent inhabitants. Thus, the upper classes—that is, senators, the cavalry, and local deputies—did not exceed 150,000, representing together with their families 1% of the total population. At the top of the hierarchy was the emperor.

From the time of Augustus, a man acquired the title of *emperor* (*imperator*) and was considered a *prince* (*princeps*), that is, first citizen. That person concentrated in his face the supreme military, political, judicial, and religious power, since he was proclaimed the *high priest* (*pontifex maximus*, meaning "greatest bridge builder," so that the contact would be declared, something that his presence restored with the divine world). After his death, the proclamation of a new emperor was formally made by the Senate, but on many occasions the succession was already a foregone conclusion, either by inheritance or by adoption. On several occasions, such as after the assassination of an emperor or his death in a war, the army, and in fact the select imperial bodyguard, called the Praetorian Guard, played a special role in the succession. After Octavian (Augustus), all emperors were honorably called *augusti* (meaning "respected"), while those destined for succession often took the title of caesar.

The emperor based his power primarily on the control of the army. At the beginning of the monarchy, the army did not exceed 350,000 men, organized into legions and auxiliary corps, and was scattered in many provinces. Two centuries later, it had reached 400,000 men. Commanders were appointed to command the approximately 40 provinces, some from the Senate and others from the emperor, mainly in areas where the military presence was more intense. Those commanders had overall responsibility for order, protection from raiders, and the administration of justice. Death penalty was usually their responsibility. To exercise his power, the emperor used senators and horsemen, but he also had a personal administrative service staffed by his house (*familia Caesaris*), which included his slaves and freedmen, many of whom gained great power.

The central administration and the large landowners were deprived of much of the productive surplus through taxation, rents, extensive contributions, and forced labor (*angaria*). When Roman power was stabilized, official taxation was no higher than in other times, and so the empire entered a period of relative prosperity. The integration into the same political territory of numerous cities and entire kingdoms, which for centuries were in competition with each other and often in open wars, facilitated movement and trade; moreover, production and the development of art were increased. For long periods piracy was almost extinct. Despite the deadly wars that continued on the empire's borders, Italy and most of the provinces lived safely—although, apart from the Jewish uprisings, there was no shortage of civil wars, especially in the 3rd century, to impose emperors. A single Roman currency was officially recognized everywhere, while the tax system promoted the circulation of money and contributed to financing the economy to the most remote areas. A small portion of what the central administration received went back to the provinces for the army's payroll, so that emergencies in times of famine and earthquakes and the construction of temples, public buildings, aqueducts, and other large projects as benefits could be dealt with.

The empire was inhabited by many nations, each with its own language, culture, and religious customs. All forms of worship were generally accepted, unless they violated law or good morals. The administration did not employ many employees and relied heavily on written evidence. Laws and decrees were always in writing, and a constant correspondence connected the capital with the provinces. For the calculation and collection of taxes, population censuses were made periodically in various provinces, lists were drawn up, and certificates were issued. However, the general illiteracy rate in the empire always remained very high. Only 10% of the population may have been be proficient in writing. Even in the imperial capital, it unlikely to have been higher than 20–30%. However, there were professional scribers available for all jobs, not only in the big cities but also in many villages.

In 212 AD the emperor Caracalla (198–217)—formally known as Antoninus (Marcus Aurelius Antoninus)—granted Roman citizenship rights to almost all free inhabitants of the empire with the so-called *Constitutio Antoniniana*. This measure may have served a variety of purposes, even purely fiscal; nevertheless, it did contribute to the much-needed sense of unity the empire. Wherever a free man lived, whatever people he belonged to, whatever social status he belonged to, he could and should feel Roman.

Under the ecumenical conditions created by the empire, many traditional languages were transformed and evolved. In oral societies even a numerically small group could retain their idiom, even if they did not have writing. The important thing was that, in parallel with the local languages, throughout the territory, Latin and Greek as the languages of the administration prevailed, Latin in the western part and Greek in the eastern, with a greater momentum than in the Hellenistic era. Large crowds of locals became familiar with either Latin or Greek, depending on the region in which they lived, and used them as a second language. From the Atlantic Ocean to Rome a traveler could communicate adequately speaking Latin, and from Rome to the Euphrates speaking Greek. These two dominant languages, used by the administration, commerce, high intellect, and the common people, were mutually influential upon and influenced by local dialects to varying degrees. Latin of the imperial years borrowed many words and terms from Greek philosophy and literature to enrich itself in areas that lagged behind. In turn, the Greek language of the time was borrowed from Latin military and administrative terms.

Rhetoric, philosophy, historiography, and poetry in the Latin language had made great strides since Rome dominated the Mediterranean for about two centuries. However, the Greek tradition in letters had always been an object of great admiration in Rome. Every educated man had to know Greek. Many Romans, even military ones, spoke Greek fluently. On the contrary, few Greeks learned Latin, and they did so more out of necessity and less to watch the progress of Latin letters. Suring his break from his wars against German invaders, Emperor Marcus Aurelius, who was very close to the model of the king-philosopher, recorded his personal thoughts in Greek.

With the gradual rise of Christianity, a new literary genre was created, the value of which was neither exactly biographical nor abstractly moral. The *evangelion* or *gospel* (which literally means "good news" and "joyful message") was a narrative of Jesus' life, action, and especially his teaching through a saving perspective—in the light, that is, the path to its believers' salvation. The "good news" brought by this new literary genre was not summed up in a philosophical theory of the structure of the world and the position of man, nor was it limited to the simple biography of an individual sacred person. While presenting the message of salvation on the basis of a specific historical event that could be placed with relative accuracy in historical space and time (in Roman Judea during the first thirty years of the 1st century), the Gospels were opened, with their prophetic and revealing tone, with the parables they contained, the miracles they described, and especially the symbolic value of the narrated events, in a dimension that could interest all people. It was the first time in the history of Antiquity that an historical event acquired such universal and monumental significance—inversely proportional to the value attributed to it by most of his contemporaries. Few historians have been interested in mentioning Jesus, who was crucified on the orders of the Roman governor Pontius Pilate. However, in his death sentence, his followers and disciples saw the opening of a new era. Gradually, a new notion of historical time and its flow was established: the notion of linear progress that reveals a hidden pattern.

From a place of pure conjuncture and human chance that was until then or, in other words, a field in which the cosmic god always manifests its fullness, history acquired for the first time a center, the coming of Jesus Christ, who, although within history, it was also outside of it, in the mind and the eternal economy of God that had created the world. All past events were considered to point to this central event in history and all future ones to acquire their value from the triumphant course of the Catholic Church. Erasing from their consciousness the cyclical and recurring time of traditional societies—the very one that the phenomena of nature signify through the processes of birth, growth, maturation, and decay—Christians developed the concept of a one-dimensional and evolving time with a specific principle (the creation of the world), a specific goal (the incarnation of the Word of God) and a specific future (the second coming of Christ and the judgment day). In an unprecedented way for the facts of Antiquity, the gaze of Christians turned to the future and became eschatological: they envisioned the end and the end of history, and awaited the embodied resurrection of the dead.

The early Christians awaited the second coming of Jesus during their lifetime. As this event moved away from the immediate horizon of the present, the end of history shifted to an indefinite future that would come when the Church completed its mission. In the 2nd century the Christian Church acquired a clear organizational structure, mandated to protect the flock from external enemies and internal devils. At the top of each local community was the bishop, and below him the priests and deacons who carried out his instructions. The authority and power of the bishops was used to reduce discord and disagreement among the faithful. However, the conflicts were not avoided. The most important were the exact content of the Christian sermon and the way it was understood by the people. In contrast to other interpretations of Christianity that were condemned as heretical, the one, holy, apostolic, and catholic Church emerged which marched to conquer the empire. However, disputes had already arisen over the authenticity of some books. The sacred texts that circulated and spread among Christians were numerous, and often had significant and deliberate differences between them. Most were written to correct a version of the actions, words, and passions of Jesus or his disciples that their authors thought were wrong. Few of these "occult" works have survived—although new significant specimens are constantly being discovered in the Egyptian desert. Many of these come from Christian circles who called themselves Gnostics.

As their name implies, Gnostics were those religious inhabitants of the Roman universe, mostly Christian, who claimed that redemption was a matter of *knowledge* (*gnosis*, in Greek). They considered *faith* as a preparatory stage to achieve real knowledge. According to the Gnostics, the source of human suffering was ignorance, not sin, and fundamental ignorance took three forms: it was ignorance of the self, ignorance of the world, and ignorance of God. The knowledge they had in mind was not, of course, the theoretical contemplation of an object, but the experienced release of the mind that led to an inner transformation. The mythic-philosophical systems developed by the Gnostics were numerous. Their orthodox accusers rightly said that each of them had the freedom to propose his own worldview. The Gnostics felt strangers in the world, strangers in society, and strangers in their own bodies. Their experience was summed up in a radical alienation—perhaps the first that the ancient world experienced in such intensity. The cities in which they lived, the culture of their cultured fellow human beings, and the politics of the ruling class, senators, and emperors left them indifferent. They declared war on all the forces of the present world, even though their war was purely spiritual. Especially in the field of eroticism, they developed two seemingly opposite but essentially compatible tendencies: extreme freedom and complete abstinence. The common denominator of the two tendencies was the opposition in the present world and the disposition to abolish it—by exaggeration or denial. All of them agreed that the perceptible universe is the result of the irrational action not of the first divine Being, but of a second God-creator, who departed from the Father, forgot his wisdom, and created the world to prove his dominion. During the cosmogenic process, no matter how complicated it was considered, a few molecules of the first God were trapped in the world of matter. These constituted the human spirit and they sought liberation and return to the paternal bottom.

Behind the diversity of cognitive myths and concepts lies the anxiety to give satisfactory answers about exactly how the transition from the all-good God to the created universe is caused. There is also a total denial of the goodness and beauty of the sensible world, and an unrelenting tendency to move away from everything that involves and binds the spirit. Two opposite tendencies were combined in the birth of the gnostic phenomenon. One, Greek both in origin and in character, emphasized the value of knowledge not only to other ends but also as the *end* (*telos*, in Greek) ("goal") of human life. Knowledge of self, world, the divine were dominant concerns of Greek philosophy from its earliest beginnings. The other tendency, of Eastern and perhaps more specifically of Iranian-Persian origin, considered the world to be fundamentally evil and therefore could not be the work of a good god.

Christianity spread along the paths of the Jewish diaspora, and along with the great paths of trade and administration. It traveled rapidly both in the Mediterranean and beyond the borders of the empire, especially to the East. The first news about Jesus' story did not require much preparation or many organized missions to reach a new place. Merchants, pilgrims, and travelers of all kinds told what they had been informed. One of the first major administrative and commercial centers in which the new teaching was established was Antioch. There, according to tradition, the faithful first began to call themselves Christians. However, in a very substantial way Christianity was early, and remained throughout the era a matter primarily of the Roman Empire.

From the moment Christ's disciples opened to the Jewish diaspora, they communicated mainly in Greek, which some spoke as their first and others as their second language. Even in the city of Rome, Greek remained the official language of Christianity until the end of the 2nd century. With Latin the new religion spread to Africa and the western provinces. From the 3rd century the basic bilingualism of the empire was also reflected in Christianity. However, a very important development took place. Latin-speaking Christianity insisted on preserving the scriptures in Latin (*Vulgate* or *Biblia Vulgata*), even when addressing a low-educated population. On the contrary, Greek-speaking Christianity encouraged the translation of the Scriptures into all the languages of the East. It also became a vehicle for empowering local dialects—even the local alphabets. In Egypt, a new script was used (based on the Greek alphabet) and was inextricably linked to the so-called Coptic culture. When monasticism appeared in Egypt and Syria at the end of the 3rd century, Egyptian (Coptic) and Syriac became two of the most powerful languages of Christianity.

Focusing on Antioch, Ephesus, Smyrna, and Alexandria (cities with a strong Greek-speaking element), some of the strongest tendencies of early Christianity were confronted. The disputes concerned the repercussions of gnostic ideas, the organizational structures of the Church, and the timeliness of the prophetic gifts as well as matters of worship, such as the celebration of Easter. To resolve the issues, discussions were held, memoranda were drafted, letters were exchanged, and local councils (synods) were convened. In short, the foundations were laid for the formation and operation of the Catholic Church. The other great center of Christianity was the imperial capital. The Christians of Rome showed great organizational talent. They communicated with all the provinces and exercised their influence, making use of their wealth and connections. From a very early age they maintained strong ties with Corinth, which always remained an important trading post and transit hub. The Christian leadership of Rome also played an important role in establishing and disseminating the "canon" of the New Testament.

Emperor Constantine the Great, through the Decree of Milan in 313, gave Christians the opportunity to have complete freedom to practice their religious beliefs and a few years later with the emperor Theodosius (379–395), Christianity became the dominant religion, and with it the religious policy became more intransigent. For the first time, Christian leaders were fired upon by Christian emperors for their dogmatic deviations, as were those who believed in traditional worship until then. Except for a tolerance of Judaism, Christianity was now the only accepted religion of the empire. Everyone was officially invited to embrace it, and in fact in the version that was considered correct. The Olympic Games, with their strongly religious element, were ended. The Greek people had to accept at a rapid pace a single manifestation of religious worship—one and only one religion and, therefore, one and only one ecclesiastical authority which exercised foreign and domestic policy, and decisively determined the consciences and the culture of the time.

Theodosius bequeathed the Roman Empire to his two sons: the eastern part of Arcadius and the western part of Honorius. The empire had been ruled many times in the past by two or more emperors, but that, as it turned out, was its final division. The eastern part of the empire continued to exist for a thousand more years. Modern historians have become accustomed to calling it the Byzantine Empire, while its inhabitants considered it a continuation of the Roman Empire, with Christianity as its official religion and its seat in Constantinople. The western part was catalyzed by the Goths. According to Duby (2019), one day the chariots of the barbarian peoples broke the barrier set up by the Roman armies on their way. Then the Middle Ages began. It commenced with the meeting of two societies with a similar structure. Both societies—the society of the invaders and the society of the natives—were rural, both accepted slavery, and both were dominated by powerful aristocracies and by an almost equal savagery. They mixed without difficulty. The Christian Church accelerated this reconciliation and crosses appeared in German cemeteries. But the church was also barbarized.

In the western part of Europe and around the monarch, there were the clergy. They sought to convince the king that his mission was the rebirth of the empire and the Roman establishment. But inspired by the Bible and especially by the Latin texts of the time, they mainly tried to form not only an overall representation of society—a representation so solid that it would be imposed on the collective consciousness for centuries—but also a hierarchical requirement of manipulation and control of worldly political acts based on the ecclesiastical co-possession of both spiritual and secular power, something that is a reality that is representative of the European Middle Ages.

Behind the show, there was a material reality. The church became an important feudal lord. And in the East, there were similar developments. As early as in the middle of the 5th century, the number of monks and regular clergy must have risen to several hundred thousand. In the 6th century, there seem to have been more than 80 monasteries in the territory of Constantinople and, in the Great Church of Constantinople alone, far more than the fully recognized 525 various clergy (from priests to lead singers and porters). De Ste Croix (1981) reports an incident where even a small-town bishop like St. Theodoros Sykeonos, as Bishop of Anastasiopolis, is said to have received the annual amount of 365 solidus for the expenses of his household. And a great hierarch, such as the metropolitan Bishop of Ravenna, around the beginning of Justinian's reign, received 3000 solidi, a little more than the highest-paid governor of the province, according to the salary scale established by Justinian a little later. Even in Merovingian Galatia, just before the middle of the 6th century, the Bishop of Iniuriosus of Tours is said, by Gregory of Tours, to have a fortune of over 20,000 solidi. According to his biographer, St. John the Merciful, the Patriarch of Alexandria in the early 7th century, stated in his will that when he took office, he found about 8000 pounds of gold (over half a million solidus) in the bishop's house and that the revenue from the contributions of Christophiles (people who loved Christ) was almost beyond human comprehension. Each city had a bishop, who received the average salary of a provincial governor, and the metropolitan bishops of the provinces, as the known figures show, were paid on the same scale as the vicars (representatives of the chiefs of the Praetorian Guard) of (urban) dioceses. In the West, too, papal supremacy over canon law was directly related to the establishment of a papal government mechanism with direct administrative, financial, judicial and executive powers. It is a predominantly bureaucratic organization with a centralized-hierarchical structure.

A little later, the competition between the masters (feudal lords and the church) for profit dissolves the cohesion that until then united the secular with the ecclesiastical aristocracy, which would henceforth be opposed and competitors. However, similar competitions occurred in the eastern part of medieval Europe—and at the same time, common interests and a complete social representation that wanted and managed to impose itself, but without ceasing to have opposing patterns of thought.

But consciousness does not develop in a vacuum. The social context of medieval times was specific and clear. Poverty, misery, disaster, and the vast majority of people were forced to struggle daily to survive. An impoverished western Europe with an economy that does not exceed the limits of survival cannot support the burden of great powers. They did not manage to be created, and they immediately collapsed and degraded. The Carolingian Empire, which was formed so quickly, disintegrated shortly after the death of the emperor in 814 AD. The Holy Roman Empire of the German nation would soon become like a torn house. Thus, Western Europe was fragmented into a heap of small hegemonies. The feudal system retained some units that were more theoretical than substantive, within the various kingdoms of the West, some of which were being modernized at a very slow pace, such as the Kingdom of the Franks, while most of them remained very archaic. And yet, all this troubled world that was going badly inside was being knocked down outside, and was already a culture with obvious homogeneity. Behind all its diversity there was a feudal culture which faced, wherever we encounter it, the same big problems often under similar conditions and gave them solutions that often also looked alike. This culture was the creation of multiple ethno-racial economic conflicts, successive struggles, common beliefs, and above all the creation of these very riots for which it strove to find ways of healing. Feudalism built Europe in both East and West.

Feudalism was the natural consequence of that disaster. The feudal regime was born with the need to have no captives in general, but absolute autonomy in all small units. Yet it took many centuries to establish itself. However, that was by nature a reaction of defense and, at the same time, a reaction of a local character. The castle, built on the hill, with the village or villages that it protects at a short distance around it, is a defense system. But feudalism is not just that. According to Braudel (1993), it is also a society based on interpersonal relationships of the people in a whole network of dependencies, an economy where land may not be the only but the most common means of paying for services. The feudal lord had received from the king, who was his sovereign or from some other lord superior to him, a manor, which is an area of land, with the obligation to provide certain services, mainly to contribute financially to marriages, wars, and ransoms.

And in the East, the confirmation of the feudal structure of society was the understanding that the source of economic power of the "strong" was the ownership of the large quantities of land. This also explains the decline of cities during the early Byzantine period, as the society became rural with few large city centers (e.g., Constantinople, Antioch, and Thessaloniki). During the mid-Byzantine period, the provincial cities flourished, but now they were feudal centers of the powerful landowners (feudal lords) who lived in them. This attachment to the land would create an economic introversion, giving room to the Italian naval forces of Venice and Genoa to appropriate and control the maritime trade and, finally, the economy of the Byzantine Empire.

The long recession experienced by Europe led to a terrible degradation of cities in the 10th century. At that time there was an increase in agricultural production everywhere, both in the new northern countries where the three-year crop rotation method spread from Germany and Poland, and in the southern regions of Italy and France where two-year crop rotation method was still the norm. When the course of the economy changed direction with the material recovery that took place between the 11th and 13th centuries, a lively renaissance of the cities began, with the free states in Italy. Toward the end of the 12th century the civilization of the West underwent a fundamental change. The rural western civilization had been dominated by the urban phenomenon. And from now on, everything had been organized around the city: wealth, power and spiritual creations were completely new and the discovery of a secular education (the education of knights who wanted to be independent of the church). That time in the East was the beginning of the end, as with the occupation of Constantinople by the Crusaders in 1204, the prosperity of the Byzantine Empire practically ended and the period that followed was simply an attempt to survive a geographically, economically, and socially mutilated empire.

At the same time, however, that era was characterized as a time when a discipline was established that sought to exclude and to punish all those whom the regime of the church considered dissidents. The 12th century was a time in which the economic and cultural prosperity of Western society was transformed into a capitalist repressive society. It developed a persecution mentality and criminal exclusion practices. Judicial and administrative institutions imposed or ratified discrimination and used violence. The systematic condemnation of heresies or Jews as well as the condemnation of lepers, homosexuals, and prostitutes after 1100 AD cannot be explained with the presence of any real threat, but by the fears they caused in the dominant culture. The persecutions were not popular initiatives, but came from institutions staffed by literate professionals who sought to eliminate "competition" and act as "ethics crusaders" who managed and strategically used available minority discourses to serve specific interests and goals.

De Ste Croix (1981) reminds us that repression and discipline have always had a class element from the beginning of this period and, more specifically, from the Antoninus period (138–193 AD), where the legal rights of the poorer classes were gradually curtailed and were reduced to the point of extinction in the Severan period (193–235 AD). In various ways, members of the lower classes accused of crimes were at a disadvantage compared to the affluent classes. For example, it was much more difficult for them to escape pre-trial detention—to be released even on bail, as we would say today. And prison conditions could be very unpleasant for humble people. More important is the fact that the testimony made in court by members of the lower classes, in both criminal and civil cases, was given less weight than in the testimony of their socially superior ones. In imperial Rome a witness was valued according to his wealth: the number of his slaves, the extent of his estates, the size and quality of his tableware. His character and manners came last—his words were believed depending on the number of coins he had in his safe. In the field of private law, we find that offenses committed against a member of the upper class by a member of the lower class were considered more serious: such an offense could automatically become an *atrox iniuria* (horrible damage), for the assessment of which special regulations were applied. And *actio doli*, or *de dolo malo*, the lawsuit for deceit, could not be accepted by members of the lower classes against even distinguished members of the upper classes. In criminal cases the situation was even worse, because the defendants, if they did not have either an honorary status themselves or a strong enough patron, could have spent long periods in prison, sometimes in horrible conditions. The culmination of misery was that you had to pay to find your right, because no one would hear a wrongdoer unless he paid the judge and his assistants. About twenty-five years after the death of Constantine, during the time of Julian, an inscription found in Timgad, indicating the order of priority in public functions in the province of Numidia (which is about present-day Algeria), determined a formal valuation of the tips that may formally require the officials of this province: these are expressed in *modii* of wheat, from two to one hundred. The situation continued in the following centuries, with an example given by De Ste Croix (1981). A 6th-century civil servant, Ioannis Lydos, tells us that during his early years as an exceptor in the Praetorian Guard, a lower position earned "without overdoing it" 1000 soldius, thanks to the care of his great patron, Zotikos, the leader of the Praetorian Guard. It was a time when slavery had now ceased to produce a surplus as large as in the brightest days of Rome, and the affluent classes had been forced to increase their pressure on the free poor to lead to the production of the villeins (or "tied tenants").

2. The rural population of medieval Europe was largely dependent on natural forces and luck, with a great inability to change their material conditions and with a narrow margin from their eternal companions, such as famine and epidemics. Usually, the similarity of their interests did not create any community, no national association and no political organization, as it had only one local reference. The basic core of rural life was the family. All these structures and processes were defined by words that meant both family and home. Their life revolved around routine and intimacy, while from a young age and—with the telling of

fairy tales such as "Little Red Riding Hood," "Puss in Boots," and "Tom Thumb," "Mother Goose"—they learned what would happen to one who broke the routine and put one's trust on one who was not closely associated with the kin.

And yet in this society, there was never a lack of controversies, uprisings, and revolutions, already from the Roman Empire, with secession from the "barbarians," and indifference to its dissolution. There are numerous testimonies that from the 2nd to the 7th centuries there were instances of escape or surrender to the "barbarians," or that they appealed to the "barbarians," or they were helped by them. In Byzantium there was a history of popular uprisings, which was relatively unknown. The lower social strata were not mere spectators of imperial power, but sometimes actively participated in the political life of the place. In November 601 AD, the royal procession of Emperor Mauritius was attacked with stones and the intervention of the bodyguard was needed to save Mauritius. The repression that followed not only failed to calm the spirits, but made them even worse. Riots broke out in Constantinople, with the people setting fire to the luxurious houses of the senators and with the emperor secretly popping it. The power vacuum was filled by the insurgent troops led by Phocas. With the help of the pro-democratic municipality of the Greens, the centurion Phocas became the first non-aristocratic heir to the throne and ordered the execution of the emperor and his sons. The new emperor inaugurated a regime of terror against the aristocrats by executing courtiers and officials as well as the widow of Mauritius, Empress Constantina, and her daughters. Phocas also proceeded with the mass deportations of senators. The aristocratic faction responded with "economic sabotage," causing widespread famine in the capital that led to the first frictions of the new regime with the poor. The transformation was completed when Phocas approached the most prosperous and pro-aristocratic municipality of the Venetians. An open rift then developed between the pro-democratic municipality of the Greens and the former rebel emperor. When the Greens attempted to set fire to a Venetian district, Phocas ordered the savage repression of the rebels. In 609 AD, after a personal insult launched by the Greens against the emperor at the hippodrome, Phocas ordered the "punishment" of the crowd, which was clearly disproportionate: mutilation, beheading, and hanging. This savagery led to a new uprising with the Greens setting fire to the Praetorium and the prisons, facilitating the escape of the prisoners. Eventually, Phocas was overthrown in a military coup by Heraclius in 610.

In Great Britain, the nobles' revolts against the king's rule led to the development of an alternative representation to the legal phenomenon. Magna Carta was named the charter of rights that King John of England was forced to grant to nobles, the clergy, merchants and the peasantry. If one considers the time and the way in which power was exercised, one understands that this is a pioneering text that is essentially the beginning of a great journey toward democracy and its freedoms. On June 15, 1215, on the banks of the Thames near Windsor, King John marked the beginning of a new era that led to the consolidation of parliamentarism. Magna Carta was originally a compromise text for the consolidation of the rights of feudal barons against royal arbitrariness. Gradually and through a slow and painstaking process, the benefits it bestowed and established were extended to all the people. One of the most important provisions of Magna Carta are those that refer to respect for the individual freedom of the person, which means in practice the legal prohibition of arrest, imprisonment, exile, or imposition of any other sentence without a prior court decision. It is the cornerstone in the history of individual freedoms. Actions, such as turning barons against kings, was a common tactic suffered by all kings after William the Conqueror (1028–1087). This time, however, the barons did not rally behind a would-be monarch who would claim the throne. On the contrary, without—here too the fundamental difference lies—the barons moved against the oppressive rule of John, focusing on changing the very model of power management. Magna Carta articles were not originally numbered, which was done much later for better supervision and understanding of the text. Article 17 of Magna Carta states that ordinary trials will not follow the royal court in its movements, but will take place in a fixed place. Article 20 states that for minor offenses a free person will be required to pay a fine commensurate with the seriousness of the offense, and for serious offenses, respectively, the fine will not be so severe as to deprive one of one's livelihood. Article 34 states that in the future no warrant will be issued for any person in connection with any possession of land if in this way a free man can be deprived of the right to a trial in the court of his lord. Article 38 states that in the future no official will judge a person based on his own statement without presenting a credible witness to his truth. Article 39 states that no free person shall be arrested, imprisoned, or deprived of his rights or property, nor shall he be declared illegal, nor shall he be exiled, nor shall he be deprived of his position in any way, nor shall we move (the barons) against him, nor will we send others for this purpose except on the basis of the law of the land. Article 60 mentions that all these customs and freedoms which we have granted will be observed in our kingdom as far as our relationship with our subjects is concerned. And all our citizens, whether clergy or laity must observe them similarly in their relationship with their own citizens. Magna Carta was initially accepted by John, but as soon as the barons left London, the king renounced the text.

The forerunner of the Magna Carta was the famous Charter of Freedoms, a text written in 1100 in which King Henry I was obliged to observe certain rules toward nobles, the clergy, and individuals. Already from the first article, this text acknowledges that the kingdom has been oppressed by unjust taxes. Article 8 states whether any of the barons or men who commit a crime will not be obliged to pay the arbitrary fine determined by the king, but will pay compensation only according to the extent of the crime committed. The production of official texts restricting the arbitrariness of power in the judiciary continues—with struggles in the centuries to come. In 1628 the Petition of Right was drafted by the English Parliament, which was submitted to Charles I of England and asked for the restoration of law on a number of issues, while in 1679 the Habeas Corpus Act was passed, which protects the citizen from illegal detention by prohibiting the trial of persons detained illegally. In 1689, during the reign of James II, the English Parliament passed the Declaration of Rights, a law that guarantees the rights of citizens.

During the Middle Ages, in both the West and the East, rural family collectives revolted and led to social banditry, as injustices against blood kin provoked acts of revenge, with the result that certain groups could be trapped in the identity of the fugitive, where they were marginalized and engaged in hostilities against the rich, aiming to plunder and mythologize in a conscious effort in the protection of the poor. But at the same time under these circumstances, the attacks against feudalism were also attacks against the church, with the result that all revolution-ary social and political dogmas inevitably evolved into theological sects. In order for existing social conditions to be challenged, they had to be stripped of the halo of sanctity. And this became even more pronounced when historical circumstances allowed the papal political power to be challenged in the West and the iconodule Orthodox doctrine in the East.

In the West, revolutionary movements of the poor, led by "living saints" and inspired by the prophecies of the Last Days, occurred with increasing frequency from the end of the 11th century onward. The Caputiati movement proclaimed the equality of all men and insisted that all had the right to freedom they had inherited from Adam and Eve. The movement was violent and began to kill nobles, act upon defending the teachings of the Christian religion itself. Within the same context, the doctrine of the Free Spirit with militant supporters in whose eyes the Church was at best an obstacle to salvation and at worst a tyrannical enemy—in any case an outdated institution that must now be replaced by their own community. At the beginning of the 13th century, the doctrine of the Free Spirit was elaborated into a totally theological and philosophical system. That was the work of a more interesting group, the Amaurians, consisting of men who had been trained at the largest school of Orthodox theology in Western Christianity at the University of Paris. Their philosophical teacher was Amaury of Bene, a Lecturer in Logic and Theology at the University of Paris, who died condemned by the Pope in 1206–1207.

According to Duby (2019), in the 14th and 15th centuries, a crack isolated those centuries from the previous ones. Mass unrest, a chain of popular uprisings, and riots that upset the lower social strata spread from one end of Europe to the other during the 14th century. Peasants revolted, took their tools, plundered the homes of the nobles, and slaughtered the officers of the rulers. In the suburbs of the cities, groups of workers were rising up, as in Florence, claiming their participation in the management of the urban community.

In the East the most famous uprising was that of Thessaloniki which led to the creation of a short-lived People's Republic in the city. In 1341, Emperor Andronikos died and his advisor Katakouzinos tried to take power by staging a coup. When he failed to do so in Constantinople, he went to the cities of Thrace, and proclaimed himself emperor. He was supported by the great feudal lords. The peasant masses, however, revolted and beat the noble feudal lords in several cities of Thrace and Macedonia. Especially in Thessaloniki, the second-largest city after Constantinople in the Byzantine Empire, which had developed significantly since the beginning of the previous century, important events took place and for a period a People's Republic was established from 1342 to 1349. In this city there had already been intense class conflicts in previous years, and the legislation and the judicial system helped the great feudal power in the oppression of the rural and city's populations. In texts of the time, the above position is confirmed. Kavasilas states in a manuscript that those who practiced usury believed that they did not wrong anyone, since they were protected by the laws, but they had reached such a point of inhumanity that even when the debtors from misfortune often suffered and still lost their whole life, not only were they not moved, but they also gradually became tougher claimants and avengers.

Similarly, Nikiforos Houmnos mentions in another document that similar events occurred at the time, stigmatizing the judicial paralysis. The poor, he says, did not find their right in the courts. Rich people, strong as they were, did what they wanted. Judges sold their consciences, while lawyers were fraudsters. But in Thessaloniki in those years there was an organized political party, the party of zealots, that had a program and fought to bring the popular masses from behind the scenes to the forefront of political life. Its main leaders were seafarers working in the port of Thessaloniki. The feudal class of Thessaloniki recognized Katakouzinos as its leader. The uprising did not take long to come. In 1342 the zealots revolted, overthrew the feudal lords' principles, and set up a revolutionary committee. The People's Republic abolished the privileges and legislated major reforms that concerned all manifestations of economic and social life. The new Byzantine emperor, although he had declared Katakouzinos an enemy, who was supported by the feudal authorities of Thessaloniki, he was concerned about the movement of the zealots in the city. He sent an army and established a new regime. However, the People's Republic of Thessaloniki continued to exist and carried out political acts such as the legislative establishment that all citizens were equal before the law and had the same rights. All people aged 18 and over could be appointed to government posts and have an opinion in popular assemblies. Judges would be elected by the people. The people's power abolished all the old laws and institutions that protected and secured the privileged position of the nobles and the clergy. Locals equated with the foreign then belonged to the lower strata of the population. It confiscated large fortunes. In essence, a state based on equality and justice was legally established. Eventually, the Byzantine Emperor Palaiologos was led to reconciliation with Katakouzinos, in the face of the danger posed by the People's Republic of Thessaloniki. The zealots were not afraid and continued their struggle until their military defeat seven years after the founding of the People's Republic.

In the West, uprisings aiming to establish a society without discrimination based on wealth were common too. In 1381, the English peasants revolted under the influence John Ball's sermons that in the beginning all people were created free and equal. Bad men were those who, by unjust oppression, had originally introduced slavery, against the will of God. But now was a time given by God when ordinary people could, if they only wished, throw away the yoke they had carried so much and could gain the freedom they had always desired. Therefore, they must have a good heart and act like the wise husband in the Scriptures who gathers the wheat in his barn, but uproots and burns the tar that had almost drowned the good wheat. The tar represented the great lords, judges, and lawyers, who were the real criminals of the time.

Within the same context, in Central Europe, radicalism found mass support among the peasants and, through uprisings, led to short-lived people's democracies, such as that in Bohemia and elsewhere. There the Taborites clearly showed their will for all the lords, nobles, and knights to be cut down and exterminated in the forests. At the beginning of 1420, they set up convents in some areas, under the control of Taborite priests. The first of these communities was established in Pisek in southern Bohemia in the early 1420s. Their influence extended as far as France and Spain. When the peasants in and around Burgundy revolted against their ecclesiastical and secular rulers, the French clergy immediately attributed the uprisings to this influence. Thomas Müntzer and the "League of the Elect" in the German peasant uprising of 1525 became a giant symbol, a hero in the history of that "class war," while Martin Luther condemned the "murderous gangs of farmers" in a special pamphlet. Hans Hut, a follower and disciple of Müntzer from Thuringia, became the first propagandist of the Baptist movement, saying that Christ would return to earth and put the double-edged sword of righteousness in the hands of the restored Saints. The Saints would judge the priests and shepherds for their false teachings and, above all, the great ones of the earth for their persecutions. Kings and nobles would be thrown in chains. Eventually, Christ had to establish a community which seemed to be characterized by a community of goods. Hutt was arrested in 1527 and imprisoned in Augsburg, where he died. In 1567, a generation later, Jan Willemsen gathered around 300 fighters, some of whom survived the days of Müntzer, and founded another New Jerusalem-Community state in Westphalia, that time in the area around Wesel and Cleves. At the same time, in 1520, Domenico Candela from Friuli, also known as Menocchio, argued that there is no life after death, that there was no future punishment and reward, that heaven and hell are on this earth, and that body and soul were a mortal whole. All of the above were not temporary and occasional phenomena, but parts of a larger uprising by the excluded who were experiencing in their lives the social tensions and the injustice of power. According to Palmer (2000), another 66 riots were recorded in Germany between 1525 and 1789, with similar quantitative results in China, Russia, and Japan.

In the East after the fall of the Byzantine Empire (1453), there were also corresponding uprisings and revolutionary movements of a radical character in the territory occupied by the Ottoman Empire. The movement of Dionysius Skylosophos (or the Dog-Philosopher) took place from 1600 to 1611, an agrarian uprising fueled by the anti-feudal ideology of a priest, who, as his name suggests, was influenced by Cynic philosophy. That uprising, which had a democratic and anti-feudal character, was violently suppressed by the nobles of Venice who occupied the island of Zakynthos (or Zante) together with another uprising that broke out in 1642, of the same character, which was drowned in blood, too.

3. The individual's political and economic freedom, self-determination of the states, the indirect representative democracy as an ideological whole, even the nation state were neither born in the era of the European Enlightenment, nor were they privileged conquests of the 19th century. They were ideologically fermented and expressed radically during the late Middle Ages, from 1250 onward, a period during which the first new secular power, the Totalitarian State and the National Monarchy, were painfully conceived as its state manifestation. Black (1992) explicitly expresses this modern dimension of the Middle Ages, and so did Merry Wiesner-Hanks in *Early Modern Europe, 1450–1789* (2006), Joseph Canning in *A History of Medieval Political Thought, 300–1450* (1996), Janet Coleman in *A History of Political Thought, from the Middle Ages to the Renaissance*, (2000), Takashi Shogimen in *Ockham, and Political Discourse in the Late Middle Ages* (2007), and Annabel Brett, who emphasizes the pioneering character of the work *Defensor Pacis* by Marsilius of Padua (1324) (Brett, 2005).

In the Late Middle Ages, Europe was rocked by calamities that decimated peoples, political unrest intensified, and the foundations of the church building creaked as never before. Corruption within the Church was increasingly alienating believers. The crisis of medieval feudalism, the development of cities due to the abandonment of the countryside, the weakening of papal power, and the creation of strong monarchies composed the new political and territorial situation of Europe in the 14th century. The old feudal and peasant society of the Middle Ages had begun to transform into a society with a strong economic and commercial oligarchy, which exerted tremendous pressure on the feudal lords to grant more privileges and rights. This development and qualitative upgrade of the sciences of the time led, on the one hand, to great scientific achievements and to the formulation of theories that are still widely accepted, such as those by Nicolaus Copernicus (1473–1543), Johannes Kepler (1571–1630), and Galileo Galilei (1564–1642), and on the other hand to a significant growth of trade thanks to the rapid development of the science of geography and navigation with the travels of Marco Polo (1254–1324), which opened up the trade routes of the West to the Far East, and seafarers who discovered America (Americo Vespucci [1451–1512], who first realized that it was a new continent, and Christopher Columbus [1451–1506], who first arrived there). However, it also led to the development of social and political institutions with the creation and prevalence in Italy of a new form of democracy, similar to that of modern bourgeois democracy, based on the economic power of the merchants. At the same time, however, the uprisings in the rest of Europe and the Franco-German and Anglo-Saxon recruitment of the king as "first among equals," as well as the feudal right of the nobles to advise him, caused the emergence of parliaments.

The transition to a new bright era was marked by the action of two artistic movements of the Renaissance and Humanism that brought man/human being to the center, who with the right education would harmoniously develop all his potential. Renaissance and Humanism emphasize respect and the greatness of humanity and praise the human spirit and power. At the level of the intellect, the ideal is the ecumenical man. Humanist scholars clearly challenged the tenets of medieval scholasticism with literary creation, which in turn brought about a new European scholarship. While the man of the Middle Ages accepted the Pope of Rome as the absolute authority, the man of the Renaissance made his spiritual activity independent from the authority of the Pope and began to think more liberally and Prometheus-like. The humanist movement became an opponent of a church which was being shaken by corruption and obscurantism. The works of both Erasmus and Rabelais are characterized by humanistic education that is certified by the breadth of knowledge, the unceasing effort to enrich knowledge, the impeccable handling of languages, and, of course, are the forerunner of new narrative means: of rhetorical irony and parody respectively, perhaps imitating Lucian of Hellenistic times. Their common feature is that they inaugurated and marked a new era for the development of literature. They came into direct rupture with all the establishments of the time, praising the true values of man and faith. In *In Praise of Folly*, Erasmus satirizes the degeneration of a corrupt era, the flaws of both clergy and laity. In *Gargantua and Pantagruel*, the unbridled freedom of speech but also the peculiarity of Rabelais' writing is a pioneer in modern fiction.

Erasmus satirizes the degeneration of a corrupt age and the shortcomings of the clergy:

> People are so disgusted with them, that it's a rotten luck to find any of this enclave in front of them. Their dirt, their illiteracy, their roughness, that's all.

Erasmus dares and hints at the action of the sacred examination that leaves no room for freedom:

> Terribly grumpy and irritable enclave; they have nothing to throw at me in groups, with seven hundred findings, to force me to recall, and if I refuse, to quickly make me a heretic.

The conflict and the constant tension that exist between the humanists and the Catholic Church is pervasive in both texts. The words of both *In Praise of Folly* and *Gargantua and Pantagruel* are critical, harsh, ironic, and vulgar, with an emphasis on removing the clergy who have stopped speaking to the human soul and have indulged in impunity:

> More ungrateful, not admitting the good I do to them, I have not found. Alas, they say to anyone who writes "Teacher" without a capital letter. And people, who preach apostolic love, raise their voices and spoil the world for a robe worn upside down or for a darker color.

While the above works were being written in the first decades of the 15th century, Humanism had already triumphed over Florence, and was spreading to most of Europe. The context within which literature would develop and give us complete samples is delineated. An important feature of the cultural development that took place was the educational secularization that enabled man to criticize the evils of political and religious life. Lyric poetry continued to exist, drawing its themes from the poetry of the troubadours and the chivalry novel; however, it started to be based on a new technique that highlighted the natural music of words. The poet now became a well-known author with political power. The autonomy of the written word led to the emergence of prose, which was initially based on the technique of transcribing the prose of medieval texts, while over time new narrative genres such as short stories and novels emerged, new lyrical forms were cultivated, and the theatrical activity developed wider use of vernacular languages written in national languages. We should remember that one of the greatest creations of Italian literature, *The Divine Comedy* by Dante (1265–1321), was produced at the beginning of the 14th century (1308–1320), during which Petrarch (1304–1374) and Boccaccio (1313–1375) wrote poems in Italian, and Geoffrey Chaucer (1343–1400) developed the literary use of English. All the aforementioned cultural developments were becoming widely known to the public through the new art of typography, which was undoubtedly the innovation of the time. The spread of cultural renaissance and humanistic education would have been almost impossible without the discovery of typography.

Braudel (1993) tells us that with the word "humanism," we can define an ethics of the nobility of human being. Turned simultaneously toward the dual direction of study and action, that ethics recognized the greatness of human spirit and its robust creations. The most important thing is the individual's effort to develop within himself, thanks to a strict and methodical discipline, all those human forces so that he does not let anything be lost from what can calmly idealize the human existence. Humanism established an individual and a collective ethics. It established a law and an economy, it reached at a policy, it provided food for an art and a literature. However, humanism is also against absolute submission to God, against any theory that may neglect or seem to neglect man, against any system that may weaken man's responsibility. It was a constant claim—the fruit of arrogance. It was a momentum, a militant attitude that aimed at the gradual emancipation of man, a constant search for the possibilities that man has to improve and change his destiny. For this reason, it integrated the wider movement of humanism and the religious-protesting humanism, which sprang up between the 15th and the 16th centuries and was established when Luther nailed the 95 theses to the doors of the palace church in Wittenberg in 1517. Reformation began by raising the banner of freedom and revolution, but it was not long before it sank into the same intolerance for which it blamed its opponents, and for this reason the first fighting Protestantism turned into a victorious and established Protestantism.

In the 17th century, an entire philosophical system was strengthened, starting from the thinking person. This situation coincided with the collapse of traditional values which were increasingly imposed by the creation of a market economy in the 16th and 17th centuries. At the same time, however, compliance and repression were intensified—the alarming increase in the number of the poor, which was related to the demographic increase observed throughout the 16th century, and the economic crisis that began at the end of that century and worsened in the 17th century, the increase of those poor that meant begging, vagrancy, and theft made repression necessary in the eyes of political and economic power. This society of outcasts would become the enemy of an already bourgeois capitalist society passionate for order and efficiency. The needy, the sick, the unemployed, and the mad were treated mercilessly and thrown into jail. Many institutions were being created for this purpose. In a world where freedom was already the prerogative of only a few, the 17th century helped to further restrict that basic right. At the beginning of the Enlightenment, the quality of life in Europe had reached its nadir.

References

Black, A. (1992). *Political thought in Europe, 1250–1450*. Cambridge Medieval Textbooks. Cambridge University Press.

Braudel, F. (1993). *Grammaire des civilisations*. Flammarion, edition Champ.

Brett, A. (2005). *Marsilius of Padua: The defender of the peace*. Cambridge University Press.

Canning, J. (1996). *A history of medieval political thought, 300–1450*. Routledge.

Coleman, J. (2000). *A history of political thought, from the Middle Ages to the Renaissance*. Blackwell.

De Ste Croix, G. E. M. (1981). *The class struggle in the ancient Greek world: From the archaic age to the Arab conquest*. Duckworth.

Duby, G. (2019). *Hommes et structures du Moyen âge: Recueil d'articles*. De Gruyter Mouton.

Palmer, B. D. (2000). *Cultures of darkness: Night travels in the histories of transgression*. Monthly Review Press.

Shogimen, T. (2007). *Ockham and political discourse in the late Middle Ages*. Cambridge University Press.

Wiesner-Hanks, M. E. (2006). *Cambridge history of Europe: Early modern Europe 1450–1789*. Cambridge University Press.

3

Medieval Philosophy

Two misconceptions are frequent and common to medieval philosophical thought in Europe. The first is the belief that a scholar of the historical development of philosophy could, without losing anything, jump straight from Plato and Aristotle to Francis Bacon and Descartes, without even examining the Greek thought that appeared after Aristotle or medieval philosophy. Medieval philosophy was believed to be dependent on Christian theology in such a way and to such an extent that it was objectively impossible to conceive of genuine philosophical thought at the time.

Today we know much better than ever before that there was a continuum between ancient, medieval, Renaissance, modern and contemporary philosophy. More specifically, at the time we are referring to, the Greco-Roman philosophy fueled the philosophical thought of the Middle Ages and managed to integrate itself, to varying degrees, in the philosophical and theological systems of the time. At the same time, during the early period that we call "modern philosophy," the use of Latin continued; let us remember, for example, Descartes (1596–1650) and Spinoza (1632–1677), while we can detect specific links between the medieval philosophy of law and that of John Locke (1632–1704). Clearly one of the

S. Georgoulas, *The Origins of Radical Criminology, Volume III*,
https://doi.org/10.1007/978-3-031-05925-4_4

distinctive features of medieval thought was undoubtedly the dominant position of Christian theology. On the one hand, the choice of the philosophical theme was indeed determined to a very large extent by theological preconditions; even if religious beliefs did not dictate the conclusions to which the philosophers "should" have reached, but it certainly did dictate, at least in some fields, the conclusions to which the philosophers should not have reached. For this reason alone, the autonomy of philosophical thought during the Middle Ages was extremely limited. On the other hand, and especially in the case of the philosophical approach to the "criminal" phenomenon, we see that the modern positivist dominant criminal approach has greater respect for the medieval scholars of metaphysics (such as Augustine or Thomas Aquinas), who did whatever they could to formulate with precision and clarity what they wanted to say, than for some much later metaphysical scholars, whose obscurity of thought and ambiguity in expression are now renowned.

The second misconception concerns the belief that the whole of medieval philosophy belonged to a pre-critical age, to a world that has passed, and we can by no means look for sources of a radical conception of the criminal phenomenon there. If by the term "critical philosophy" we mean the philosophy of Immanuel Kant (1724–1804), it is above all true that medieval thinkers belong to a pre-critical period. If, however, by saying that medieval philosophy is pre-"critical," we mean that medieval thinkers were unable to call into question the conditions of their theories, then the characterization of their thought as pre-"critical" is not applicable. Obviously, philosophical questions arise within a context, and in the Middle Ages that context was often of a theological nature. But as we shall see later, especially in the late Middle Ages, a number of comprehensive epistemological views were recorded (often at the personal cost of those who recorded them) that did not hesitate to question the prevailing philosophical paradigm and to highlight aspects of an early radical view on issues related to law and the view on the criminal phenomenon. Issues—such as the critique of authority that defines the view of "evil" as a transcendental phenomenon, while recognizing conflicting interests that express different perspectives and boundaries on the "criminal" phenomenon that conflict with authority, but also the impact of a changing historical and social context that had to define by changing the dominant reasons for the criminal phenome-non—were/are some of these elements which in turn, if studied in more detail in the development of the same argument, will enrich the arsenal of modern critical thinking about crime.

Medieval philosophy was developed within a context that had been initially formed, under the domination of the views of St. Augustine (354–430 AD) in the West and (Pseudo)—Dionysius of Areopagite (circa 500 AD) in the East, through the prism of the phrase *philosophia est ancilla theologiae*, that is, "philosophy is the helper of theology." The approach to God (hence the Good) can only be achieved in a way that is contrary to human reason and, accordingly, the approach to Evil, which is synonymous with the Devil. Therefore, crime is an act under the influence of the latter, sin with an illogical explanation.

1   Augustine

Augustine was born in Tagasti, Nudeidia (present-day Algeria), on November 13, 354 AD His father was a pagan and his mother a Christian, and thanks to her he embraced Christianity. Through his major epistemological work *Contra Academicos* (*Against the Academics*, which he wrote to refute the arguments of the sceptics of the Platonic Academy in 386 AD), Augustine formulated his proposal on which the foundations of philosophical and theological epistemology were laid, an epistemology that dominated medieval and Western Europe for ten cen-turies (mainly through its influence on Bonaventura and Aquinas). The influence of Augustine's epistemology on modern and contemporary philosophy is still the subject of intense research activity by numerous scholars, who find several similarities with Hegels' epistemology (1770–1831), but, certainly, has a clear impact on the dominant/mainstream conventional criminological thought (see Chadwick, 1986).

In this work (i.e., *Contra Academicos: Against the Academics*), Augustine aims to counter the attacks against the possibility of the existence of the truth of the Skeptics (the Platonic Academy under the guidance of Arcesilaus or *Arkesilaos* [circa 315–241 BC] and Carneadis [circa 213–129 BC]) had sharply criticized the doctrines of Stoicism and Aristotle). The epistemological reduction that Augustine proposed is not only a response to the Skepticism of the Academics, but also to the most systematic and modern for his time skeptical theory of Sextus Empiricus (circa second–third century AD). He argues that even the strongest skeptical arguments cannot undermine the certainty of truth of the subjective conception of reality.

Trying to address the problem of how we conceive certain knowledge in his theory—that is, how we approach eternal and unchangeable truths from a changeable and finite mind, like that of human being—Augustine (based on the Scriptures and being influenced by Neoplatonic approaches) proposes the theory of enlightenment or "epiphany," according to which God enlightens the human mind with the unchanging and eternal light of His wisdom. This enlightenment is not an implantation of knowledge, nor is it due to our own intellectual abstraction, but it needs God's help, who helps us to understand what is right and true by the grace of Divine Grace in our judgment.

Augustine's theory of the soul presents the same systematicity: the human soul is a being which uses a perishable body, creating a psychosomatic being, in the form of a person. Thus, the soul, in order to perceive the world around it, uses the body. However, it is not material and perishable and can survive even after the death of the body. The substantiation of the soul on a systemic philosophical level that Augustine proposed had a catalytic effect on the development of the philosophy of mind in medieval and modern philosophy.

Augustine's moral and political theory is also manifestations of the systematicity of his thought. In his moral philosophy he places the freedom of the human will in a central position. Human being is free to do evil and good. Both evil and good lead to a form of happiness. Human being, however, using his logical and mental abilities, must choose the lasting and true happiness that can be found only close to God (and it is essentially good) and avoid the ephemeral and perishable pleasures that are created by the corrupted sense of happiness (which leads to evil). Thus, the choice of good is based on the mental and logical abilities and possibilities of the human mind to distinguish the true from the false, true happiness from its ephemeral and perishable manifestations. In this way, the unquenchable thirst for truth, which plays a leading role in Augustine's intellectual development, now acquires a more practical content. Moreover, when Augustine expresses the view that a hedonistic framework (hedonism is the moral theory that one should act upon the pursuit of what gives one the greatest pleasure), it can be misunderstood and can lead to extreme inhuman behavior very easily; in his anthropological theory he introduces the strong motivation of love that should be inherent in every judgment concerning our fellow human being and God. Our will is transformed by our love for our neighbor and God, and protects us from many temptations that, instead of leading to indestructible and true happiness, cause us to deviate from its perishable and ephemeral effects. Our rational judgment, aided by the intense consciousness of love, always chooses actions that lead to God. So, not only do we judge and do good, but we also want to do it. Our love for God draws His help into the form of His mercy, which helps us to judge what is right and what is false, and not to be trapped in the elements of our senses, which can easily deceive us.

Augustine's political philosophy is an extension of his moral ontology. The difficult struggle between the desire for ephemeral and perishable pleasure and the desire for eternal and indestructible happiness results in people sometimes choosing perishable and ephemeral pleasure. Because this choice is directly related to the lack of love for God and fellow human beings, it inevitably leads to controversy between people who seek to enjoy their own ephemeral pleasures. Because this choice is directly related to the lack of love for God and fellow human beings, it inevitably leads to controversy between people who seek to enjoy their own ephemeral pleasures. Thus, the states of this world are nothing more than unholy criminal gangs operating for the purpose of their common survival. In contrast to the cosmic states, Augustine in his work *De civitate Dei* outlined a state that can be shaped by principles borrowed from the Gospels and dominated by love, mercy, justice, and the Law of God. In the field of public life as well as in that of the Church, he recognized the existence not only of perverted people but also people who choose to live according to the principles of the Gospel. He believed, however, that worldly power, by institutionalizing the violence and injustice it represented, had become a constant threat to the moral lives of those who relied on the principles of the Gospel and belonged primarily to a heavenly state. The Church must strive to be transformed into a form of earthly state whose operation will be regulated by the principles of the heavenly state. The dynamic and exemplary influence of ecclesiastical life in this way penetrates the cosmic state and reshapes it in order to gradually turn it into a heavenly state.

The Church is proposed to be a society with a higher spiritual dimension than that of the cosmic state (although this, according to Augustine, did not have in its time the spiritual dimension of the State of God) and the cosmic state must look to it for guidance, as well as and to protect it from its enemies, both internal (heretics) and external (the unfaithful).

For the first time, philosophy with Augustine acquired a new role: the scientific and systematic exposition and support of basic theological truths, such as the existence of evil in the world and the very existence of the Christian God. At the same time, his views on the existence and functioning of the soul and spirit (basic elements of his anthropology) were a point of reference for medieval debates and made it easier for the Pope to deal ruthlessly and harshly with intellectuals who were in conflict with him and his politics. The human body was considered to be dirty, so corporal punishment and torture became legal. The ecclesiastical committee called the Holy Inquisition would ensure the purification of the souls of the faithful, the salvation of their souls, and the coexistence of the secular state with the heavenly state of the Papal Roman Catholic Church. Finally, Augustine's views on the definitive, unequivocal, and universal distinction of justice from injustice, both secular and ecclesiastical, as well as on the relationship between the Church and the secular state, gave the Pope the opportunity, with the help of Augustine's Latin texts that were spread in the Middle Ages, to transform his power from purely ecclesiastical (until the sixth century) into political and ecclesiastical at the same time (after the seventh century). With the system of Ceasaropapism, the Pope made obedience part of the doctrine to his political and ecclesiastical will and, thus, created a de facto center of political power in his person. The consolidation of Christianity in Western Europe (which had been achieved to a large

extent thanks to his efforts) meant at the same time a bloodless consolidation of papal political power and its influence on the European space
without the negative consequences of the use of force.

2 (Pseudo)-Dionysius of Areopagite

During the same time in the first centuries of the Middle Ages, in the
eastern part of the Roman Empire, the view of (Pseudo)-Dionysius
of Areopagite and his texts prevailed (these texts were written by a
monk in the fifth to sixth centuries, who appropriated the name of
the Disciple of the Apostle Paul and Archbishop of Athens). These
texts are influenced not only by the Neoplatonism of the fourth and
fifth centuries (mainly Plotinus [205–270 AD], Proclus [418–485
AD] and Iamblichus [circa 245–325 AD]), but also from the theology
and philosophy of the Church Fathers of the first four centuries and,
more specifically, from works of Titus Flavius Clemens, also known as
Clement of Alexandria (circa 150–211/216 AD), of St. Basil the Great
(circa 333–379 AD), of St. Gregory of Nyssa (circa 335–394 AD) and
St. Gregory the Theologian (329–389 AD). In the Middle Ages and
Byzantium those texts were used in parallel with the comments of St.
Maximus the Confessor. Their titles immediately predispose the scholar
to their content: Divine Names (Περὶ Θείων ὀνομάτων), Celestial
Hierarchy (Περὶ τῆς οὐρανίου ἱεραρχίας), Ecclesiastical Hierarchy
(Περὶ τῆς ἐκκλησιαστικῆς ἱεραρχίας), and Mystical Theology (Περὶ
μυστικῆς θεολογίας). These texts, together with those by Augustine,
laid the foundations for the development of the Christian Mysticism
movement and had a catalytic effect on the development of Mysticism
in the Middle Ages and Byzantium (see O'Rourke, 1992).

For Pseudo-Dionysius, the true nature of God is covered by a veil
of darkness: the gloominess of ignorance (or otherwise the darkness of
ignorance) that surrounds God's nature can be broken only by God's
power and will, who reveals His nature only to whomever and when-
ever He wills (*On Mystical Theology*, 2). With this emphasis on the
ignorance that surrounds God's nature together with the widespread
use of symbolism and metaphors, the author of these texts endued the

philosophical and theological development of both the Middle Ages and Byzantium in a form of mysticism. However, these texts influenced medieval philosophy and theology, and their positions on the otherness and unity of the persons of the Holy Trinity and the nature of evil. Moreover, the view that evil is a denial of good was put on a new basis in these texts. God—full of goodness and ecstatic (i.e., outside of Himself) love and affection for creation—is attracted by it and creates only good and good in it (*On Divine Names*, 4 and 8–11). Therefore, the existence of a being can only do good, since it was created by Almighty God. Thus, evil is nothing but the denial of good, and evil is he who deprives a being of his existence or one who is not in a harmonic relationship with the existence of good in the world. Even demons in this theory are good in terms of their existence, and their evil is found in their voluntary turning away from virtues, that is, from their voluntary moral mutilation, and in the reduction of their existence and goodness. Natural evil, like death and natural disasters, forbids natural beings from fulfilling their natural purposes, which is the perfection of good inherent in them—that is, natural evil is a form of reduction of good and benevolence. These two positions expressed in the Areopagite texts—that is, that evil is the deprivation of existence or good (the famous position in the Middle Ages, known as *privatio boni*) and that the phenomenon is distant from the essence—are perhaps the ones that exerted the greatest influence on the Middle Ages and beyond. They also define the dominant view of criminological analysis to date.

In the centuries immediately following Augustine in the West, the period was philosophically characterized by an intense attempt to search for the cultural identity of Western Europe. Communication with the East, where the empire's administrative center was located, and its political and military power was difficult due to pirate raids and the often-conquering attacks of hostile peoples. Trying to maintain his influence over the political and military development of Western Europe, the Pope placed emphasis on ecclesiastical power and the support of theological research. The cultural distance from the East, instead of giving a boost to the culture of Western Europe, marked its cultural (and mainly educational and philosophical) decay for almost three centuries. That decay (which in Western European literature was called the

Dark Ages, that is, the Black Age or the Age of Darkness) was so felt in education, philosophy, and theology that until the time of John Scotus Eriugena or Johannes Scotus Erigena or John the Scot (circa 800–877) in the ninth century, nothing remarkable was recorded. After all, before Charlemagne, Western Europe was a theater of political and military confrontations, and violent and destructive conflicts—in short, a theater of inhuman violence. With Charlemagne there was pacification and unification of a large part of it. At the same time, the East would find in Platonism and mysticism arguments to develop its philosophy and theology. The mystical theological tendencies in the ninth and tenth centuries would take the form of Hesychasm.

3   John Scotus Eriugena or Johannes Scotus Erigena or John the Scot

During the ninth century in the West, a particularly remarkable philosophical system was created, by a philosopher and theologian who expressed in a new form the important cultural rearrangements of his time and renewed Augustine's dominant epistemological paradigm: John Scotus Eriugena or Johannes Scotus Erigena or John the Scot (circa 800–877). In his work *De Divisione Naturae* (*On the Division of Nature*), he tried to map all levels of reality. He saw the whole creation as a mirror that reflects God. Human nature, when it is far from God due to sin, does not exist, while when man approaches God through his faith and works, he exists.

John's epistemological views on the omnipotence of human speech also had a very significant effect on the late Middle Ages. John argued that any authority that is not supported by man's rational capacity (reasoning) is not strong, while man's rational capacity (reasoning) does not need any authority to be supported. This view of the omnipotence of human reason had a profound effect on the development of science in the late Middle Ages. In this particular work he tries to make a logical description of nature and the relationships that exist in it, based on theological and philosophical principles and direct observation of its processes. Knowledge, according to him, exists in the doctrines of faith; however, what is required is a full understanding and systematic exposition of it. The main instrument for this understanding is the right reason (*recta ratio*). Here, faith and reason are complementary. This is especially evident in his position on authority: authority derives from true reason, while true reason never derives from authority.

John, influenced by the writings of (Pseudo-)Dionysius of Areopagite and the Platonism of Augustine, could not ignore the existence of evil. Evil, for John, lies in the corrupt will of the angels and men who are far removed from God's will. The evil man and the demon will eventually return to God, but they will be tortured in the following way: they will not be able to stabilize their will in the images of these evil wills they desire. This unfulfilled will of theirs (which before their union with God was fulfilled and thus committed sin or evil) will be their eternal punishment. In this way all creation will return to God, but only the elect (people who have lived voluntarily close to God) will reach the stage of deification (*De Divisione Naturae*, 5, 26–36). It is characteristic of the influence of John's system that political theory in the Middle Ages, especially after him, considered the deterministic concept of secular power to be self-evident, on the basis of which all monarchs in the particularly violent period of the ninth and tenth centuries supported absolute power. Secular power can commit heinous crimes against the people. Its existence, however, is imposed not by some agreement between the people and the monarch, but by the will of God and by the model of human society which imposes the medieval model of secular power with the absolute monarch and the absolute power of the rulers. John's theory tended to lead to political exaggerations in the late Middle Ages. This differentiation of the Middle Ages from ancient times (which mainly concerned political theory and practice) was not based only on John's theory, but also on that of Augustine, who formulated (mainly in his work *De Civitate Dei* or *The State of God*) the view that the human state operates in a completely different way from the state of God. In the human state we have violence and power, because man, due to the primary sin and disobedience of Adam, is in full estrangement from God's will. So to rule over sinful people requires ruthless power and the absolute use of force. With this differentiation he allowed (if not imposed) the full estrangement between the existing and the proper state of secular power (that is, the estrangement in secular power between what is and what should be): secular power is violent and cruel because it does not serve divine laws, but human laws and people's weaknesses. So, any change is completely useless and utopian. In this way the theology and metaphysics developed on the basis of the conceptions of Augustine and John greatly contributed to the political and social stability of the Middle Ages. Pope Gelasius I laid the foundations of the union between secular and ecclesiastical power as early as the fifth century: the two powers with which this world is mainly governed (ecclesiastical or *auctoritas* and political or *potestas*) must work together to manage society in a way that allows for the coexistence of both. This theory of the Two Swords was a generally accepted theory throughout the Middle Ages and pre-dated state–church relations at a time when neither the rulers nor the Popes wanted to come into direct conflict to assert their power.

4   Giacomo Bonaventura

The development in the following centuries of the Middle Ages of the dominant Augustinian view of philosophy and, consequently, the demarcation of evil and crime followed two paths. The first, the most faithful, was expressed by the texts of Bonaventura (1214–1274), whose view of the relationship between philosophy and theology is part of the Augustinian Neoplatonism. To the possible objection that the pagan and the unbeliever do not possess this truth, Bonaventura replies that they do, but prefer not to acknowledge it due to their erroneous conclusions about natural phenomena and the state of beings; for example, the unbeliever or atheist mistakenly believes that the lack of justice in everyday life can lead to the conclusion that there is no God.

Evil is, for Bonaventura, the defective state of a being in relation to the archetype; that is, the evil that governs human relationships is not due to its existence in an archetype, but to people's very will not to approach the relevant archetypes in the ideal way of behavior and relationships. This knowledge of God is of a different nature from that of good (he calls it *cognitio visionis*). Bonaventura accepts Augustine's view that the only evil in the world is sin. Bonaventura tried to prove the immortality of the soul with other reasonings, two of which are most valuable, the proof from the figurative cause and the proof from the divine justice. In the second proof he argues that it is generally accepted that God acts with the rule of the ultimate form of justice, according to which good is always rewarded. Therefore, according to the divine command, man should prefer to die than to be unjust. If, however, all people preferred to die rather than do wrong and did not have an immortal soul, any effect of their goodwill would be annihilated. So, the soul must be immortal.

The second path of the development of the dominant philosophical perspective is more complicated. It begins with the dialogue (in opposition and under the influence) with philosophical figures of Islamic-Arabic and Jewish philosophy that developed in Europe and reaches up to Thomas Aquinas and John Duns Scotus.

5   Islam and Arab Philosophers

Islam, after the sixth century, presented a serious cultural challenge for Europe, which was under the constant siege of barbaric peoples. After all, the Arabs got to know the ancient Greek philosophy and science with the help of the Greeks of the Byzantine Empire, and especially with the help of the Nestorian Christians of the Syrian school. In the eleventh century, four universities in the Arab regions were famous throughout the Mediterranean: Fez (or Fes) in Morocco, Cordoba in Spain, El-Azar in Cairo, and Baghdad in Persia. Thus, the confrontation between Western Europe and the Islamic East took place not only at the military level but also at the cultural level (Leaman, 1985). Many of the Aristotelian arguments—for example, those by Averroes—were considered by many Western European Christian thinkers to be entirely hostile to the Platonic arguments of the Latin Fathers, and prominent philosophers of the eleventh, twelfth, and thirteenth centuries aimed to deal with them using all the philosophical arsenal at their disposal.

It should be noted that the Arab philosophers did not copy the Byzantine or Syrian composition of Aristotelianism and Neo-Platonism, but proceeded to a further composition of them with their own tradition of Qur'an.

Avicenna or Ibn Sina–Ibn Sina (Persian: ابن سينا, also known as Abu Ali Sina [ابوعلى سينا], Pur Sina [پورسينا], of Persian descent, who was named Avicenna from the Hebrew form of Aven Sina's name), is perhaps the most systematic philosopher of Islamic philosophy, a tendency he expressed as Islamic scholasticism. His main philosophical work is *Al-Shifā'* which in the Middle Ages was known as *Sufficientia*. According to this work, a connection of Ontology with Epistemology leads us to a complete questioning of Ontology, while, if we connect Ontology with Metaphysics, we preserve the value of Ontology in supporting the most scientifically sound theories and theories (see Afnan, 1958). We can also see Avicenna's profound metaphysical reflection on the notion of necessity. This notion is very important not only for Islamic philosophy and culture (which accepts, in the form of kismet or fate, the notion of necessity as a notion with absolute power), but also for the medieval intellect, since it is related to the debate about the necessity of evil and the freedom of man and God, and also the fundamentally scholastic problem of the relationship between the existence and the essence of beings (issues that have occupied the Western intellect from Augustine's time up to the present day). Avicenna considers necessity a primary notion (as basic as the notion of existence) and supports the common understanding of the time that evil does not have an independent existence, but is a lack of good and just or *privatio boni*. So, because God is Absolute Good and because God's all attributes are interwoven in His absolute essence, it implies that God is both Truth and Love and Life (these are the manifestations of the Good in knowledge, the relationship with other people and personal situation).

On the other hand, according to Averroes (or Ibn Sina), the raw material is eternal, self-existent, and by its nature contrary to God's nature. The creation and use of this Raw Material took place out of time, and to accept its creation in time would mean an a priori change in God's immutability. In this way, Averroes went against any claim that the motion of bodies is eternal and that time has no beginning. He argued that the motion of bodies has a beginning and an end in time, which began to exist from the creation of the world (Kogan, 1985).

Another position of Averroes that became the focus of much criticism and controversy is the famous medieval theory of double truth about the relationship between philosophy and theology. With this theory, the philosophy from *ancillae theologiae* (that is, the maidservant of theology) supported by the Church Fathers, was now becoming one that is closer to truth than theology. In other words, with the theory of double truth, truth of philosophy took the lead in practice and philosophers started becoming independent of religious authority and dogma.

At the same time, Moses Maimonides (1135–1204), a Jewish philosopher who was born in Cordoba and died in Cairo, where he had been granted asylum after the persecution of philosophers in Arab Spain, wrote his work *Guide of the Perplexed*. In it, he sought to establish Jewish theology on rational and Aristotelian foundations (Colette, 1985). He follows Averroes' theory of dual truth and argues that we must accept the data of our senses and the conclusions of our rational reasoning. If any truth of the Old Testament is in conflict with our observations or with the method of reasoning dictated by Aristotle's logic, then this truth must be interpreted allegorically, and in fact allegorically, so that to the controversy can be eliminated in favor of Aristotle's philosophy (whom Maimonides respected like the Prophets) and the facts of our observations.

Maimonides' belief in the independence of philosophy from theology created a huge problem not only for the Arabs, but also for the fanatical Jewish and Latin theologians who saw in his thought the retreat of dogmas to the ancient Greek philosophers. Maimonides' flight to Cairo, as well as the strong criticism of his theory by Latin theologians, was the result of the hostile climate toward the independence of philosophy that was prevailing at the time. With his radical views, Maimonides is now considered the Jewish thinker who brought the revolution not only to Jewish but to all medieval and especially to scholastic philosophy, who talked to the current of nominalism, and who influenced the development of the radical movement of Occamism (or Ockhamism), which will be discussed below. His arguments, however, did not leave Thomas

Aquinas at all indifferent, who, together with John Duns Scotus, constituted the dominant philosophical paradigm (an evolution of Augustine's paradigm) in the late Middle Ages.

6   Thomas Aquinas

As we have discussed earlier, Bonaventura (expressing the mainstream Augustinian evolution) considered that any truth which does not come from doctrine directly or indirectly is doomed to error and uncertainty. Thomas Aquinas (1225–1274), however, takes a distance from this view, and accepts that "unbelieving" philosophers may be right in their judgments of the world, man, and God. The true knowledge of unbelievers or pagans may be characterized by Aquinas as imperfect and incomplete (due to the fact that it is not part of man's general thirst for theological truth), but never fallacy.

But let us look in detail at Aquinas' philosophy with an emphasis on the view of evil and, consequently, the criminal phenomenon (Davies, 1992; Kenny, 1980; Martin, 1997). Man, according to Aquinas, consists of body and soul, and, according to his hylomorphic theory, man's rational soul is the specific substantive form that is directly united with the raw material in the creation of the human body. This substantive form is one and we call the body and the soul "human" in their unified form. The union of soul and body does not follow, according to Aquinas, the Platonic Gnostic conception of the enslavement of the soul to the body and of the body as a sign (or tomb) of the soul. The soul is united with the body because only in this way can it exercise its functions and abilities to the fullest.

This view of Aquinas has direct implications for his theory of free will, the relationship between the active and the passive mind, and the epistemology he developed in conjunction with his theory of the mind and man's perceptual capacity. Thus, for Aquinas, because desire is determined by the good that man wants to acquire with it, human will (which differs from desire as to the breadth of the object) is determined by the theory of good that has been accepted and guides us in life. In this way, will can be distinguished into free (that is, there must be freedom in the choice of means) and non-free (that is, there can be no freedom in the choice of means). Therefore, the freedom of will or *liberum arbitrium* depends on the choice of means and, as such, is directly connected with the rational ability of the human soul. The animal cannot have freedom of will because its desire is determined by its instinct, and the choice of means is a result of its natural and mechanistic ways of behaving. However, man—freely judging the means that he will choose to achieve what he judges as good every time—exercises his potential for free will to the fullest. Of course, there are times when man, under the influence of drugs or drunkenness or even highly addictive behaviors, falls into a position where he can no longer freely choose, but this case goes back to a previous use of freedom (where man chooses for the first time to be alcoholic, violent, and so on). It should be emphasized here that for Aquinas, freedom of will can never be freedom in terms of purposes. Aquinas accepts that although man has a natural impulse in his will to follow what he considers to be general good, he does not follow any logic or other necessity to connect the specific means in order to achieve a goal. Thus, he exercises his freedom only to choose specific means and not to choose purposes. The purpose on which the will is based is always good. And man can aim at evil only due to the fact that he does not fully realize that what he seeks is not good.

Aquinas' belief is that deep down all people seek beatitude or *beatitudo*, which can only exist close to God. Because we cannot see what specific action can serve as a means to an end, and because we cannot judge exactly where we need to go in order to draw near to God, we find misery (using the freedom of will in an evil way).

For Aquinas, man seeks with his moral actions to achieve his completion and the purpose of his life—happiness. Both of these can be achieved with man's moral act moving toward God. The only point in which Aquinas differs from Aristotle in the general form of teleological ethics and ethics of blessedness is the content of blessedness. On the one hand, Aristotle claimed that it consisted of knowledge of how the world works (theory), whereas Aquinas argues that it is God's view, the Absolute Good (beatitude, *beatitudo*). It actually divides blessedness into two types: (a) blessedness that we can achieve while we are in life, with free actions (which are ultimate moral acts) that move toward the natural knowledge of God (that is, natural theology) and the works of love for God (imperfect blessedness); and (b) blessedness that we are going to attain in the sight of God Himself after death (perfect blessedness). The two kinds of blessedness are related and interdependent: the second kind is the result and the natural continuation of the first. Man by nature turns to the ultimate goal of blessedness; the drive to achieve blessedness is something completely natural, and his very will is a drive to achieve general good. And while the attainment of imperfect blessedness is something natural and within the power of every human being, the attainment of perfect blessedness is something that requires divine intervention and grace. Based on the above principles, Aquinas forms a whole moral system which is distinguished for its elaborate structure and logical consistency. Thus, all man's intentional actions are divided into moral (good) and immoral (evil). All intentional actions that are designed and accomplished, that are based on logic, and that serve the ultimate goal of bliss are good, while all others are evil. The only acts that cannot have a moral character are involuntary acts, i.e., unintentional acts. Man is responsible for all his intentional acts, even those that have become a habit that can hardly be stopped. Aquinas emphasizes that man's virtues (as well as vices) that characterize him as a person are essentially the habits according to which he lives and for which he is fully responsible. In this way the moral good is connected with God and is something positive and complete in terms of its existence. But does something similar happen to evil? Here, Aquinas opposes to the followers of Manichaeism (a sect in which there is absolute evil and absolute good personified in Devil and God, and that both have absolute power and equality) who believe that, as there is an ontology of good, there is also an ontology of evil, and formulates the well-known medieval position that evil is *privatio boni*, that is, simply absence of good. Thus, evil is parasitic on good and does not exist as a separate entity. God did not create evil, nor is this something that man can ever desire. Because it is something without an entity, that is, something that does not exist by itself, but parasitically, that is why man who always desires good can never desire the absence of good, that is, evil. The man who does evil does it without knowing it.

In other words, there is natural law or *lex naturalis*, which is the basis and condition of moral law in the finding of which our rational abilities help. Moral law is thus in constant interdependence and interaction with natural law, and this interdependence protects human life from exaggeration in the use of logic. Just as natural law is one (since man as nature never changes), so moral law is one and timeless. The only thing that changes from season to season and from culture to culture is the specific circumstances of the implementation of moral rules (*mutatio materiae* in the Middle Ages). However, in no case should the implementation of moral rules be opposed to the spirit and logic of moral law that imposes them. This law that never changes, even in the specific circumstances of its implementation, is the divine or transcendental law. Divine or transcendental law, according to Aquinas, is the guide both for the natural law (God only knows man's nature completely, since He created it, so only He can lead us with certainty to true natural law) and for moral law (God is the only one who can have absolute knowledge of general and specific conditions of our moral actions and therefore can help us to achieve virtue). Whereas divine law was originally given to man to make him turn to natural law (the Laws of Moses in the Old Testament), in the post-Christ era, He leads man to his transcendental course and to the manifestation of his truly natural desire for his union with God. In this way divine law is the safeguard of the whole moral system of Aquinas: any differences and conflicts between natural and moral law are dissolved through the existence of divine law and its absolute and general power. Divine law is above not only natural law but also moral law, which helps the man who follows natural and moral law to achieve his ultimate goal: the perfect blessedness in the sight of God Himself.

Aquinas also differs from Augustine in his general view on political power. As we have discussed, Augustine viewed secular power as something negative and separated the secular state from God's kingdom. Aquinas does not separate the two, but unites them in his system. Thus, ecclesiastical power is different from and of greater importance than secular power, not because it is completely opposite in terms of methods, but because of its higher purpose. The exercise of state power aims at citizens' good and the realization of their imperfect blessedness, but the exercise of ecclesiastical power aims to fulfill perfect blessedness after death. As such, the ecclesiastical power is superior and must immediately guide (with the creation of certain moral predispositions) the state power so that it does not become oppressive and tyrannical.

Consequently, Aquinas argues that there are four kinds of law: eternal law, natural law, divine ordained law, and human law. The first two kinds of law are those which God Himself has created and which He alone knows perfectly. Of the other two kinds, the first kind (that is, divinely ordained law) is the law which God has revealed to men (imperfectly to the Jews in the Old Testament and perfectly to the Christians in the New Testament). The human laid law is law created by the rulers of political and judicial power. The purpose of the human laid law is to implement natural law in the specific circumstances and to guarantee its observance with the appropriate prohibitions and punishments. Thus, if human law is contrary to divine law or natural law, then it is perverted and the citizen cannot (or must not, if it is disobedience to divine law) follow it (although Aquinas believes that the citizen/subject should in some cases obey laws that are contrary to natural law if disobedience can lead to serious malfunction or chaos in world power in these cases). Thus, the political ruler must obey divine and natural law, and must create the appropriate human law, which will not force the citizens to rebel against him. The aforementioned political theory of Aquinas not only strengthened the sense of law in the late Middle Ages (it is a characteristic of this time that many small towns in Central Europe did not have a doctor, but they had a court), but it was the source for all European constitutional reflection of Europe after the Middle Ages and helped create an entire school of political theory for the fair use of political power. Although teleological and utilitarian in its inspiration, it managed to set legal and moral barriers to political power and make the latter respect the personal dignity and freedom of the subject-citizen.

7   John Duns Scotus

A few years after Thomas Aquinas, John Duns Scotus (1266–1308) followed his point of view with reference to the role that the will has in the moral and religious evaluation of our actions (see Broadie, 1995, 1996, 1999). He observes that sin, according to the Christian doctrine, is equated with desire, the will for evil and not with its intellect. Simple intellect, the thought of evil and, especially, if we do not desire it or if we do not take pleasure in it, is not characterized as sin. On the contrary, the will to do evil, even if we do not do so, is sin. John defines the realm of ethics as the realm of free action. A free act is morally good when it conforms to the right reason. The object or purpose for which the act is performed has a primary role in determining the moral act. Not only the purpose and the object of the act, but also the means that will be chosen to achieve the good purpose and the acquisition of the good object must be appropriate and consistent with the correct reason and these in order for the act to be characterized as a good. John's specific position shows that he is trying, here too, to achieve his own immediate solution to the problem of the criterion of moral practice. Thus, the criterion for morally correct judgment is made not only the right judgment on the basis of purpose, but also on the basis of all other specific facts of the act. To the question of what exactly are the standards on the basis of which this criterion can work, John answers by formulating a doctrine on the relationship between moral and divine law: the divine will, as imprinted in the divine law, is the cause of good in the world. God's will is necessarily good because by His nature, He cannot want evil. The moral law that man must obey with his free will is God's will for man, which will bring with it God's all wisdom and prudence. Human moral law is the definition of divine law in human space. Man voluntarily accepts divine law and turns it into moral law and rule of his life because he sees in it the absolute good. His right reason aids his decision to remain faithful to moral law and any disagreement is considered unreasonable. Because moral law that man has chosen to follow is divine will in relation to him, disobedience is also a sin. The right reason helps in the observance of divine and moral law because with his correct judgment, man sees that the opposite act to that which divine law allows is also opposed to natural law—that is, it is contrary to man's very survival. Even if divine law seemingly contradicts man's right judgment about his survival (as in the case of Abraham's wil to sacrifice Isaac), man must obey, because God has expressed His will to him in divine law, and man has freely accepted it with his moral law. In this way (and in contrast to the intellectual moral theory of Thomas Aquinas), although correct judgment is ancillary to the observance of moral law, it cannot prevail in the event of a conflict. Within John's moral system, divine law along with moral law, natural law, and the written law of the courts creates a compact and uniform body of law in which any conflict gives way to the omnipotence of divine will expressed in divine law inherent in the Scriptures and the tradition of the Church. At the same time, in the field of political theory, John argues that political power has nothing to do with parents' authority and power over their children, which obeys natural law (which was a commonly accepted position in the political theory of the latter Middle Ages). Obedience to political power is not related to natural, moral, or divine law, but is simply the result of citizens' consent and their desire to live in relative peace and without the worries of political power. Because this agreement of citizens to obey a ruler does not have the indisputable and universal force of moral, divine, or natural law, the ruler and the courts must decide on the basis of divine or natural law, and on the basis of these they should create written laws as well.

8 The School of Chartres and John of Salisbury

The views of Thomas Aquinas and John Duns Scotus would seem, for their time, to be the closest to a radical epistemological paradigm (with the proposal to put limits on power and authority in the field of law) if there were not two other movements that developed between the twelfth and fourteenth centuries. Those were the School of Chartres and, especially, John of Salisbury (1115–1180) and the much more emphatically Occamism (or Ockhamism) movement which, at least in the field of medieval universities, would be a strong epistemological counter-paradigm shortly before (and during) the advent of the Renaissance.

The School of Chartres was essentially the first attempt to have a philosophical paradigm rival to Augustinian philosophy and, with its main views, the introduction of Aristotelian hylomorphism and the view of barriers to political power by natural law (under the influence of radical Stoics of the Hellenistic period); it was one of the sources of radical thought about crime in the Middle Ages. After all, the idea was developed in the early twelfth century (as we saw in the previous chapter) that special socio-political developments facilitated the development of that different epistemological paradigm.

In general, representatives of the School of Chartres follow in their metaphysics the theory of exemplarism (*exemplarismus*), according to which the forms of beings are copies or examples of the form in which God created them. Undoubtedly, the most famous representative of that School in the Middle Ages was John of Salisbury and, especially, the political theory and the theory of law that he developed in his *Polycraticus*, a very famous work in the late Middle Ages. John of Salisbury is one of the few philosophers and theologians of the Middle Ages who viewed the social and political problems of his time more as political and institutional and less as metaphysical (Taylor, 2006). Such a direction in the political theory of the Middle Ages went against the tradition, since until the tenth century there was only one main political theory that prevailed: that of Augustine.

Just a century before John of Salisbury, Manegold of Leutenbach (circa 1030–1103) had written that the ruler has entered into a contract with his subjects, the contempt of which gives to the latter the right to revolt and replace him (in his *Liber ad Gebehardum*, 30 and 47). John of Salisbury, using the writings of Augustine as well as *De Officiis* by Ambrosius, argued that the ruler's power has moral, political, and legal barriers, which he must respect if he wants to act as a ruler and not as a tyrant. These barriers have their origin in the Stoic theory of natural law, according to which all enacted laws (i.e., decisions and decrees made by the ruler and his representatives) must comply with the rule of law which transcends persons and situations and has timeless power. This rule of law can be no other, according to John, than Roman law, customs of the place and the Gospel. In other words, John does not propose a kind of contract between the subjects and the ruler, which the ruler should observe (since every citizen would not be able to comprehend Roman law and other sources of natural law), but he does hold the leader accountable to the entire human race, thus creating the basis for the establishment of barriers with intercultural and timeless power. In fact, the sanctity of these barriers for John was so great that it could fully justify the revolt against the tyrant, and even his physical extermination for insulting the sense of justice of the whole human race.

9 Roger Bacon

At the beginning of the thirteenth century, critical thought was dominated by Roger Bacon (1219/20–1292) or Doctor Mirabilis for his disciples (not to be confused with Francis Bacon, whom he preceded two centuries earlier), who was born in Ulster, in around 1219/20. In 1250 he became a monk in the Franciscan order and taught at Oxford until 1257, when he was ordered to stop teaching in public due to the fact that he was suspected to teach "new beliefs." His most important work is *Opus Maius*. In it he lists four causes of human failure to conquer the truth—man fails in his attempt to conquer the truth due to: (a) his submission to a non-credible authority; (b) his habit; (c) his prejudices; and (d) the presentation of positions of an authority in a subject out of his inability to support his own. There are two kinds of experiences: there is the experience of the bodily senses aided by instruments and reliable recordings of others, and the experience of spiritual things that needs the intervention of divine grace. The first kind of experience can, among other things, be used to prolong life (with medicine), to generate new forms of energy, and to transform lower metals into gold with the help of the philosopher's stone. With the second kind of experiences, man is led toward a mystical union with God. In this way Roger was one of the first to promote the "authority of experimentation" (i.e., no theory should be accepted without validation in a series of successful and relevant experiments).

10   Henry of Ghent

At about the same time, the critical thought of Henry of Ghent (1217–1293) is important, who observed that metaphysical knowledge of God (which is achieved in physical theology) presupposes a concept of the existence of beings themselves, both for the existence of God and for the existence of creations. This is necessary because otherwise we would never be able to formulate concepts that could describe Him (and obviously the acceptance of the Christian doctrine requires us to have such concepts). Regarding Henry's view on the dual meaning of existence (one for God and another different for creations), he considered that it limited the possibilities of knowledge of existence only in creations and condemned us to a kind of agnosticism in relation to God.

11   William of Ockham or *Venerabilis Inceptor*

However, the dawn of the fourteenth century brought with it the most brilliant epistemological paradigm of critical thinking in philosophy and in the discussion about evil and crime: the spiritual movement of the Occamism (or Ockhamism) that marked the development of medieval skepticism (see Spade, 1999).

William of Ockham or *Venerabilis Inceptor*, the pre-eminent skeptical empiricist and agnostic of the late Middle Ages, was born in around 1290, deposed by the Pope and took refuge in Munich, under the protection of Louis of Bavaria. He died in 1349 from the Black Death (a deadly form of febrile disease which spread rapidly in the cities of the late Middle Ages due to poor sanitation and exterminated hundreds of millions of people).

In general, Ockham sought to overthrow essentialism and, especially, the powerful essentialist realities of his time: those by Scotus and Aquinas (which the followers of Aquinas and Scotus had succeeded in introducing to and strengthening at the Universities of Paris and Oxford) using Aristotelian logic and epistemology. Ockham believed that the two main points of Christian doctrine—God's omnipotence and God's absolute freedom—could not be reconciled with the essentialism and realism of his time, which was based on the philosophical theories of the ancient Greeks. Thus, he tried to prove that all kinds of realism of his time are misunderstandings and erroneous interpretations of Aristotelian metaphysics, and, at the same time, to give a new impetus to nominalism.

Ockham's distinctive personality, as a philosopher who was not afraid to break with the authorities of his time, is evident even from his fundamental position on the subject of metaphysics. If there is no possibility of substantial or accidental resemblance and analogy between creation and God, then all philosophical and theological endeavors to know God from prominent figures of his time (such as Aquinas and John Duns Scotus) are a priori destined to fail.

According to Ockham, we must separate the oral term (*terminus prolatus*) and the written term (*terminus scriptus*) from the concept they indicate (*terminus conceptus* or *intentio animae*). Although words are conventional and belong to a dialect or language, and are impossible for someone unfamiliar with that dialect and language to understand, the meaning that these words signify is the same regardless of language or dialect. Ockham called this concept (*terminus conceptus*) the "natural sign" to indicate that the experience of a thing by a human naturally creates (as opposed to the conventional way of being expressed) a corresponding meaning. The natural sign is the same for two people in different languages, but the conventional ways of expressing it (i.e., the words to be used) are different and depend entirely on the cultural environment of each person. Logical terms also belong to the conventional forms of expression of natural signs and function as a *suppositio* only within a sentence. "Universalis" (or, in other words, general categories of beings, i.e., general and universal meanings of beings) are terms which, using *suppositio*, signify "a particular" (i.e., particular beings that can be perceived by the senses). Thus, universals concepts do not exist and cannot exist in reality; their existence is conventional and depends on the cultural context to which they belong. To claim that universal concepts exist is essentially a contradiction: if universal concepts exist, then, by their very existence, they are simultaneously transformed into particulars. With this reasoning of Ockham, all the general categories of beings (colors, time, biological species) are transformed to non-existing and dependent on an actor who perceives them. That is, the color red does not exist, there is only a red tomato that I see in front of me, and time generally does not exist, there is only one object that moves in relation to another (*Primum Sententiarum*, 2, 8, Q and 2, 4, D and 2, 6, B and 2, 6, E, *Summa totius logicae*, 1, 63, *Quodlibet*, 4, 19).

Ockham's view on evidential knowledge (as he calls it) is typical: by adopting the Aristotelian definition ("proof is a reasoning that produces knowledge"), he proceeds to formulate the position that proof is essentially proof of properties or characteristics of a subject and not of the existence of the subject himself. In essence, we see in Ockham the foundation of knowledge of the experience of the existing world, a limitation of ontology to beings that actually exist and a contempt for any sophisticated theory of the existence of beings (such as by Bonaventura, Aquinas, or even Scotus), because it deviates from the correct use of language. The above principle is the basis of the deductive method (the bottom-up method) and is also called "Pluralitas non est ponenda sine necessitate," or the "Ockham's razor" (*novacula Occami*) (i.e., the minimization of ontological requirements of a scientific or philosophical theory), which as a philosophical principle has had a significant influence on modern philosophy.

In his moral and political theory, Ockham consistently adopts his metaphysical opposition to realism as expressed by Scotus and Aquinas. He refers to absolute freedom a man has and for the sake of which it makes sense that there are moral and legal sanctions for his actions (*Tertium Sent.*, 10, H). In fact, Ockham defines this freedom as the power of man to become the cause or the non-cause of an effect which he has the power to achieve (*Quodlibet*, 1, 16).

Absolute freedom, however, in creation implies an absolute sense of duty and obligation to the one who created it. Thus, according to Ockham, moral law owes its existence and is based on the will of God and the Creator for its rules (*Tertium Sent.*, 13, U). This authoritarian and volitional (in relation to divine will) moral theory was a point of intense controversy with the traditional Aristotelian schools of his day and even pushed him to support the view that if it were God's will for man to commit sin, it would be moral for man to commit it (*Secundum Sent.*, 19, P and O). However, beyond this basic (and perhaps extreme) position, Ockham accepts the common belief in his time that in every-day life we follow the principles of right reason (*Primum Sent.*, 41, K, *Tertium Sent.*, 12, C); that is, although he is in stark contrast to Aquinas' intellectualism, although he is more extreme in his intellectualism than John Duns Scotus, Ockham's view that in everyday practice we must obey the right reason of commonly accepted standard places him in the tradition of the Aristotelian rationalists of his time.

Thus, although Ockham accepted God's will as an absolute moral rule, he did not consider the Pope's will to have the same effect. True to his general moral position, he opposed the will of Pope John XXII, who had condemned as heretical the Franciscans' basic position that the clergy should be poor (this decision of Pope John can easily be understood as a consequence of the intense theological and philosophical contrast between the Dominicans and the Franciscans at that time). In fact, in 1332, Ockham published a political and ecclesiastical treatise, the *Opus nonaginta dierum* (*The Work of Ninety Days*), in which he supported this position of the Franciscans and, especially, the view of Michael of Cesena, the general of the Franciscan order who was excommunicated by Pope John. Ockham, along with Michael of Cesena and other Franciscans (especially the Franciscans of Munich), who began to react to the totalitarian and strongly anti-Franciscan spirit of Pope John, turned to Emperor Louis of Bavaria. The Pope, affected by the Franciscans' disobedience and their strong criticism of ecclesiastical property, issued the decree *Quia vir reprobus* in 1329 in a highly critical manner, to which Ockham responded in detail three years later with the aforementioned treatise. This treatise is a systematic elaboration of the relationship between statute law and natural law, as well as the legal status of property in the Middle Ages. In his writings, Ockham tried to prove this position of the Franciscans and distinguished between the statutory right of adverse possession and the moral obligation to maintain one's life; that is, according to him, although one has no right to possess material things, one can use them for one's survival if this is God's command. The Pope, because he foresaw a general questioning of his power in this view, condemned and persecuted Ockham, and did not succumb to the appeals of his friends, until Ockham signed his final repentance a year before he died. With this treatise as well as with other

relevant treatises, Ockham brought about a real revolution in the political and ecclesiastical affairs of the Middle Ages, and he annulled the
officially accepted by the papal church dogma of the subjugation of politics to ecclesiastical power.

12   Nicholas of Autrecourt

Ockham's vision was perfected by Nicholas of Autrecourt, who was
born in 1300 in Verdun and studied at the Sorbonne from 1320 to
1327. In 1346 he was ordered by the Pope to burn all his books in
public and revoke his positions. He obeyed to the Pope's orders and
was expelled from Paris. He died in 1350 in the city of Metz. Few of
his writings have survived, most notably his letters to opponents and
friends. From these few writings and from the knowledge of his contemporaries, we can outline his work and clearly include him in the radical Occamists of his time.

According to Nicholas, the basic premise of all epistemological reasoning and the only proposition that is absolutely certain and true is
that neither a proposition nor a contradiction can both be true at the
same time. The above principle affects the way in which we perceive
reality. He therefore adopted the view that both the direct conception
of reality (which another Occamist of the time, John of Mirecourt, calls
evidentia naturalis, the direct natural reflection) and the logical truths of
the type of the principle of non-contradiction (or, according to John of
Mirecourt, *evidentia potissima*) are the two most certain and true objects
of an epistemology. In the final analysis, what Nicholas actually managed to do is to call into question all things that are not directly perceptible and do not depend on or are not related to the principle of
contradiction. In this way Nicholas' extreme challenge included all philosophical, theological, and scientific knowledge of his time (which in its
true form he considered only to be possible because causal relations are
not directly related to the principle of contradiction).

Undoubtedly, the influence of radical Occamists and, especially, that
of Nicholas of Autrecourt was great, especially in terms of university
studies. Indicatively, we can mention that in 1389 it was decided in

Vienna that some original works of Occamists (those that were not forbidden by the Pope) could be taught at the university. Nominalism conquered most of the universities founded in the late 1300s in Germany
and the University of Krakow in Poland. The nominalists, who were
mostly Occamists, also dominated Paris, from where they were expelled
because of the Hundred Years' War (it was so called after a series of
bloody conflicts between the British and French from 1337 until 1453,
under the pretext of the succession to the throne of France and with
deeper causes, including claims over political, commercial, naval, and
economic sovereignty in Western Europe) during which religious zeal
for the Pope prevailed in Paris. In 1474, King Louis XI of France forbade the teaching of all the works of the Occamists and the destruction of existing books, but in 1481, after strong reactions, he revoked
this prohibition. As a result of these developments, nominalism prevailed not only in both Oxford and Paris, but also at most universities
in the Central European countries (with the notable exception of the
Universities of Cologne, Leuven, and Heidelberg, where Aquinas' and
Scotus' theories remained in a strong position) in the fifteenth century.

The same period saw the development of a modern political philosophical thought that radically expressed the political and economic
freedom of the individual and representative democracy as an ideological whole. In 2006, Mary E. Wiesner-Hanks wrote about early
European modernity to agree with Black (1992) that processes that
are considered modern were already initiated in the Middle Ages and
Antiquity. There are mainly ideas that favored the emergence of the
modern state and allowed the formation of an alternative approach in
terms of contract, consent, and common benefit; within this context,
these ideas gradually discredited the papal claims of validity and power
in the field of law and the identification of the criminal phenomenon,
and this is recorded primarily in the field of collectivity (*universitas*), as
well as in the sphere of *civitas* as a term expressive of this state community in general. This undertaking encompasses a series of subordi-
nate notions, on which the goal attributed to political communities is
reflected; that is, these are the medieval notions of common good, freedom, the individual's relationship to existing superior collectivities, and
ultimately the subordination of political governance to the operational

validity of principles, rules, and legal commitments. At the level of the preconditions for the political formation of the community, the influence of the earlier Roman political tradition and, especially, that of Cicero becomes decisive. The significance of Cicero's political thought for the formulation of medieval political theory is twofold: on the one hand, the notion of *civitas*, as a fundamental dimension of the public affairs of collective coexistence, as a predominant derivative of human rationality, reciprocity, and reasonable debate, with a view to securing peace, property, justice, and other legal property. The notion of political community as a product of human nature and social skill, and ingenuity and its philosophical familiarity in the thirteenth century is obviously influenced by Aristotelian political philosophy, aiming to construct an alternative political proposal to papal hierarchy and the power of theological traditions, whereas the rule of common utility is also based on the fair distribution of individual burdens to the whole social body.

13   Azonne of Bologna or Azzo or Azolenus

Thus, we have, on the one hand, the Church of the medieval Western European tradition which was promoting the universal claim of its proclamation as a pre-eminently political society, the fullness and perfection of which (*societas perfecta*) automatically elevates it as the highest and most inclusive human society. Contrary to this dominant view, reasonable controversy was gradually developing. Azzone (1198–1230), referring to the legislative function and its exercise body, observes that the assignment and transfer by the Roman people of such a right to the ruler was never complete. It is certainly recognized that the ruler has the jurisdiction (*juris dictio*) and the dictation of new laws (*merum imperium*); nevertheless, the people had never relinquished the exercise of this right, even though it had become useless over time. Therefore, the legal status of collective associations confers on them certain rights of representation and election to office based on the principle of self-government, but does not make them autonomous political entities.

Claiming the organizational autonomy of Italian city states vis-à-vis the imperial power does not automatically give them the status of political sovereignty. This is made possible by the consolidation of a new political reality in northern Italy. The right of legislative self-determination is now recognized by the legal interpretive intelligentsia in the autonomous cities, who, in the fourteenth century, acquired the theoretical legitimacy of enacting laws that were not necessarily compatible with Roman law, but were clearly not contrary to the concept of natural law, in accordance with the principle that each *civitas* determines its own political law.

14 Bartolus de Saxoferrato

According to Bartolus de Saxoferrato (Italian: Bartolo da Sassoferrato) (1314–1357), the principle of legal sovereignty is not limited only to its legal content, but also extends to the conception of cities as independent budgetary entities that are not dependent on overriding political entities. These positions are of particular importance for the formulation of a rational public law, capable of carrying out the identification of any legal political sovereignty with the possibility of self-determination of the conditions of collective coexistence by local communities. These findings, when transferred to the political field, led to the radical distinction between a legislative supervisory authority and the enforceability of the implementation and enforcement of these laws. The real legislator, the primary and pre-eminently competent legislative principle is the whole of the social body, the *Universitas* of the citizens, considered as a single whole. This is the famous principle of *civitas sibi prìnceps* (the city constitutes a prince [or Emperor] unto itself).

The shift in favor of the inherent value of collective coexistence is based on the overthrow of the dominant Augustinian hypothesis that every form of legal authority was imposed by divine command as a simple antidote to the treatment of human sin and disobedience to divine law. On the contrary, this specific medieval political question arises from the fundamental axiom that every possibility of collective well-being is a natural tendency of humanity, and that the formation of a political community to ensure fundamental existential needs emerges by nature and is imposed on social coexistence.

15   Marsilius of Padua

Marcilius of Padua (circa 1280–1342/1343) would go one step further. In his work, the problem of popular sovereignty would be given special emphasis (Brett, 2005). Each form of government consolidates its own claims of validity only when it is in line with the popular will, and he clearly articulated a radical dimension of a "criminal" phenomenon based on an anomic status quo: in the coupling of the criteria of the common good and the need to formulate the popular will, the lack of which leads to the pathological operation of the state (Marcilius of Padua, *Defensor Pads*, 1.8.2). The chief work of Marcilius, a figure who overshadows all others in fourteenth-century political thought, was *Defensor Pacis*, which was first published anonymously. Aristotelian philosophy played a decisive role in its intellectual composition, which Marcilius elaborated in an original way. Typically, he considered the state as a self-sufficient and perfect community whose goal is prosperity. But, unlike Aristotle, Marcilius believed that not only city states, but also all forms of state were part of the physical order. Sovereign role and supreme power in political society is held by all citizens, which Marcilius identified with the human legislator.

In the fourteenth century, the constant fluidity of socio-political formations and the ongoing processes in the politico-economic sphere contributed to the progressive release of political power from the supremacy of the Western Church and the gradual formation of a concept of power that was autonomous from its previous theological pre-determinations. This development was, to a significant degree, a consequence of the gradual secularization of the collective representations of the criminal phenomenon that emerged in the ecclesiastical sphere. Within this context, both the theories of Ockham and his followers and the modern political thought as reflected above were an important epistemological counter-paradigm which began to gain visibility and power. After all, it was the dawn of a new philosophical age: that of Humanism.

References

Afnan, S. M. (1958). *Avicenna, his life and works*. George Allen & Unwin.

Black, A. (1992). *Political thought in Europe, 1250–1450*. Cambridge Medieval Textbooks. Cambridge University Press.

Brett, A. (2005). *Marsilius of Padua: The defender of the peace*. Cambridge University Press.

Broadie, A. (1995). *The shadow of Scotus: Philosophy and faith in pre-reformation Scotland*. T&T Clark.

Broadie, A. (1996). Duns Scotus on sinful thought. *Scottish Journal of Theology, 49*, 291–310.

Broadie, A. (1999). Scotus on God's relation to the world. *British Journal for the History of Philosophy, 7*(1), 1–13.

Chadwick, H. (1986). *Augustine*. Oxford University Press.

Colette, S. (1985). *History of Jewish philosophy in the middle age*. Cambridge University Press; La Maison des Sciences de l'Homme.

Davies, B. (1992). *The thought of Thomas Aquinas*. Clarendon Press.

Kenny, A. (1980). *Aquinas*. Oxford University Press.

Kogan, B. S. (1985). *Averroes and the metaphysics of causation*. State University of New York Press.

Leaman, O. (1985). *An introduction to medieval Islamic philosophy*. Cambridge University Press.

Martin, C. F. J. (1997). *Thomas Aquinas: God and explanations*. Edinburgh University Press.

O'Rourke, F. (1992). *Pseudo-Dionysius and the metaphysics of Aquinas*. E.J. Brill.

Spade, P. V. (Ed.). (1999). *The Cambridge companion to Ockham*. Cambridge University Press.

Taylor, Q. (2006). John of Salisbury, the Policraticus and political thought. *Humanitas*, XIX (1 and 2), 133–157.

Wiesner-Hanks, M. E. (2006). *Cambridge history of Europe: Early modern Europe 1450–1789*. Cambridge University Press.

4

Byzantine Thought

During the Enlightenment, generalized underestimation of the Eastern Roman Empire focused not only on the intellect, but also on every aspect of Byzantine existence, as well as on the imperial institutions. The prevailing view was, on the one hand, that Byzantine society remained stagnant and unchanged over the centuries, and, on the other hand, that the Byzantine Empire did not influence the formation of the modern world. More specifically, Byzantine intellect was marginalized by philosophers such as Voltaire, Montesquieu, and Gibbon, who saw the historical course of Byzantium as a far-reaching decline of the Roman state. This attitude resulted in the Byzantine intellect continuing to be treated, because of its religious orientation, as a philosophy of lesser value, or even a negative moment in the history of the ideas.

Byzantine philosophy still remains *terra incognita* as we have not yet explored to a sufficient degree and in a way that ensures the conditions for a valid overview of the performance of the Byzantines in philosophy and science. And yet, the intelligentsia in Byzantium was nurtured and acted in socio-historical terms that, at least in relation to the medieval West, seem familiar to modern reality (see Benakis, 2002, 2013), and this had an impact on the context in which it was developed and

© The Author(s), under exclusive license to Springer Nature Switzerland AG 2022
S. Georgoulas, *The Origins of Radical Criminology, Volume III*,
https://doi.org/10.1007/978-3-031-05925-4_5

printed, as we shall see below and in relation to the dominant paradigm of conceptualization of the criminal phenomenon and the development of its radical counter-paradigm. After all, every philosophical system is part of dialectics. Within it, every philosophical theory pushes the intellect and reality toward the discourse and its realization. Moreover, the dialectic of history is reflected in the dialectics within the being. Every being or idea contains negation in its definition: the definition of being derives from the definition of non-being, and positivity derives from negativity.

We must first say that in the specific case of the Byzantine Empire, the concepts of state and justice are closely related both to each other and to the concept of religion. The rational state is the ultimate body of power, the Rule of Justice. The state is indeed the reality, to the extent that only within it is any attitude or change possible. The educational system was also well organized by the state or the church, and, in general, there was never in Byzantium any autonomous "guild" of the teachers of philosophy toward the state or ecclesiastical power, as in the Western Middle Ages.

In the Byzantine paradigm, the Hegelian identification of state and justice finds its most widespread implementation. In the medieval West, autonomous communities appeared in the people's courts, self-organized around unions; on the contrary, in the Byzantine area, everyone was under the orders of the emperor, the reflection of God on earth. However, it is an historical fact that in Byzantium the use of the link between state and religion for selfish purposes led to political disputes and attempts to social development, resulting in religious conflicts, which were almost always resolved by violent conflict.

But let us look in a little more detail at what we could claim that in Byzantium and especially in later Byzantium we have in miniature the whole later intellectual history of the West, with "humanism," "Counter-Reformation," and the utopia by Georgius *Gemistus Pletho*.

1 The Justinian Code or *Codex Justinianus* or *Corpus Juris Civilis* ("Body of Civil Law")

One of the greatest cultural achievements of Byzantium concerns the field of legal science: it is the codification of Roman law, due to an order of Emperor Justinian. The resulting text was published in 533 A.D. with force of law over the whole empire. Thanks to this codification and its subsequent adoption by the West, the influence of Roman law extends to the present day. From the beginning of the Byzantine Empire, the already wide power of the ruler following the establishment of hegemony was further strengthened. The period was characterized with the name "despotism," and he (the ruler) became formally the sole body of legislative power. The influence of Christianity on the formulation of law extends to the content of the regulations with their harmonization of legislation with the Christian teaching in many matters of private and public law. During the reign of Constantine the Great, the concept of the Christian kingdom was formed, according to which the basic legitimizing element of the form of the state but also of the person of the specific emperor was each ruler's close relationship of with God. Thus, the criterion for the ethical evaluation of the laws was henceforth whether they coexisted with the content of the divine commandments (divine law). As far the criminal policy pursued by the first Christian emperors is concerned, there was a significant increase in the strictness in terms of punishment of criminals, which is incompatible with the leniency and philanthropy taught by Christianity. From the fourth century and under the influence of St. Basil the Great, the purpose of punishment was addressed in its overall dimension, that is, in the fields of both the state and the church, repelling its retribution character since, as St. Basil writes, no way has been devised so that the facts can be eliminated, emphasizing its value mainly as a means of improving lawbreakers.

2   The Isaurian Dynasty

In the mid-Byzantine period and, especially, in the Isaurian dynasty, there was a new legislative innovation in the form of the *Election*, which was the first Byzantine legislation that defined the purpose of punishment: cleansing, improvement, and general prevention by intimidation. The reform of criminal law was carried out with the following measures. First with the almost complete abolition of the inhuman ways of execution of the death penalty and, at the same time, with the noticeable limitation of its scope of implementation. Secondly with the usually precise determination of the imposed punishment and the introduction, in this way, of barriers to free assessment, and, therefore, to arbitrariness of the criminal judge. Thirdly, by restricting the differentiation of sentences as much as possible on the basis of class criteria and by partially adapting the criminal treatment to the personality of the perpetrator. However, it should be noted that even at that time, the criminal punishment measures were the following: death, extermination, mutilation, flogging, exile, and confiscation of property. At the same time, there was an expulsion of the convict, who was thus subjected to public humiliation. There were no penalties of imprisonment except for the incarceration of the perpetrators of certain crimes, especially women in a monastery. The prisons were used only for the detention of defendants or public debtors.

3   The Macedonian Dynasty

At that time, there was also an historical paradigm of the creation of a law, a product of a compromise between secular and ecclesiastical power, indicative of the relevance of "values" and the influence of specific interests. Emperor Leo VI, known as the Wise or the Philosopher, after three marriages, acquired a successor in relation to whom he was forced to enter into a fourth marriage in order to legitimize. The fourth marriage led to the rupture of the emperor's relationship with the ecclesiastical leadership. In order for the church to grant forgiveness and for it to accept the legal consequences of his fourth marriage—that is, the recognition of his newborn successor and his mother as co-regent—Leo agreed to pass a law which would henceforth prohibit fourth marriages. The regulation of the issue by a special law would require the terms of the issue to be set out in its preface, something that would force Leo to disapprove of his own action. The ban was therefore introduced indirectly. In other words, a new legislative collection was published, the *Draft Law* (*Procheiron*) (907) as a revised version of the previous legislation, *Introduction*, in which the prohibition of the fourth marriage was included. Another point of interest was that those laws were written in Greek, not Latin, and they were organized by subject for ease of reference by judges and lawyers.

4   The Late Byzantine Era

In the late Byzantine era, the enhanced presence of the clergy and the church in general in all areas of legal science, both theoretical and applied, was due to the fact that with the overthrow of the state structures with the Sack of Constantinople by the Crusaders in 1204, a countervailing force within the church was developed to fill the void that had been created.

The most important legacy was the rescue of the ancient Greek literature, which was a multidimensional scientific object. The preservation of the Greek language in a living, vibrant form, the tradition of texts, and the preservation of historiography, rhetoric, and art were a valuable legacy, which fed the later European thought and art in the most productive way. However, above all, Byzantine civilization saved ancient Greek philosophy, both as an autonomous object of study and as a latent way of thinking, which influenced every branch of modern science. Almost all of the ancient Greek literature that we have at our disposal nowadays has been saved thanks to the copiers of manuscripts of the Byzantine schools and monasteries. In Byzantium—and not in the Latin West—the tradition of Greek antiquity found its natural continuation. There, and not in the West, the great works of the ancient Greeks continued to be read, studied, commented on, and copied.

As far as Greek philosophy in particular is concerned, we must realize that the established perception that it was to find a tragic end in the fateful year 529 is a conventional myth without any real basis. In 529 Emperor Justinian issued a decree which completely forbade the teaching of philosophy in Athens. This meant the closure of the Platonic Academy, which until then, for almost 900 years, has continued uninterrupted in the hands of Plato's successors. The last partners of the School were forced to flee to Persia, while the property of the School was confiscated. However, Greek philosophy did not expire in 529 after a course of 1000 years, but, on the contrary, it had before it a second millennium of further development. This second great phase, Byzantine philosophy—a direct, living continuation of Greek philosophy was in dialectical interaction with Christianity.

Neoplatonic-Byzantine philosophy (from the middle of the third century to the middle of the fifteenth century) was characterized by the dominance of Neoplatonism and Christianity. Neoplatonism manages to synthesize in a single system the key points of the philosophical and religious tradition, creating a system governed by a new metaphysical principle, with a combination of Plato and Aristotle. In Neoplatonism, however, the synthetic elements do not change freely, but are organized on the basis of a fixed framework, a fixed order, which is basically the separation between the sensible world and the supersensible world. This intense dualism is removed within a monism, which is achieved by considering the One as a principle, from which the Mind derives, from which then flows the soul of the world, from which the world of phenomena emerges in a final phase.

Neoplatonism from its very beginning presented points of contact with Christianity. The theology of the ancient Church borrowed many concepts from Neoplatonic philosophy. The most important of these was the concept of substance. Closely related to the concept of substance is the concept of being in ancient Christian theology, which is also borrowed from Neoplatonism.

The first clear demarcation of these dogmatically crucial categories is found in the minutes of the anti-iconoclastic Council of Nicaea (787). In the great iconoclastic controversy, the above fundamental philosophical-dogmatic concepts once again played an important role.

When Emperor Leo III (717–741), in order to facilitate the religious conversion of Jews and Muslims to Christianity, banned the worship of icons, demanding their removal from the churches or their covering, the controversy took on a political character (in 730). The reign of Empress Irene (780–802) marked a major political turning point: under the leadership of Patriarch Tarasius, the iconophiles (friends of icons) convened the Seventh Ecumenical Council at Nicaea in 787, which restored the veneration of icons. The importance of this conflict is crucial apart from its political context, for its philosophical one and its extensions in the field of analysis of the criminal phenomenon.

Iconoclasts started from the premise that a real image must be identical with its original. Thus, they concluded that Christ's representation can only include a representation of His divine nature, which is impossible. They accused the iconophiles (or iconodules) of Monophysitism, that is, that the latter believed that the representation of Christ's human nature represented the divine at the same time. Such a view, they argued, inevitably led to confusion between the two natures. The only co-essential image of Christ, they stressed, is Holy Communion. Contrary to these views, the Synod of 787 proclaimed that Christ is depicted only in His visible, human nature, while the divine is invisible and incomprehensible. The visible depiction of Christ's human nature does not presuppose or imply an acceptance of the possibility of depicting the divine. The error of the iconoclasts—according to the decision—is attributed to the inability to distinguish between original (*principale*) and illustration (image/icon, *imago*). This distinction, which is the key point of the theology of icons, was particularly emphasized by the iconophiles. Behind this ontological gradation, it is not at all difficult to recognize the basic structure of the Platonic theory of the two worlds. The world order of phenomena is a tangible representation of the highest order of ideas, in the fullness of which the things of the visible world participate only imperfectly. By analogy, the icon is not a metaphor, a sign or a symbol, but an ontological *methexis* (i.e., a relation between a particular and a form) in the essence of the represented thing. It is this *methexis* that makes the icon an object worthy of respect and veneration. The veneration given to it "goes to the original." He or she who bows before the icon venerates the being of the depicted. There is a unity between the original and the icon, which is not physical but substantive. This is how the Orthodox Christian Church established the veneration of icons, which is another chapter in the history of the survival of Platonic idealism.

But the conflict over the nature of the illustration/iconicity also means that the body is not excluded from the realm of the divine effect. On the contrary, Byzantine theologians, such as St. John of Damascus, expressed through many writings and emphatically their negative attitude toward the devaluation of the corporeal element vis-à-vis the spiritual one. Thus, in the dominant Byzantine theology, the final personification of the ancient concept of energy took place alongside the conceptual formation of the Christian religion within the context of the Byzantine intelligentsia, as well as the political expansion and realization of the new idea in the historical reality of Byzantine Empire. The process of the objectification and institutionalization of spiritual worship and community, which expanded and constituted the Church, was being legitimized in the mainstream philosophical paradigm. Therefore the leagalization and essentialism became the dominant explanation for the phenomena that take place in both the human and social body.

This dominant paradigm had its counter-paradigms and, after the iconoclasm of the eighth century, these took the form of social movements which violently clashed with the power of the Byzantine Empire, were suppresed materialy and symbolically with official history to record them as heresies.

The main argument (within the context that the material and spiritual conditions allowed to be imprinted) of these heresies was that Byzantine theologians and philosophers of the dominant paradigm, while elaborating philosophically the Christian principles, had falsified the primordial message of Christianity, and the expression of Christian teaching went beyond the limits of the first, genuine historical form of Christianity. Therefore, it was said that it was necessary to return to the primordial purity of Christianity, that is, to the Word of God as it was delivered to us in the books of the New Testament. In the rival dominant view, the text of the New Testament, being the way of the first historical appearance of Christianity, could not explicitly include the content of the fundamental elements of the Christian worldview.

Two such examples are the "heresies" of the "Paulicians" and the "Bogomils" (see Garsoian, 1967; Lambert, 1977) as they were redefined by the official historical record. It should be understood that both "religious sects" did not limit themselves to theological disputes, but put forward a full-fledged challenge to the earthly and heavenly order, as perceived by the official Church and the social and historical terms that challenged the two powers (secular and ecclesiastical), but the consequences of the widespread spread of "heresies" also show that they posed a more serious threat to the existing order of things and, therefore, were one of the most complex social problems.

These two social movements put forward an alternative worldview and ethics to the official worldview that acted as a rejection and subversive of the status quo. It is a general worldview based on different intepretations for the material world and the heavens. Evil as a moral category is now visible as a social condition. This works contradictorily in all spheres of society: it is projected not only as a confirmation of the unreliability of the official Church and the state, but also as proof of the presence of the devil who had to be exorcised.

As in any dynamic confrontation of social groups, the winner imposes his or her own version of events and eliminates the presumptions of the other point of view, namely the version of his or her opponents. In other words, he or she tends to impose his or her own presumptions as the only valid historical evidence. In the case of "heresies" this principle proves to be decisive. Few of the texts of the "heretics" themselves were spared, as they were burnt as a political act of power (like the Bible of the Bogomils). From the beginning, ecclesiastical and political power were opposed to the "heretics" and even acted together, as the "heretic" was treated as an enemy of the Church but also as an "apostate" and, therefore, an enemy of the state. The ecumenical synods that were convened during the first centuries instituted measures how to deal with these heresies. At the same time, most emperors passed laws to punish the heretics with repressive measures, including physical extermination. But let us see in more detail what the Paulicians and the Bogomils stood for.

5   The Paulicians

The Paulicians appeared in the seventh century. They rejected the birth of Christ from the Virgin Mary, while they did not believe in Jesus' crucifixion and, therefore, did not pay homage to the symbol of the cross. They rejected the veneration of saints and prophets, and belonged to the iconoclastic current of Christianity. They rejected the Old Testament,[1] as well as a large part of the New Testament. They did not accept the existence of the clergy and the hierarchy; they accepted only a class of non-privileged initiated teachers (associates and notaries). They had the same rights and obligations as the rest of the faithful without forming a separate privileged layer. They participated in a common and austere ascetic life, as they despised material goods and wealth.

The goal of the Paulicians, as well as of all the revolutionary sects, was the return to the "pure" early Christian communism. They rejected the Byzantine state and the Church as corruptors of society and soon clashed with them. In addition to their dogmatic differences with Orthodoxy, they rejected the Church as a body, too. Thus, apart from the Church of Constantinople itself, the Paulicians rejected the Byzantine emperor, the mercy of God appointed to rule the earth, and His power. The seemingly religious apostasy of the Paulicians took on a political character and meant apostasy against the emperor. As early as 655, they were persecuted when they clashed with the Armenian Patriarch Nersen III. They then resorted to the Byzantine lands, throwing the seeds of a social movement that, although peaceful at first, was quickly pushed into violence and social banditry. It was the constant persecutions that gradually led to the military rupture of the sect with the empire. In 688, Emperor Justinian II ordered the fiery punishment of the followers of the sect and killed the initiated Paulician Symeon-Titus. Before having joined the "heresy," Symeon was a state official of the empire and a fierce persecutor of the "heretics." He was the person who executed another Paulician

---

[1] In Pauline theology, the God of the Old Testament was the evil God (the Demiurge who created the material world). That is why they rejected the Prophets as instruments of the evil God. They only accepted the good God and Jesus, who was sent to redeem people from the Demiurge.

leader, Constantine-Silvanus. After a period of relative tolerance, in the ninth century the final rupture with the empire occurred. Emperor Michael I, at the urging of Patriarch Nikiforos, launched a new brutal persecution, killing thousands of Paulicians, until they found refuge in the territory of the Arab emir of Melitene. In 835, a new persecution was launched by Emperor Theophilus, during which Sergios-Tychikos, the moderate leader of the sect, was executed. Under a new leader, Karbeas, a former official, the Paulicians launched a counter-attack and, collaborating with the Arabs of Tarsus, carried out raids and looting against Byzantine lands. New persecutions were ordered by Empress Theodora and thousands of Paulicians were killed during the siege of Tephrike, while Karbeas was killed by the Byzantines in the besieged city of Melitene in 863. With a new leader, Chrysoheir, the Paulicians responded with raids in Asia Minor. In 870 (or 871), after a failed campaign of the Byzantines, the Paulicians took revenge by carrying out looting, reaching as far as Ankara. One year later, the Byzantines conquered Tephrike and other fortresses of the Paulicians. Chrysoheir was arrested and beheaded by Palladis, a former hostage of the insurgents. The military conflicts that followed until 873 weakened the Paulicians and put them on the margins of history. Groups of "heretics" moved to the eastern Balkans, but the Balkan Paulicians soon abandoned the armed resistance against the Empire. However, their revolutionary ideas took root and sowed the seeds for another revolutionary sect: the Bogomils.

6   The Bogomils

The Bogomils appeared in the middle of the tenth century in Bulgaria. The founder of the sect was a priest, Bogomil (Theophilos). The Bogomils had much in common with the Paulicians, rejecting not only the secular and ecclesiastical hierarchy but also waged labor. They taught their followers not to submit to the authorities, to discredit the rich, to hate the emperors, to malign their superiors, to insult the lords, to claim that God hates those who work for the emperor, and urged the slaves not to work for their masters.

The Bogomils, denying wealth and the secular or ecclesiastical hierarchy, organized their communities to the standards of a strict and ascetic communism, strongly reminiscent of the early Christian communities. The priests were not hierarchically superior to the rest of the faithful ("the laity"), while their interference in the private personal life of the "flock" was strictly forbidden. Their doctrines were clearly influenced by Paulicianism: they believed that the material world was ruled by Satan, they considered churches to be the abode of demons, they were iconoclasts, and they rejected the veneration of the cross and the sacred relics. They rejected the ecclesiastical sacraments (infant baptism, divine communion, etc.) and, as deniers of secular power, they did not pay state taxes.

The followers of the sect were recruited from the lower social strata, mainly small farmers and working cattle breeders, who were involved in intense class conflict with landowners and with ecclesiastical landowners.

Although the sect was initially unarmed and adopted a peaceful stance, harsh persecutions were soon launched against it by Emperor Alexios I Komnenos. The reason for the persecution was the Bogomils' refusal to help the empire in its campaign against the Normans in 1110. In this way, the Bogomils expressed the discontent of the Bulgarian people with the arbitrariness of the Byzantine rulers, but also with the onerous tax measures. The monk Basil, one of the leaders of the sect, was martyred in a fire and three years later, the emperor, presuming negotiations, deceived the most prominent members of the sect and proceeded to enforce arrests, deportations, imprisonments, and confiscations of their property. During the anti-heretical persecutions, the Bogomil sisters of the state official Travlos were also targeted. This resulted in Travlos leaving the service of the emperor and took refuge in Beliatova, from where he carried out looting raids against his commanders.

Despite the harsh persecutions, Bogomilism even took root in Constantinople, and reached Mount Athos in the thirteenth century. It quickly spread across almost all the Balkans (Serbia, Bosnia, Montenegro, etc.), which resulted in significant social unrest, as the Bogomils preached disobedience to the state and the Church, which led to new persecutions. Many of the persecuted and exiled "heretics" fled to France, Italy, and the Rhineland of Germany, and from there contributed to the development of other revolutionary sects, such as the Pure and the Adamites.

Bogomilism gradually became obsolete after the Ottomans conquered Southeastern Europe, but, according to some accounts, some sectarian groups could be found in parts of Bulgaria until the eighteenth century, when they merged with Catholicism. Therefore, the constant persecutions could not suppress the movement, as the sect covered wider social needs, which went beyond the narrow confines of religious insurgency.

The important aspect of both of these "heretical" social movements was that within the context of seeking a convincing explanation for their daily sufferings, they considered attributing responsibility to evil and criminal forces that ruled the Earth—not the good God, but the wicked devil and the organs that represented him, that is, the emperor and the Church, with all the hierarchy he supported. The earthly lord (i.e., the emperor) had been sent by the devil, and the state officials, as servants of the lord, also served the devil. The disobedience of the slave (the cultivator, worker, servant, etc.) to the master (the feudal lord, emperor, or the Church) was a legal and obligatory act.

7   John Italos (or Italus)

However, in addition to the above social movements that tried to express and co-shape the radical counter-paradigm, there were also specific individuals such as philosophers, who contributed with their thinking in this counter-paradigm.

In the eleventh century the philosopher John Italos or Italus (1025–1090), a student of Michael Psellos, wrote that Christian doctrines did not satisfy him and characterized them as immoral. His bold ideas and teachings at the time caused great controversy. He had fanatical supporters and admirers, but also many enemies, including the wife of General Nikiforos Vryennios and daughter of the Emperor Alexios I Komnenos, Anna Komnene (or Comnena) who wrote the history of her time and presented the philosopher's teaching as subversive, and his students and followers as dangerous and disturbing elements. John Italos did not accept the eternal hell and the veneration of icons, while he accepted the eternity of matter. He took it for granted that one could philosophize freely, and drew a distinction between the philosophical and the theological field, believing that one could have different views on each. His teachings made ecclesiastical authority unnecessary even for matters of good and evil. Emperor Alexios I Komnenos himself issued a treatise to refute John's beliefs. John's anti-conformity was finally condemned in both various ecclesiastical synods and courts, with the punishment being the denunciation and destruction of his work and his confinement in a monastery. However, at that time, his ideas met with a popular response. At the same time, an anonymous satire *The Patriotic* presented a discussion between a Christian and a pagan. With a very subtle satire, the playwright reveals all the court intrigues, and the ugliness and greed of the clergy. In other words, this is a satire written by a free thinker who criticizes social ills, imitating Lucianus. In addition, a text signed by Christopher of Mytilene from the same period refers to similar perspectives.

Christopher of Mytilene was a patrician and general of the Paphlagonians, who was alive in the first half of the eleventh century. He was a free thinker and a poetic satire who wrote about the monks, the mire of religion and greed in which they were immersed. Among the verses of this particular satire, he mentions that the monks and the church in general (which was the measure of good and evil, legal and illegal, as we saw above) are "bone merchants."

In the years of the emperors of Komnenos, Ptochoprodromos (1115–1160) was also known for the political lyrics he wrote in the vernacular of his time. In his poems he mocks, and he expresses his complaint about the social misery around him.

8   Georgios Gemistus Pletho

In Byzantium in the fourteenth and fifteenth centuries, a new trend was presented in the science of philosophy and literature that has much in common with humanism. This movement was led by Manuel

Chrysoloras, but much more strongly by Georgios Gemistus Pletho (Woodhouse, 1986). Before them, however, there was the well-known philosopher Barlaam (1290–1348), who opposed the dominant movement of Hesychasm and ridiculed the Hesychasts and their ascetic method, characterizing them not only as *omphaloskopous* or "umbilical" and *omphalopsychoi* "men with their souls in their navels," but also as heretics. Barlaam's views were condemned by an ecclesiastical synod, with the result that the philosopher fled to medieval Italy, embraced Catholicism, and joined Humanism as a teacher of Petrarch. As for the dispute over hesychasm and, especially, with Gregory Palamas, who was the most important supporter of hesychasm, Barlaam should rather be considered an exponent of objections that were lurking in a part of Byzantine society that did not agree with his hesychastic theology rather than a promoter of the controversy. The following century (the last of the Byzantine Empire) was characterized by the personality of George Gemistus, Pletho (1355–1452) and his philosophy that formed an important and radical counter-paradigm vis-à-vis the mainstream paradigm of Byzantine thought. He had already developed serious reservations about the intellectually and politically degenerated Byzantium, while rejecting the Christian religion and its conservatism. Because to his teachings and having been accused of paganism and polytheism, he became the target of ecclesiastical circles of the Patriarchate of Constantinople, who hunted down and killed his student Juvenal. He then fled in a hurry and settled with the help of his friend, Emperor Manuel II Palaiologos (or Palaiologus), in the Despotate of Mystras in 1393. But these persecutions did not stop him. In a detailed memorandum to Emperor Manuel II Palaiologos in 1416 and in a second memorandum to the son of the despot of Mystras, Theodore, in 1423, he formulated a series of pioneering proposals (land reclamation, to be given to the farmers, improvement of their working conditions, strengthening of trade, administrative reorganization, more balanced taxation, more spending on education, nationalization of the army instead of foreign mercenaries, and the abolition of torture). In the winter of 1437/1438, despite his advanced age, he took part in the Council of Florence for the union of the Churches of the East and the West. There, he accompanied Emperor John VIII Palaiologos. A member of that mission to the Council of Florence was his student, the human-ist scholar and metropolitan of Nicaea, Bessarion Trebizon. During his almost two-year stay in Italy, Plethon was brought into contact with the most famous humanist scholars and intellectuals of the West. It is worth noting that Pletho did not write a book until 1437. At that time, he wrote his great work *Nómōn syngraphḗ* (*Νόμων συγγραφή*) or *Nómoi* (*Νόμοι, Book of Laws*)[2]—a work that had clearly utopian tendencies regarding the foundations of state organization, culminating in a polit-ical and social reorganization, from which a state based on a reformed version of ancient Greek polytheism would emerge and in which the people "lived well and to the best of their ability." On this project, a discussion was opened up with Patriarch Gennadius (Scholarius), who condemned it. After his death, Theodora, the wife of the despot of Mystras, Dimitrios Palaiologos, considered it right to hand over the manuscript *Nómōn syngraphḗ* (*Νόμων συγγραφή*) or *Nómoi* (*Νόμοι, Book of Laws*) to Gennadios Scholarius. After having read it, he did not refute it, as he had originally said, but burned it publicly, as he consid-ered it "pagan" and "satanic," containing, as he wrote, "the putrescent of Greeks' silly talks." Only excerpts from this work have survived, includ-ing specific ones that reveal aspects of a radical approach to the conflict with the dominant authority, and Pletho's reflections on the omnipo-tence of determinism. Indicatively, following points can be mentioned:

"On the difference between the greatest human glories," where he analyzes that although all people by nature want to be happy, everyone has the right to find a unique way. So everyone can approach virtue differently.

"About destiny," where he claims, like the Stoics, that everything happens for a reason, the will of Zeus, everything finally finds its place and is guided by the wisdom of Zeus (of the "Most Caused"). However, although everything is predetermined, the freedom of will of every human being remains and each of us chooses the life we live ("mortals, even they are ruled, rule").

---

[2] Available at https://mathgenealogy.org/id.php?id=131575.

References

Benakis, L. (2002). *Texts and studies on Byzantine philosophy*. Parousia.

Benakis, L. (2013). *Byzantine philosophy B*. Parousia.

Garsoian, N. G. (1967). *The Paulician Heresy: A study of the origin and development of Paulicianism in Armenia and the eastern provinces of the Byzantine empire*. Mouton.

Lambert, M. D. (1977). *Medieval Heresy: Popular movements from Bogomil to Hus*. Holmes & Meier Publishers.

Woodhouse, C. M. (1986). *George Gemistos Plethon: The last of the hellenes*. Clarendon Press.

5

From Humanism to the Dawn of a New Age

In the twilight of the late Middle Ages at the end of the fourteenth century, Europe was shaken by calamities that decimated its peoples, political unrest intensified, and the foundations of the church construct creaked as never before. The crisis of medieval feudalism, the development of cities due to the abandonment of the countryside, the weakening of papal power, and the creation of powerful monarchies created a new social canvas marked by the action of two cultural movements, the Renaissance and Humanism, which brought man into focus. In this context, humanist scholars clearly challenged the dominant doctrines of the Middle Ages and criticized the ills of political and religious life (Black, 1992). While the man of the Middle Ages accepted the Pope of Rome as the absolute authority, the spiritual activity of the man of the Renaissance became independent the authority of the Pope and he began to think more liberally and Prometheus-like.

However, it should be noted that the change in the worldview (that is, in the prevailing perception of the world and the man) that was brought about by the Renaissance man in comparison with the man of the Middle Ages was not so radical (some refer to the myth of Renaissance according to Burckhardt's views, as presented in Burckhardt

(1990)—see also Cassirer (1963, pp. 3–4), Parkinson (1993, pp. 1–2), Burke (1997)). Some historians of philosophy classify the Renaissance in the late Middle Ages (with a separate and distinct period of philosophy after the Middle Ages, that is, that of modern philosophy), claiming that the only different characteristic which can be attributed to the Renaissance is that the belief in the existence of God was strongly challenged and the Pope's political power was shaken (see Gilson, 1955, p. 192; Kristeller, 1972, pp. 1–21).

But changes took place and certainly these changes in the way of understanding reality have specific sources. First, the intense philosophical and theological redistribution of power in European universities from the thirteenth to the fifteenth centuries played an important role, along with the power of typography and the use of local languages instead of Latin. The Occamists and Meister Eckhart (a German theologian and philosopher, 1260–1327) used their national language (German) to develop their theories. The philosophical current of the Occamists, which was an important counter-paradigm in European universities, gradually became linked to the humanist movement.

1   Lutheran Groups, the Reformation, and the Holy Inquisition

At the same time, important religious developments took place, and, in turn, they were connected to the new cultural currents. Conflict was now required. Independence from the spiritual guardianship of the Pope as well as the general concern for the content and significance of the Christian doctrine that emerged from the ideas of the mainly Italian Renaissance thinkers resulted in the birth and rapid development of Protestant groups. These groups—John Wycliffe and his followers (the Lollards) in England in 1380, and John Hus and his followers (the Hussites, who accepted Wycliffe's view on Holy Communion, that is, that during Holy Communion they should receive the body and blood of Christ together, and not separately as the Pope ordered) in Bohemia in 1400—caused a serious crisis in Roman Catholic doctrine, which resulted in violent conflicts all over Europe, the convergence of a series of synods, as well as compromise moves by the Pope (in Council of Constance, Basel and Trento). However, the result of all these theological controversies was to prepare the ground for the emergence of the first Protestant Churches. Thus, Lutheranism appeared—that is, the Church that the humanist theologian and philosopher Martin Luther founded in Germany and Low Countries in 1517 with the publication of his 95 Theses (with which he demanded a radical reform of the papal Church and was rejected by the Pope). After Luther, Protestant Churches were founded by Huldreich Zwingli in Zurich, John Calvin in Geneva (and later by the Huguenots in France), and John Knox in Scotland. Perhaps the most important political and religious development of the time took place in England, where King Henry VIII, after failing to secure a divorce from his first wife, which the Pope did not grant him, seceded from the Papal Church and proclaimed himself Head of the Church of England. The Pope, in the face of the uncontrolled and rapid development of philosophy and science, as well as of the Protestant Churches, hastened to react with establishing new orders, which were more disciplined in papal missionary activity and excellent trained in philosophy, as well as in mathematical and natural sciences. Thus, the Order of the Jesuits ("Brotherhood of Jesus") was founded by Ignatius of Loyola in Spain in 1530. At the same time, the Pope strengthened the institutions of censorship by publishing the *Index Librorum Prohibitorum* (*An Index of Prohibited Books*) and by establishing the Council of Inquisition (which recruited important theologians and philosophers from those new military orders of the Church) in order to control the countries that were still under his influence religiously, socially, and politically.

2   Giordano Bruno

As far as the institution of the Holy Inquisition is concerned, it is worth mentioning that several important Renaissance thinkers were martyred following the orders of Holy Inquisition, including the eminent philosopher and cosmologist of the late Renaissance Giordano Bruno (1548–1600). Bruno, after experiencing relative success in the philosophical circles of the Renaissance (mainly in England, Paris, Germany, and Switzerland, but also in northern Italy) through his hermetic and occult, psychological, and philosophical works *On the Art of Memory* (*Ars Memoriae*, 1582) and *On the Shadow of Ideas* (*De Umbris Idearum*, 1582), broke with both the Roman Catholic Church and the Calvinist Protestant Church when he published his work *On the Infinite Universe and the Cosmos* (*De l'inondito, universo e mondi*) in 1584, which essentially overturned not only the Aristotelian geocentric cosmology but also all the other mainstream cosmologies in its time (he was even differentiated from the heliocentric one of the Polish Renaissance astronomer Nicolaus Copernicus (1473–1543). His confrontation with the powerful ecclesiastical authority of the time was intensified by his work *On the Exile of the Triumphant Beast* (1584), as well as by other treatises in which he argued in favor of a general secularism and which emphasized the cosmological and ethical of the heroically fighting and free-thinking man against all the authorities and powers, as well as of destiny or fortune. At the same time, in his works he was promoting a kind of pantheistic materialism that denied basic points of the Christian doctrine. Having been persecuted throughout Central and Southern Europe, he fled to Venice, where he was arrested in 1592 and, after a series of trials in Venice and Rome, was publicly burnt in Rome in 1600, and was considered by many (and is still being considered nowadays) as a martyr of the Renaissance spirit and new science (see Cassirer, 1963; Jensen, 2005; Ruggiero, 2002).

3   Byzantine Philosophers: Barlaam and Petrarch

Finally, the influence of Byzantine philosophers who left Byzantium either because they were politically and socially defeated or they left immediately after the Fall of Constantinople (1453) to the Ottomans played an important role in the rise of Humanism. An early Renaissance figure, the humanist Petrarch (Francesco Petrarcha, 1304–1374) had probably received the best Greek education of his time, at least at the beginning of his studies, alongside the Greek-speaking Italian monk Barlaam from Calabria. Barlaam was born in 1290, had considerable education and training, both in the original texts of Aristotle and Plato and in the scholastic interpretation of them, and was a strong personality. He initially dominated the spiritual world of Lower Italy, promoting a liberal and coherent revisionist interpretation of the Christian doctrine and key passages from the works of Aristotle and the Fathers, and he then sought to extend his influence to Constantinople. The result of his aspirations was the Hesychastic Dispute, with his theological and philosophical attack against the hesychastic practices of the Mount Athos monks. However, Barlaam's ideological and philosophical challenge encountered strong philosophical and theological criticism from St. Gregory Palamas, later Archbishop of Thessaloniki, and it completely failed to exert any influence on Byzantium. The result was the condemnation of his position, as well as those of his disciples, Akindynos and Grigoras, in Pan-Orthodox Synods in 1341 and 1351. Petrarch, as a true student of the liberal and revisionist Barlaam, harshly criticized the Latin philosophical texts, which he considered made both the meaning of Aristotle's works and his philosophical preoccupation with them a sterile and formalistic process of barbarism.

4   Renaissance Historians

But it was not only Petrarch—important historians, such as Flavio Biondo (1392–1463) and Leonardo Bruni (1370–1444), appeared on the scene in the independent states of northern Italy. Bruni, who published his work *Twelve Books of Florentine Stories* (*Historiarum Florentini populi libri XII*) in 1420; Francesco Guicciardini (1483–1550), with *The History of Italy* (*Storia d'Italia*) that was published posthumously in around (1561–1564), and Niccolò Machiavelli (1469–1527) in *The Florentine Stories* (*Istorie fiorentine*), which was published in 1525. Those historians, along with Jean Boden (1530–1596) and his work *Methods of a Better Understanding of History* (*Methodus ad facilem historiarum cognitionem*), contributed to the formation of a new trend in understanding history, rejecting its medieval tripartite division (in which there were the stages of Creation, Incarnation [of Jesus], and the Last Crisis), in favor of a renaissance threefold division (which included the stages of Antiquity, the Middle Ages and the modern era, which they tried to relate to the ancient). In the work of these historians, Antiquity went from being despised (which was the case during the Middle Ages) to becoming the model; the Middle Ages was considered to be a period of illiteracy and barbarism, whereas their era seemed like an era of light and a continuation of the neglected classical heritage. But the important thing in their work is that they tried to disconnect human life from the theocracy and determinism of the medieval historians, introducing other external factors that influenced human life, such as fortune (*fortuna*), and highlighting the absolute power and freedom of the will of the cultivated and educated man. The concept of destiny/fortune was of particular importance at that time, strongly reminiscent of the radical moments of Stoicism of the Hellenistic era. As can be seen in the work of the Renaissance historian Giovanni Poggio (1380–1459), Niccolò Machiavelli, and Leone Battista Alberti (1404–1472), the forces of destiny/fortune exert pressures on the freedom of human will only as long as the human remains uncultured and does not take the necessary actions to overthrow them (see Cassirer, 1963, pp. 73–122). The conflict with determinism did not come as a shock. Let us not forget that the fundamental Augustinian perception of the relationship between faith and knowledge still remained very strong. The certainty of faith (*certitudo fidei*) was based on the triple authority (*auctoritas*)— that of the Scriptures, that of the Fathers and that of the Church—and the rational elaboration of the articles of faith had to be *fidei ratio* (or *fidei intellectus*), that is, Reason that started from faith to lead, in turn, to its assertion. *Auctoritas* and *ratio*, as the two foundations of scholastic-methodological theology, also appeared in the work of Thomas Aquinas. However, the introduction of a rational method of dealing with the problems of faith (due to specific historical reasons, that is, the fact that the Catholic Church wanted to support *fidei ratio* against the *fidei irrationality* of Lutheranism, and against the tendencies of radical and skeptical agnosticism that were developing at the same time) inevitably gave rise to serious difficulties—and correspondingly great reactions. By emphasizing God's *potentia absoluta* versus *potentia ordinata*, the focus now fell not on the fact that God created our known world and our known laws, despite his ability to create others, completely different worlds. So, our world and our logical or moral laws are not necessary in the absolute sense, but rather express the randomness or contingency of Creation as a product of the uncontrollable, unexplored, and therefore potentially infinitely variable divine will. The idea of the contingency (*contingentia*) of the world implied complete certainty as to divine sovereignty, while at the same time, it was abandoned the plan to prove God's existence through a chain of causes or imaginary substances drawn abstractly from the processing of empirical data. And it was this idea that gained ground because it corresponded to central existential and social experiences of the fourteenth century (the shattering of an at least theoretically integrated *res publica Christiana* with the formation of national centers of power and the related defamation of the papacy in Avignon, a number of agrarian crises and uprisings, and the horrific event of the Black Death), and created fertile ground for the radical nominalists of the time. Thus, a critique began to grow stronger and stronger at a social and an intellectual level that pointed out of the limits of the human intellect, which, being forced to rely on the illusory data of the senses, can neither conquer absolute certainties nor expand its narrow horizon decisively. After the rediscovery of Sextus and Cicero in the sixteenth century, the subject of the limits of the human intellect in terms of its dependence on unreliable senses was gradually translated into the language and incorporated into anti-theological skepticism and into humanism. Humanism was rooted in the young and prosperous Italian bourgeois communities, and constituted its ideological world with materials taken largely from Classical Antiquity, when nominalism had already taken root. It reached its full potential and exploited the fact that nominalism remained trapped mainly in terminological trichotomies in order to claim the position of the dominant counter-paradigm in the theories of Augustine and Thomas Aquinas, and to transform theology into science (*scientia*), where the freedom of individual will have seemed to have been lost in the rigid causal definitions of a hyperpersonal (that is, divine) and equally causal intellect. Returning to Cicero's relevant positions, humanists overturned the Platonic and Aristotelian priority of philosophy over rhetoric, that is, the priority of the philosophical ideal of the one and only truth, which is conquered by reason vis-à-vis the rhetorical ideal of persuasion, which can be achieved in a way that is only probable or sophisticated. Reality that rhetoric wants to present and at the same time to influence is fluid, fluctuating and open.

The turn to rhetoric implies that things were seen in their dynamic form, in the endless process of dialogue or contradiction, of friendly or hostile communication between people. Language, as an expression of the infinite richness of human attitudes and situations, is thus a constituent element of things themselves in their dynamic formation and view. Rhetoric undermined the causal and metaphysical view in one more way. It reinforced relativism and skepticism, in the sense that the orator's ability to support (often equally well) two opposing views embodied the dependence of each "truth" on a particular point of view, specific interests, and different types of argumentation.

5   Valla

Lorenzo Valla (1407–1457) justified the above with arguments taken from everyday language use (Mack, 1993). How can one claim, for example, that inside a piece of wood there is potentially a box? And to whom does this "potential" refer, since it can be attributed neither to the wood nor to the craftsman, who, of course, builds the box, but does not create it from scratch? In fact, wood can take many forms, without any necessary relationship between power and energy. That is why everyday discourse is much more accurate when it says that a box can be made of wood and not that wood is potentially a box. The Latin language indicates the above possibility with the suffix *-ibilis*. Valla sought the conformity of our theoretical conceptions with the physical sense, as crystallized in the common use of language. Thus, since the transition from power to energy is abolished, for Valla, there is only the transition from specific actions (*actiones*) to specific qualities, which gives birth to and, at the same time, constitutes the perpetual motion of the world. In other words, the abolition of the Aristotelian distinction between power and energy means that, on the one hand, there is no longer a ready, model world (imprinted at the level of rational construction) and, on the other hand, an unprepared and incomplete world, which must be completed, thanks to the action of some teleology. The world is as it is, constantly changing and constantly complete.

6   Gianfrancesco Pico Della Mirandola (1469–1533)

Agnosticism, that is, the teaching about the limits of the human intellect and its inability to reasonably know the ultimate essence and cause of things, returned strongly many centuries after its last dynamic appearance in Hellenistic times.

Evidence is, depending on ghosts, therefore on the senses, which, as Gianfrancesco did not tire of emphasizing, are uncertain, as they differ from person to person and from moment to moment. Gianfrancesco graciously accepted the possibility to correct one sense with the help of the data of the other as well as to combine an idea from the collection of many impressions. But, he added, this is not enough, because universal concepts, without the help of which there can be no ultimate ontological evidence, are not created on the basis of many, but rather on all individual things. But everything is impossible to fall into the senses and so if we start from empirical conditions, universal concepts are impossible. Besides, evidence is impossible because definition (*definitio*) is also impossible, which, according to Aristotle, must be based on the knowledge of the gender and the specific difference. But the latter does not fall on the senses. Since Gianfrancesco denied the possibility to define and provide evidence on the basis of Aristotelian sensualistic conditions, he naturally rejected the possibility to know the substance through the knowledge of what to know the substance through senses. He states that according to Aristotle, the senses cannot go beyond what happened in order to reach the innermost space of matter. How, then, will the "ghost" be born in the intellect, that is, the image and the representation of substance?

7   Jean Luis Vives and Bernardino Telesio

Within the same context, Jean Luis Vives (1493–1540) emphasized that in no case can we break the barrier of the limits of our knowledge and, therefore, even when we talk about the existence and properties of things, we use measures and weights of our mind. Similarly, Bernardino Telesio (1509–1588), an Italian Renaissance philosopher from Calabria who had studied in Padua, rejected Aristotle's teleology, but accepted Epicureanism and considered it possible that new forms of life and beings can be created and evolved for humans. He wrote the work *De rerum natura iuxta propria principia* (*On the Nature of Things According to Their Principles*, 1565). That work had a great influence on the Renaissance and modern philosophy as a whole; it prompted Francis Bacon to call Telesius the first philosopher of the modern age (mainly because of his emphasis from the beginning of this work on the value of observation of natural phenomena, denying the role of the intellect, that is, intellectualism observed in the dominant philosophical systems up to that time).

8   Gerolamo Cardano

Agnosticism evolved into moral relativism, and that also influenced humanists' analyses of law and crime, and the dominant issue is the opposition to authority.[1] For Gerolamo Cardano (1501–1576), agnosticism refers not only to the mysteries of being, but also to the concepts of good and evil; that is, the practical orientation necessarily implies the adaptation to specific, unique, and unrepeatable situations, where rigid moral truths and their supposedly final knowledge do not help. Doesn't

---

[1] Concrete examples can be seen in *Epitome philosophiae moralis* (1538) by Philipp Melanchthon (1497–1560), who adopted the theory of natural law, arguing that moral philosophy must reveal a sense of law and ethics (Kusukawa, 1995), and in the work *De Justitia et Jure*, or *On Justice and Law* (1614) by Luis de Molina (1535–1600), which was published after his death, and in which he used ethical and political argumentation to argue for the abolition of slavery.

experience show that there is no law, custom, or opinion without an adversary? Thus, by making his theoretical agnosticism into moral relativism, Cardano radically relocated the scholastic notion of the highest good (*summum bonum*) and brought it into the measure of a life wisdom adapted to persons and situations. Every person, he wrote, considers something different as the highest good, depending on what he or she can accomplish. The connection between highest good and virtue is doubtful, since we see that the latter often implies an unpleasant self-denial, whereas evil often gives pleasure. The identification of the highest good with *sapientia* is also doubtful. Cardano emphasizes that the science of human consciousness is radically different from the other forms of consciousness—for example, from the physical form—both in its object and in its degree of attainable certainty. The knowledge of the outside world can only stop at probabilities or analogous conclusions, despite those who claim that human knowledge can at all levels be equated with the knowledge of higher spirits, which do not live imprisoned in a material body. But the human soul, as it is placed in the body and sees the world through it, is not able to penetrate into the essence of things, but wanders on their surface with the help of the senses, examining their dimensions, similarities, and activities.

9 Nizolio

In the same context, Marius Nizolio (1498–1576), wishing to project the demand for a philosophy free from all pressure and all authority, showed that the rejection of universal concepts, *universalia*, which have no real basis, come from the metaphorical use (i.e., the abuse) of language. Since metaphysics in its essence is an abstraction that is completely autonomous from the material world and is crystallized in language, it is natural for universal concepts to be at its center. Nizolio often emphasized that metaphysics stands and falls along with universal concepts, and also knew that the rejection of the latter is tantamount to the expulsion of most of its dominant philosophical tradition at the time. He also interpreted the difference between nouns and adjectives in a way that precludes the conversion of the various properties, as expressed by adjectives, into universal concepts. Adjectives come from the nouns ("criminal" from "crime") and mean a property, which exists not by itself, but in something else. Whereas nouns mean both a substance and a property at the same time, adjectives are limited to denoting a certain property. This insurmountable semantic difference between nouns and adjectives is precisely due to the fact that properties cannot exist as separate entities, independent of substances through which they are felt.

10   Zabarella

Giacomo Zambarella (1533–1589) also called constructed meanings (*cogitationes fabricatae*) logical concepts that move at an imaginary level. But he also went on connecting conceptual relativism to the war against causality. Because, he writes, whatever evidence path we take, whether we go from cause to effect or from result to cause, evidence is made by us and for us, not for nature. Initially we know the result better, but when we get to the cause in detail, then it is better known to us than the result, and we return to the result with its help to better understand it. Aristotle, Zabarella believes, defined causes or principles as the starting point of the evidentiary process not because they precede nature, but because it is the most appropriate order of our knowledge; that is, Aristotle's criterion was the distinctness of human knowledge and not the nature of things. Thus, logic is only a study of human cognitive perspective, since its object is *secundae notions* (the definition of concepts), which do not suggest things as they are, but rather as our intellect conceives them. Any objectivity of the ontological frame of reference thus becomes indifferent, since there is no way for this to be verified. Knowledge is a purely human affair not only in the (self-evident) sense, that those who know are human, but also in the sense that its limits coincide with the limits of human cognitive subjects.

11   Niccolò Machiavelli

The case of Niccolò Machiavelli and his work (and, especially, the thinkers who wrote in opposition to his views) deserves special reference as although he was less versatile than other Renaissance thinkers, nevertheless he has functioned as a catalyst in the modern political and moral thinking of Europe. In 1512, when the Medici family seized power in Florence and overthrew the Republic, Machiavelli was imprisoned for a short time, and he then retired to his estate on the outskirts of Florence, where he wrote his works, the most famous of which was *The Prince* (*Il Principe*, 1513). In this work Machiavelli shows the practical way in which a ruler can conquer but also maintain his power. It takes the form of a political textbook (and there is a great deal of literature on whether Machiavelli regarded it as such or simply as a satire of political textbooks circulating at his time; see the view on this issue by Berlin [1971] and Burke [1972]). Machiavelli's political theory is based on the doctrine that the ruler cannot be limited to exercising his power by any moral law. Calhoun calls Machiavelli's political pragmatism "political pragmatism of dirty hands" (see Calhoun, 2004). The ruler, according to Machiavelli, living in such a selfish society, should not be bound by moral rules, because then he will contribute to the development of a climate of political and social anarchy that for him (and for many of his contemporaries, as well as for our contemporaries) is the absolute evil. In other words, the ruler must support and absolutize his power as much as he can. Even in the case of an unjust, bloodthirsty, and cruel ruler, this is good, since the weak ruler is a bad one (*Il Principe*, XV). This theory advanced by Machiavelli, although expressing the commonly accepted political and moral conceptions by the rising economic and political oligarchy, came into conflict with philosophical, moral, and political theories such as those of Robert Bellarmine (1542–1621), where religious scholasticism met humanism, and had a great impact on the philosophers of the Renaissance. According to Bellarmine, the political power of rulers depends directly on the political community, which has the right to replace them. Rulers' relationship with God is only indirect. Thus, if the ruler does not exercise power according to God's law, then the citizens have the right to replace him (Bellarmine, *De summo pontifice*). At the same time, other important thinkers of the late Renaissance, such as Jean Bodin (1530–1596) and Joannes Althusius (1557–1638), promoted political and moral theories that showed a strong correlation of natural political power and—for the first time in modern times—expressed views on religious tolerance, the historical basis of the theory of law, and the theory of social contract (concepts expressed by figures such as Montesquieu, Voltaire, and Rousseau during the French Enlightenment). In this way, although Machiavelli's theory has received many different interpretations over the centuries (e.g., that his much-discussed work is a treatise on political irony in terms of the way in which absolute political power can be degenerated when it moves away from the moral and political scrutiny of natural law—views that Machiavelli promotes in his other works, such as *Discourses on the First Ten Books of Titus Livius*), the general influence that this work had is in relation to the theoretical elaboration of a moral and political egoism, with pragmatic and pragmatic tendencies.

12   The Seventeenth Century: Science and Positivism

The end of Humanism brought about the dawn of a new era. In the first half of the seventeenth century, a new dominant paradigm began to emerge, science and positivism, and this caused changes in the shaping of a potential radical and critical counter-paradigm. In the fifteenth and sixteenth centuries, skeptics denied not only the rational knowledge of metaphysical truths but also the possibility of a reliable knowledge of the natural world. The pioneers of new science adopted a dual attitude to the tradition handed down from sixteenth century skepticism: on the one hand, they accepted that human intellect is not able to grasp innermost texture—the essence of beings and, therefore, metaphysics as rational knowledge remains impossible; yet, on the other hand, they supported the possibility of acquiring reliable knowledge of natural phenomena, provided that the appropriate method is applied, and the data of experience and experiments are used in the right way. Therefore, the position that knowledge is possible as knowledge of phenomena, relations, and functions, not as knowledge of ultimate causes and substances, involves both partial acceptance and partial rejection of agnosticism and skepticism.

Galileo Galilei (1564–1642) believed that human intellect cannot grasp matter, either earthly or celestial. At the same time, although he admitted the frequent unreliability of the senses, he believed in the possibility of correcting them with (scientific) Reason. He emphasized at every opportunity that nature is a perfectly ordered whole, that it acts with necessity without ever breaking its laws, and that it always uses the simplest means. Of course, Galilei emphasizes the relativity and subjectivity of the human cognitive perspective in various cases. Thus, he claimed that concepts such as "big-small," "near-far," etc. are relevant and related to linguistic habits that depend on the perspective of some subjects, and that secondary properties are a correlation of human senses and would not have existed if the latter had been missing. Nevertheless, he did not doubt that the primary properties, that is, geometric shapes and relationships that stand behind the imaginary data of senses, not only exist objectively, but can also be known with unshakable certainty. Objectivity of human knowledge is based precisely on the priority of the rational order of beings over the rational order of knowledge. In this sense, knowledge remains submissive to being and essence.

Within the same context, Bacon makes a popular argument with those who would like to fight against the teaching of the ultimate causes in the seventeenth and eighteenth centuries without clashing directly with theology: that is, that God accomplishes His intentions precisely through physical laws and not by revoking them.

New science—although it was partly derived from the radical, critical, and skeptical counter-paradigm of the Middle Ages at the dawn of the new era—claimed the place of the dominant paradigm held by Augustine's philosophy and its developments. It simply replaced the divine and the transcendental with the positive scientific method of the natural sciences as an explanation of everything.

Thomas Hobbes (1588–1679) explicitly stated, after all, that God is either identified with the universe or is a part of it. In the first case, His existence has no practical significance, since it means nothing for the constitution of the universe, except for its name. But even in the second case, the consequences are no less important, because if God coincides with a part of the universe, then He cannot have pre-existed the universe and created it, since the part, as a part, cannot be preceded in time by everything to which it belongs.

We see similar conclusions in Baruch Spinoza's (1632–1677) work and, especially, in the abolition of the distinction between There and Hereafter, God and nature, spirit and body. But, conversely, this abolition takes place with the use of conceptual means of old metaphysics, not original ones of course, but ones radically interpreted according to the requirements of the new natural and mathematical sciences. This is how the concept of substance works, which is central to Spinoza's philosophical system. Substance is identified with a universe, the components of which are captured and described based on their functional position within a strictly law-abiding system. Substance is the unity of order and the whole, the ordered lawful whole, where the presence of the whole in the parts is manifested exclusively by the decisive effect of the same single and unchangeable necessity within all natural beings without exception. In this sense, general law determines the texture of each thing—the whole is logically and ontologically superior to the individual parts. But, as Spinoza points out, the whole or the substance is not a cause, which enters into things from the outside, but an inherent cause, since, of course, the substance and nature of the thing is from the beginning related to causality. If so, then substance, as a cause, neither gives birth to nor creates physical beings as an external force would do. Between cause and effect, there is only the relation of necessary sequence, but at the same time, this sequence must be perceived as the simultaneous development of its elements within the fixed and timeless framework of a single/integrated substance.

Positivism, causality, determinism, and the borrowings of theoretical concepts and research methods from natural sciences, which so distinguish the dominant paradigm in criminological thought and research nowadays, have their roots in that very period. If we understand how the transcendental of theocracy became a natural law, which in turn became a transcendental ontology, we will understand the profound conservatism that modern managerial criminology inherently conveys. We can see this in the following reference to Gottfried Wilhelm Leibniz's (1646–1716) thought. To understand natural phenomena themselves, metaphysical knowledge (that is, knowledge of substance) is not necessary, and, in fact, scholastics erred in using it in this field. But the independence of the mechanical explanation of the "system" of phenomena is by no means equivalent to its exclusivity, since this system can be just as well explained teleologically. Both of these interpretations are legitimate, but in two ways: not to mix with each other and, moreover, to accept that the mechanics of phenomena stands under the auspices of their metaphysics. By equating a mechanical view with mathematics and thus underlining once again the hierarchical subordination of mathematics to metaphysics, Leibniz cancels himself and relativizes his view on the possibility to a complete mechanical explanation of natural phenomena with the position that general principles of a material nature and mechanics themselves are more metaphysical than geometric—that is, they refer to some invisible forms or substances. Nevertheless, at least, Leibniz was honest and did not hide the true nature of positivism as modern managerial criminologists do.

In the first half of the seventeenth century, any radical thought about the criminal phenomenon was suppressed. The old that has yet to die (the theocratic conception), and the new (positivism) that has yet to born, which is a mirror of the old transcendental. But this radical thought would not cease to exist: on the one hand, it would just find new, innovative paths to walk on, such as utopias, myths, and literature (as it has always done), while on the other hand, it would wait a few years, at the end of the century and the beginning of the next, to find its place in philosophy in an intellectual current that came to change everything—the Enlightenment—and bring in the new era, an era of revolutions.

References

Berlin, I. (1971, November 4). The question of Machiavelli. *New York Review of Books*. http://www.nybooks.com/articles/10391.

Black, A. (1992). *Political thought in Europe, 1250–1450*. Cambridge Medieval Textbooks. Cambridge University Press.

Burckhardt, J. (1990). *The civilization of the renaissance in Italy* (S. G. C. Middlemore, Trans.). Penguin.

Burke, K. (1972, April 6). An exchange on Machiavelli. *New York Review of Books*. http://www.nybooks.com/articles/10240.

Burke, P. (1997). *The renaissance*. Studies in European History. Palgrave Macmillan.

Calhoun, L. (2004). The problem of "dirty hands" and corrupt leadership. *The Independent Review, VIII*(3), 363–385.

Cassirer, E. (1963). *The individual and the cosmos in renaissance philosophy* (M. Domandi, Trans.). University of Pennsylvania Press.

Gilson, E. (1955). *Les Idees et les letters* (2nd ed.). J. Vrin.

Jensen, D. (2005). *Renaissance Europe: Age of recovery and reconciliation* (2 Vols.). D.C. Heath.

Kristeller, P. O. (1972). *Renaissance concepts of man and other essays*. Harper & Row.

Kusukawa, S. (1995). *The transformation of natural philosophy: The case of Philip Melancthon*. Cambridge University Press.

Mack, P. (1993). *Renaissance argument: Valla and Agricola in the traditions of rhetoric and dialectic*. Brill.

Parkinson, G. H. R. (Ed.). (1993). *The renaissance and seventeenth-century rationalism* (Vol. IV). Routledge History of Philosophy. Routledge.

Ruggiero, G. (Ed.). (2002). *Companion to the worlds of the renaissance*. Blackwell.

6

Utopias

1. The inability to dream of a positive political vision for the future, according to Jameson (1982, 2005), is our failure to escape the cultural/ideological constraints that bind us to today, and discourse (scientific or not) is an important part of these constraints. In the face of the dystopia of neoliberalism and the "realistic" narrative of TINA (there is no alternative), the concept of utopia has been used as an antidote to recent social theories (Ackerman et al., 2006; Bourdieu, 1998; Bowles & Gintis, 1999; Cohen & Rogers, 1995; Eagleton, 2000; Fung & Wright, 2003; Gornick & Meyers, 2009; Roemer, 1996; Wright, 2006, 2010), whereas Malloch and Munro also study it in relation to crime (Malloch & Munro, 2012). It is a concept that has been produced within an historical context, which is its constraint, as Marx and Engels (1970), Engels (1970) and Gramsci reflected upon (*Selection from Prison Notebooks*, pp. 257–258, cited in Hoare and Nowell Smith [1971]). The utopian idea was important and progressive, but was limited by the embryonic stage at which the proletariat was at the time of the development of this idea. However, Adorno (1998, p. 32) also recorded that it is characteristic of urban utopia that it cannot perceive an image of perfect happiness without people being excluded from it. It is conspicuous

© The Author(s), under exclusive license to Springer Nature Switzerland AG 2022
S. Georgoulas, *The Origins of Radical Criminology, Volume III*,
https://doi.org/10.1007/978-3-031-05925-4_7

that when a utopian policy becomes specific, it is forced to answer the specific questions or dilemmas that are posed historically (Goodwin & Taylor, 1982), using norms and patterns that are historically familiar. But let us not be absolute with connecting history with utopia and let us pay attention to Kumar's thought (1991) who states that this connection is problematic, as the concept is timeless, a timeless type of human, social vision, which according to Wallerstein (2001) can take different forms corresponding to different historical moments. Therefore, can utopia have elements that transcend historical boundaries of a scientific discourse and be the seed for its overthrow when it is dominant in its time? And if it has such elements over time and they are primarily part of the critique of the existing model and the need for a better tomorrow, can this tomorrow have a specific value content (Levitas, 1997)? Our question—almost half a millennium after the first editions of the utopias of the late Middle Ages and the beginning of the seventeenth century (those by More, Campanella, Bacon, and Neville)—is expressed as follows: what are the elements of critique and vision for something better in the future, which are included in these works (*Utopia*, *The City of Sun*, *New Atlantis*, and *The Isle of Pines*, respectively) and can they be combined with elements contained in modern scientific discourse so as to be ruptures with dominant theoretical legitimations in the way of delimiting and dealing with the criminal phenomenon? Yet first let us look at them in detail, starting with *Utopia* by Thomas More, which was written first.

2. More than half a millennium has passed since the publication in Latin of *Utopia* by Thomas More. This particular work, which was literary and not scientific, is full of references to issues of delimitation of an act as criminal and, above all, the investigation of different criminal policy measures from those in the mainstream at the time. It was also written evidence of the emergence of an alternative holistic view of social reality, influencing theoretical and socio-political currents of an early socialist transformation of society. The work by Thomas More was named by him as "Utopia" using the letter "u", common from the two conjunctions "ou" and "eu" (in Greek) and the word "place" (*topos* in Greek) in order to state exactly this ambiguous state of the island he describes; that is, the good ("[e]u") and at the same time non-existent

("[o]u"). The author was a multifaceted historical figure, widely known for his influence on English history, both in his actions and in his work: Lord Chancellor in the reign of Henry VIII, a devout Catholic who reacted to the break of the Church of England from papal authority, a martyr of the Catholic Church since 1935 and at the same time a martyr of the Anglican Church since 1980 and an honored person in the Soviet Union since 1918, with his name appearing on the Column of Freedom erected in Moscow in the same year (the obelisk of the revolutionary scholars). But his work *Utopia* exerted a very important influence on the subsequent thinking of other thinkers. Of course, it cannot be characterized as an historical originality, except in the introduction of the corresponding term, as the idea of a place of happiness was an idea recorded in written evidence of ancient Greek and Judeo-Christian culture (to which More had access), which is also recorded and in other, non-Western cultures (Manuel & Manuel, 1979), whereas this kind of evidence was also recorded in the Hellenistic era (Georgoulas, 2021).

However, what More brought about was the rebirth—in written evidence of Western civilization from the seventeenth century—of a thought that did not hesitate to criticize the evils of European feudalism and dared to envision a social change of reality, a better tomorrow, opening the way—according to some—and in a scientific documentation of it in nineteenth-century thought. However, what should be discussed is whether the idea, terms, and specific propositions in *Utopia* can be used to revitalize social thought in modern times and in what way. It is logical to consider that this work reflects its time, the specific historical and social conditions that gave birth to it, as well as reflecting those constraints. On the one hand, we must not "read" these conditions statically, as consolidated, but as dynamic, with reference to an evolving social becoming determined by frequent social conflicts between different social groups during the era of European feudalism and similar to the context of the discourse when it is delivered, adopting well-known and dominant motifs (namely theological ones) in order to make it more readable to the intended audience. On the other hand, such written evidence acquires a relative autonomy from its birth conditions and can be used (and how?) as a guiding thought in a discussion with modern written evidence in order to contribute to a purposefulness that we have programmatically set. In response to the statement that there is no realistic alternative should we follow Jameson (2005) that today there is no other alternative than *Utopia*?

Utopia is divided into two "books" by More himself, with distinct characteristics in terms of content. The first book describes the (hypothetical) meeting of the author with the narrator Raphael Hythloday (Υθλόδαιος, whose name translates as "expert of nonsense" in Greek, which is the "safety valve" to protect More against those who may have criticized him and, consequently, threatened his position as well as his life), a meeting that will end in a discussion—criticism against the way the then state delimited and dealt with the criminal phenomenon. In the second book we have the continuous narration of Raphael about the island called Utopia that he encountered on one of his travels, with special reference to cities, officials, the way of life, social relations, art, and religion. The second book was written earlier than the first one, and in its chapters there are scattered references to how the criminal phenomenon can be delimited and be dealt with in the utopian society. On the contrary, in the first book and in the critique of the existing system, the references to the criminal phenomenon are proportionally multiple, more coherent, and diverse, from specific to those that touch on the social root of the issue.

Starting from the second book, a society of equality in the productive process is described (involving equal ownership and six hours of work for all), relative religious tolerance, while, at the same time, remaining closed, with movement of people being unauthorized. Laws are enacted by social consensus in order to ensure an equal distribution of goods. Already in the first pages of the description of the utopian society, two social "evils" are delimited. The first evil is injustice to deprive the other person of things to benefit you yourself, and the second evil is if you leave the city twice without permission. In this case, there is a sentence of slavery. Other specific references to criminal acts are made in relation to premarital relationships, adultery, seduction, and attempted seduction (because a failure to seduce does not reduce the perpetrator's guilt in any way). The specific reference to such crimes is explained, according to More, by the extraordinary importance it attaches to the concept of family and marriage as institutions that make up the essence of utopian society. It is also stated that one of the most ancient laws stipulates that no one is punished for their religion, while proselytism is allowed without reproach and violence (if there is violent proselytism, it is a crime). At the same time, however, one who believes that the soul is not immortal and that the universe is ruled by fate is not rewarded. Proponents of this theory cannot take public offices or honorary distinctions, or become civil servants, whereas priests have the unaccountable and are not persecuted.

In general, apart from the above laws, no others are mentioned. On the contrary, it is stated that they have minimal laws because their social system does not need many, and those laws they have are known to everyone and are not based on complex legislation (which is criticized). The justice system is not based on lawyers (they have none, and they even criticize lawyers for doing all they can to distort things and falsify laws) and judges. On the contrary, punishments are set within the family, and only if the offense is serious and affects the public interest does the Senate—a body elected by them—intervene, with the assembly of the people being the supreme body. The penalties are equally uncomplicated. They correspond to the gravity of the crime (e.g., for premarital relations, it is a deprivation of marriage, while for troublemakers, it is exclusion from worship), whereas the most important punishments are exile and, primarily, slavery. More specifically, slavery is essentially work in public works, and as such the sentence may be reduced or even abolished either by decision of the elected Lord of the Senate or by people's mediation and depending on the convict's conduct. Death penalty exists only in one case: when already convicted "slaves" refuse to work and are not "tamed." Moreover, euthanasia, with the permission of the priests and the Senate, is considered an "extremely virtuous choice." There is a general perception in the utopian society that complex legislation with special exceptions is not only a way of excluding many from knowledge, but also the basis—along with judges influenced by personal interests and greed—for the decadence of the state and social decline, which is why they criticize neighboring countries with similar legislation. Likewise, foreign relations of the utopian state are marked with suspicion. The utopian people do not take part in transnational coalitions and agreements; they consider injustice done under the pretext of law as a serious problem, even though they serve as judges in neighboring states.

In the first book of *Utopia*, the discussion between the author and the narrator Raphael is described, in which elements of criticism are found in relation to the existing (of the time) system of delimitation and confrontation of the criminal phenomenon. On the one hand, these excerpts are just as important (if not more so) than the detailed formulation of a "utopian" criminal policy given in the second book, although they are not only elements of a negative critique (what is bad and why), but also contain elements of an alternative view of the criminal phenomenon, thus giving specific content to utopia. In support of our argument, we will group the excerpts into two categories, with the first focusing on specialized criticism of ineffectiveness of criminal policy measures and the second on radical alternative views associated with subsequent reflections and scientific formulations of "another" criminology.

The first category includes proposals for the need that sentences should be proportionate to crime committed, as not all crimes are equal, and there is also an opposition to the death penalty because "nothing in the world is worth as much as human life." The mismatch between sentences and the gravity of the crime is ineffective and creates new problems because "by terrorizing thieves too much, we make them killers." At the same time, the effectiveness of alternative punishments, such as the victim's compensation in the case of theft and work in public works as a punishment, is discussed, and it is explicitly stated that crime prevention is a better policy than repression and that restorative justice is effective. The effort to reconstruct the arguments in support of the austerity of sentences, as supported by a lawyer (in the text) is interesting. The narrator responds, on the one hand, by invoking the ineffectiveness of the strict treatment and the need for social protection measures of the poor. When the argument from the lawyer is that there is care for the poor and that they simply, because of their free will, choose to become loafers, the narrator responds that poverty and unemployment come as a result not of a personal choice, but of objective conditions, such as a war that leaves behind the crippled whom no one takes to work anymore. If we want to talk about loafers, why not talk about many nobles who, inactive as drones, live off the toil of others, off the sweat of their collars that literally squeeze them in order to increase their income.

As far as the second category of excerpts is concerned—those that touch on the root of an alternative view of the criminal phenomenon—we can note the following:

(a) The way of life of deviants and no deviants is no different. The relevant example that More used is in relation to thieves and soldiers, and the existing possibility that one role can become the other and vice versa. It becomes conspicuous that with this position, the constitutive differentiation of the deviant is questioned and consequently, the positivist search for the causes that led to this differentiation is also questioned.

(b) First you make them thieves and then you punish them. This is where the reversal of the construct of the positivist approach to crime focuses. Instead of emphasizing the causes, the center of gravity goes to the operation of the mechanisms of formal social control (controlled by the socially and politically sovereigh) that attribute the stigma of deviant.

(c) Following the previous two elements, More clearly raises the issue of how a justice system that ultimately attributes the stigma of the criminal operates. He calls it "inhuman", explaining in great detail how it worked in his own time. He cites old laws that have lain inactive for years, completely forgotten, and that have been violated by all, which are then dug up in order for the relevant fines to be imposed and the king's income to be increased, under the most elegant emphasis of law enforcement and administration of justice. Similarly, advisers can propose new laws that criminalize misdemeanors, while, at the same time, legislating exemptions for gross remuneration, thus filling the coffers twice over. Judges can always find "a window into the interests of the throne", and when there is a dispute between judges, the king's authority gives the opportunity to interpret in his own interests. So, both legislation and the administration of justice are processes that are part of the problem, which is why a system where laws are minimal is proposed.

(d) The root of the problem is clear to More and it is called property: he believes that no society will be fair and happy as long as it exists and everything is judged by money; it will not be happy because much will belong to the few as long as there is property, and there can be no equal and fair distribution of wealth. Laws do not work in a society that rejects communal ownership, says the narrator in *Utopia*. In fact, More makes a specific and detailed report on a cause of the criminal phenomenon in feudal England. This is the expansion of the pastures, when nobles, landowners, and even the holy abbots are not content to live in luxury without offering the slightest thing, but are now set to harm it as well. These unscrupulous vanguards arbitrarily decide to plunder thousands of hectares of land, evict their owners and co-workers using scams, intimidation, and systematic abuse.

What we call crime, according to More, is the inevitable consequence of the aforementioned. But he goes one step further. No reform policy in the above will work. The point is to tackle the root of the problem and the only cure is community ownership. As he states in this regard, laws could be made or the maximum amount that everyone is entitled to hold and laws that place a limit on the property of the king. Laws could also be made to block human impunity and prevent party appointments to public office, which should not be sold. Such laws have a similar effect to dieting and monitoring a serious illness: they relieve and alleviate the symptoms, but they can neither cure the problem nor restore the health of society as a whole. As long as there is property, it will create constant complications.

3. Tommaso Campanella (1568–1639) was an Italian Dominican friar, philosopher, theologian, astrologer, and poet. He was prosecuted by the Roman Inquisition in 1594 and was placed under house arrest for two years. In 1599, he was tortured and sent to prison, where he spent 27 years. He wrote his most significant works during this time, including *The City of the Sun*, a utopia describing an egalitarian theocratic society where property is held in common, clearly inspired by Iambulus or Jambulus' *Islands of the Sun*.

The City of the Sun was written in Italian in 1602. A Latin version was written in 1613–1614 and was published in Frankfurt in 1623. The book is presented as a dialogue between a Grandmaster of the Knights Hospitaller and a Genoese Sea-Captain.

According to Campanella, the citizens of the City of Sun "have to a greater extent surrendered their private property. I think truly that the friars and monks and clergy of our country, if they were not weakened by love for their kindred and friends or by the ambition to rise to higher dignities, would be less fond of property, and more imbued with a spirit of charity toward all, as it was in the time of the apostles" … "Wherefore among them neither robbery nor clever murders, nor lewdness, incest, adultery, or other crimes of which we accuse one another, can be found. They accuse themselves of ingratitude and malignity when anyone denies a lawful satisfaction to another of indolence, of sadness, of anger, of scurrility, of slander, and of lying, which curseful thing they thoroughly hate. Accused persons undergoing punishment are deprived of the common table, and other honors, until the judge thinks that they agree with their correction" … "men and women wear the same kind of garment … and both sexes are instructed in all the arts together."

There is no jealousy among them or disappointment in that one who has not been elected to a magistracy, or to any other dignity to which he aspires, because "no one wants either necessaries or luxuries. Moreover, the race is managed for the good of the commonwealth, and not of private individuals, and the magistrates must be obeyed."

Most importantly, "each one receives what one is in need of" and "every man who, when he is told off to work, does his duty, is considered very honorable. It is not the custom to keep slaves." "In the City of the Sun, while duty and work are distributed among all, it only falls to each one to work for about four hours every day. The remaining hours are spent in learning joyously, in debating, in reading, in reciting, in writing, in walking, in exercising the mind and body, and with play."

"Commerce is of little use to them" … "The people of the City of the Sun refuse to take money, but in importing they accept in exchange those things of which they are in need, and sometimes they buy with money; and the young people in the City of the Sun are much amused when they see that for a small price, they receive so many things in exchange. The old men, however, do not laugh. They are unwilling that the State should be corrupted by the vicious customs of slaves and foreigners."

In the third and last part of *The City of the Sun*, Campanella describes the justice system of this ideal city. Judges do not have a specialization, but a connection with the mode of production, laws are few, simply written and accessible to all, sentences have elements of compromise and mitigation, the purpose is forgiveness, and the greatest crime is that against the freedom of democracy and its symbols. As Campanella specifically states:

> everyone is judged by the first master of his trade, and thus all the head artificers are judges. They punish with exile, with flogging, with blame, with deprivation of the common table, with exclusion from the church and from the company of women. When there is a case in which great injury has been done, it is punished with death, and they repay an eye with an eye, a nose for a nose, a tooth for a tooth, and so on, according to the law of retaliation. If the offence is willful the Council decides. When there is strife and it takes place undesignedly, the sentence is mitigated; nevertheless, not by the judge but by the triumvirate, from whom even it may be referred to Hoh, not on account of justice but of mercy, for Hoh is able to pardon. They have no prisons, except one tower for shutting up rebellious enemies, and there is no written statement of a case, which we commonly call a lawsuit. But the accusation and witnesses are produced in the presence of the judge and Power; the accused person makes his defense, and he is immediately acquitted or condemned by the judge; and if he appeals to the triumvirate, on the following day he is acquitted or condemned. On the third day he is dismissed through the mercy and clemency of Hoh or receives the inviolable rigor of his sentence. An accused person is reconciled to his accuser and to his witnesses, as it were, with the medicine of his complaint, that is, with embracing and kissing. No one is killed or stoned unless by the hands of the people, the accuser and the witnesses beginning first. For they have no executioners and lictors, lest the State should sink into ruin. The choice of death is given to the rest of the people, who enclose the lifeless remains in little bags and burn them by the application of fire, while exhorters are present for the purpose of advising concerning a good death. Nevertheless, the whole nation laments and beseeches God that his anger may be appeased, being in grief that it should, as it were, have to cut off a rotten member of the

State. Certain officers talk to and convince the accused man by means of arguments until he himself acquiesces in the sentence of death passed upon him, or else he does not die. But if a crime has been committed against the liberty of the republic, or against God, or against the supreme magistrates, there is immediate censure without pity. These only are punished with death. He who is about to die is compelled to state in the presence of the people and with religious scrupulousness the reasons for which he does not deserve death, and also the sins of the others who ought to die instead of him, and further the mistakes of the magistrates. If, moreover, it should seem right to the person thus asserting, he must say why the accused ones are deserving of less punishment than he. And if by his arguments he gains the victory he is sent into exile and appeases the State by means of prayers and sacrifices and good life ensuing. They do not torture those named by the accused person, but they warn them. Sins of frailty and ignorance are punished only with blaming, and with compulsory continuation as learners under the law and discipline of those sciences or arts against which they have sinned. And all these things they have mutually among themselves, since they seem to be in very truth members of the same body, and one of another. This further I would have you know, that if a transgressor, without waiting to be accused, goes of his own accord before a magistrate, accusing himself and seeking to make amends, that one is liberated from the punishment of a secret crime, and since he has not been accused of such a crime, his punishment is changed into another. They take special care that no one should invent slander, and if this should happen, they meet the offence with the punishment of retaliation. Since they always walk about and work in crowds, five witnesses are required for the conviction of a transgressor. If the case is otherwise, after having threatened him, he is released after he has sworn an oath as the warrant of good conduct. Or if he is accused a second or third time, his increased punishment rests on the testimony of three or two witnesses. They have but few laws, and these short and plain, and written upon a flat table and hanging to the doors of the temple, that is between the columns. And on single columns can be seen the essences of things described in the very terse style of Metaphysic--viz., the essences of God, of the angels, of the world, of the stars, of man, of fate, of virtue, all done with great wisdom. The definitions of all the virtues are also delineated here, and here is the tribunal, where the judges of all the virtues have their seat. The definition of a certain virtue is written under that column where the judges for the aforesaid virtue sit, and when a judge gives judgment, he sits and speaks thus: O son, thou hast sinned against this sacred definition of beneficence, or of magnanimity, or of another virtue, as the case may be. And after discussion the judge legally condemns him to the punishment for the crime of which he is accused--viz., for injury, for despondency, for pride, for ingratitude, for sloth, etc. But the sentences are certain and true correctives, savoring more of clemency than of actual punishment.

4. *New Atlantis* is an incomplete utopian novel by Sir Francis Bacon, published posthumously in 1627 by William Rawley, Bacon's secretary, the year after the author's death. It seems to have been written in about 1623, during that period of literary activity which followed Bacon's political fall. Sir Francis Bacon, Viscount St. Albans (1561–1626), was an English philosopher and statesman who served as Attorney General and as Lord Chancellor of England in the late sixteenth and early seventeenth centuries. He is considered to be the father of empiricism, and he developed the scientific method and remained influential through the scientific revolution.

In *New Atlantis*, Bacon portrayed a vision of the future of human discovery and knowledge, expressing his aspirations and ideals for humankind. The novel depicts a mythical island, Bensalem, which is discovered by the crew of a European ship after they are lost in the Pacific Ocean, somewhere west of Peru. The plot gradually reveals the island and its customs, but, most importantly, its state-sponsored scientific institution, Salomon's House, "which house or college … is the very eye of this kingdom."

In the more than 15,000 words on his utopia, Bacon does not mention the words "crime" and "criminal" even once. On the contrary, it is stated that:

> "we entered into a good haven, being the port of a fair city...There reigned in this land, about nineteen hundred years ago, a king, whose memory of all others we most adore; not superstitiously, but as a divine instrument, though a mortal man; his name was Solamona: and we esteem him as the lawgiver of our nation. This king had a large heart, inscrutable for good; and was wholly bent to make his kingdom and people happy."

Overall, Bacon's utopia, a utopia dominated by natural law, is character-ized in relation to the philosopher's contemporary societies in the fol-lowing passage:

> But hear me now, and I will tell you what I know. You shall understand that there is not under the heavens so chaste a nation as this of Bensalem; nor so free from all pollution or foulness. It is the virgin of the world. I remember I have read in one of your European books, of a holy her-mit amongst you that desired to see the Spirit of Fornication; and there appeared to him a little foul ugly Aethiop. But if he had desired to see the Spirit of Chastity of Bensalem, it would have appeared to him in the likeness of a fair beautiful Cherubim. For there is nothing amongst mor-tal men more fair and admirable, than the chaste minds of this people. Know therefore, that with them there are no stews, no dissolute houses, no courtesans, nor anything of that kind.

5. *The Isle of Pines*—a book by Henry Neville, which was published in 1668—is considered one of the early utopian narratives, along with More's *Utopia* and Bacon's *New Atlantis*. The book presents its story through an epistolary frame: a "Letter to a friend in London, declar-ing the truth of his Voyage to the East Indies" written by a fictional Dutchman "Henry Cornelius Van Sloetten" concerning the discovery of an island in the southern hemisphere, populated with the descendants of a small group of castaways. The book explores the story of these cast-aways—the British George Pine and four female survivors, who were shipwrecked on an idyllic island. Pine finds that the island produces food abundantly with little or no effort, and he soon enjoys a leisurely existence, engaging in open sexual activity with the four women. Each of the women gives birth to children, who in turn multiply to produce distinct tribes, which view Pine as the patriarch.

However, the book is far from being a utopian fiction and could be considered as a political allegory that uses the framework of a utopian literature. Neville was an anti-Stuart English republican, and as a polit-ical exile he was clearly conscious of the socio-political concerns of the end of the early modern period. He opposed Oliver Cromwell, against whom he wrote some political pamphlets. Starting in the 1650s, he developed a close relationship with the philosopher James Harrington, who wrote *The Commonwealth of Oceana*, a work of political philosophy, an exposition on an ideal constitution designed to allow for the existence of a utopian republic. After the Restoration, he was arrested for treasonable practices in October 1663; he was suspected of involvement in the "Yorkshire rising" and held in the Tower of London.

In the light of this and the failure of Harrington and Neville's political democratic plan to control large private estates and draw lots as the main mechanism for taking positions in administration and justice, Neville wrote the work during the Second Anglo-Dutch War, an island narrative that was framed by the story of the Dutch explorers who were more organized and better equipped than the English voyage of three generations earlier, and who were needed to rescue a small English colonial nation state from chaos.

The island's society is finally dystopian (perhaps the English society of Neville's area?) and, thus, we should look at justice as described by Neville along with the basic argument that supports and legitimizes it:

> Now as Seed being cast into stinking Dung produceth good and wholesome Corn for the Indentation of man's life, so bad manners produceth good and wholesome Laws for the preservation of Humane Society. Soon after my Father with the advice of some few others of his Counsel, ordained and set forth these Laws to be observed by them.

1. That whosoever should blaspheme or talk irreverently of the name of God should be put to death.
2. That who should be absent from the monthly assembly to hear the Bible read, without sufficient cause shown to the contrary, should for the first default be kept without any victuals or drink, for the space of four days, and if he offends therein again, then to suffer death.
3. That who should force or ravish any Maid or Woman should be burnt to death, the party so ravished putting fire to the wood that should burn him.
4. Whosoever shall commit adultery, for the first crime the Male shall lose his Privities, and the Woman have her right eye bored out, if after that she was again taken in the act, she should die without mercy.

5. That who so injured his Neighbour, by laming of his Limbs, or taking anything away which he possesseth, shall suffer in the same kind himself by loss of Limb; and for defrauding his Neighbour, to become servant to him, whilst he had made him double satisfaction.
6. That, who should defame or speak evil of the Governor, or refuse to come before him upon Summons, should receive a punishment by whipping with Rods, and afterwards be exploded from the society of the rest of the inhabitants.

The Dutch came to the island when an inter-racial crime had created the conditions for a civil war. The above laws (and their theoretical legitimacy) obviously could not have prevented the situation, which is ultimately resolved by force by an external factor:

Henry Phil, the chief Ruler of the Tribe or Family of the Phils, being the Offspring of George Pines which he had by the Negro-woman; this man had ravished the Wife of one of the principal of the Family of the Trevors, which act being made known, the Trevors assembled themselves all together to bring the offender unto Justice: But he knowing his crime to be so great, as extended to the loss of life: fought to defend that by force, which he had as unlawfully committed, whereupon the whole Island was in a great hurly burly, they being too great Potent Factions, the bandying of which against each other, threatned a general ruin to the whole State. The Governour William Pines had interposed in the matter but found his Authority too weak to repress such Disorders; for where the Hedge of Government is once broken down, the most vile bear the greatest rule, whereupon he desired our assistance, to which we readily condescended, and arming out twelve of us went on Shore, rather as to a surprise than fight, for what could nakedness do to encounter with Arms. Being conducted by him to the force of our Enemy, we first entered into parley, seeking to gain them rather by fair means then force, but that not prevailing, we were necesitated to use violence, for this Henry Phill being of an undaunted resolution, and having armed his fellows with Clubs and Stones, they sent such a Peal amongst us, as made us at the first to give back, which encouraged them to follow us on with great violence, but we discharging off three or four Guns, when they saw some of themselves wounded, and heard the terrible reports which they gave, they ran away with greater speed then they came. The Band of the Trevors who were joyned with us, hotly pursued them, and having taken their Captain, returned with great triumph to their Governour, who fitting in Judgment upon him, he was adjudged to death, and thrown off a steep Rock into the Sea, the only way they have of punishing any by death, except burning.

References

Ackerman, B., Alcott, A., & van Parijs, P. (2006). *Redesigning distribution: Basic income and stakeholder grants as cornerstones of a more egalitarian capitalism.* Volume V of the Real Utopias Project Series. Verso.

Adorno, T. W. (1998). *Beethoven: The philosophy of music.* Polity Press.

Bacon, F. (1626). *New Atlantis.* https://www.gutenberg.org/ebooks/2434

Bourdieu, P. (1998, January–February). A reasoned Utopia and economic fatalism. *New Left Review, I,* 227.

Bowles, S., & Gintis, H. (1999). *Recasting egalitarianism: New rules for accountability and equity in markets, states and communities* (Vol. III). Real Utopias Project Series. Verso.

Campanella, T. (1602). *The city of the sun.* https://www.gutenberg.org/ebooks/2816.

Cohen, J., & Rogers, J. (1995). *Associations and democracy* (Vol. I). Real Utopias Project Series. Verso.

Eagleton, T. (2000, July–August). Defending Utopia. *New Left Review, 4,* 173–176.

Engels, F. (1970). *Socialism: Utopian and scientific.* Progress Publishers.

Fung, A., & Wright, E. (2003). *Deepening democracy: Innovations in empowered participatory governance* (Vol. IV). Real Utopias Project Series. Verso.

Georgoulas, S. (2021). *The origins of radical criminology, Vol II: from classical Greece to early christianity.* Palgrave Macmillan.

Goodwin, B., & Taylor, K. (1982). *The politics of Utopia: A study in theory and practice.* Hutchison.

Gornick, J., & Meyers, M. (2009). *Gender equality: Transforming family divisions of labor.* Verso.

Hoare, Q., & Nowell Smith, G. (1971). *Antonio Gramsci: Selection from prison notebooks.* Lawrence & Wishart.

Jameson, F. (1982). Progress versus Utopia, or, can we imagine the future? *Science-Fiction Studies, 27,* 153.

Jameson, F. (2005). *Archaeologies of the future: The desire called Utopia and other science fictions.* Verso.

Kumar, K. (1991). *Utopianism.* Open University Press.

Levitas, R. (1997). Educated Hope: Ernst Bloch on abstract and concrete Utopia. In J. Owen Daniel & T. Moylan (Eds.), *Not yet: Reconsidering Ernst Bloch.* Verso.

Malloch, M., & Munro, W. (2012). Crime, critique and Utopia. In S. Georgoulas (Ed.), *The politics of criminology* (pp. 45–62). LIT Verlag.

Manuel, F., & Manuel, S. (1979). *Utopian thought in the Western world.* Basil Blackwell.

Marx, K., & Engels, F. (1970). *The communist manifesto.* Pathfinder.

More, T. (2005). *Utopia.* https://www.gutenberg.org/ebooks/2130

Neville, H. (1668). *The Isle of Pines.* https://www.gutenberg.org/ebooks/21410

Roemer, J. (1996). *Equal shares: Making market socialism work* (Vol. II). Real Utopias Project Series. Verso.

Wallerstein, E. (2001). *Unthinking social science: The limits of nineteenth-century paradigms.* Temple University Press.

Wright, E. O. (2006, September–October). Compass points. *New Left Review, 41.*

Wright, E. O. (2010). *Envisioning real Utopias.* Verso.

7

Myths and Fairy Tales

A common feature of medieval Europe was exploitation and extreme poverty as a result of conditions and policies imposed on the majority of the mainly rural but also urban population at the time. A frequent feature was also the strict nature of a repression, which complemented the imposition of a routine life, restricted to the limits of kinship, where nothing changed and nothing should change, repression as punishment for everything that escaped the control of such a material reality. Evil and crime as both a collective and an individual action were often the breaking of this routine, and such action involved a conflict with the dominant value model imposed within the context of maintaining and reproducing the status quo. The farm children of the Middle Ages learned through oral narrations the stories of Little Red Riding Hood, Puss in Boots, Hop-o'-My-Thumb, and Mother Goose, tales that warned of what would happen if they broke the routine and trusted people who were not closely associated with their kin, which also provided tips for avoiding infringements. But they often learned some other stories, through popular poetry, stories about people or groups of people who challenged the socio-economic and political order of things by challenging those who held the claims to power, law, and control

S. Georgoulas, *The Origins of Radical Criminology, Volume III*,
https://doi.org/10.1007/978-3-031-05925-4_8

over resources. And the corresponding historical figures may not have existed, or their real-life counterparts may have been completely different from the myth—the oral history recordings may be a very slippery source as they were being altered by the way stories were passed down from generation to generation. However, it is worth noting these for the following reason: because the same stories and myths themselves about people who challenged elements of the established order, did justice, and redistributed social wealth through heroism, violence, or humor were persistently repeated throughout Europe, East and West, or across the whole globe as Hobsbawm (2000) tells us, and were the raw material for the heroes of medieval literature that we will encounter in the next chapter. It is a common feature of an alternative to the dominant representation, which then gradually acquired the character of a counter-paradigm.

The heroes of the myths portrayed in songs and oral narratives who initially refused obedience and were beyond the reach of power were themselves potential agents of power, and therefore potentially rebellious. When they became outlaws and possibly subject to punishment, this was due to a crisis with the external criteria of law and order. They were considered illegal by the authorities, but at the same time they remained a part of society and the people considered them heroes, protectors, avengers, fighters for justice, maybe even liberators, and definitely people who deserved admiration, help, and support. Their program, as reflected in their stories, was to defend and restore the traditional order of things as it should be. They corrected wrongs, punished oppressors, and avenged injustices, especially between the rich and the poor, and between the strong and the weak. Nevertheless, regardless of their ideas or goals, they had to be politically realistic. The best-case scenario was for them to maintain a degree of autonomy and, without committing themselves to either side, to sell themselves as protectors to the higher bider. But in the end, they were obliged, if they did not want to be lost, to compromise with any centers of higher power. This can be seen from the fact that their main target was the local representative of the government and not the government itself. They were not an enemy of the king or emperor, who was the source of justice, but only an enemy of the local aristocracy, the local clergy, and other oppressors.

They were, in essence, reformers with modest goals that, according to Hobsbawm (2000), allowed the rich to exploit the poor without exceeding the limits of what was traditionally considered fair. That hero does not require a world without masters. And yet all his life and action in his myth, he was clashing with the dominant (albeit locally) code of values and, especially, with representatives of law, supporting (even at an ideal level) another world with equality, brotherhood, freedom and above all justice. After all, the subjects of most medieval myths that refer to "illegal" nobles and knights (or dames) began their careers as victims of injustice or due to the fact that they were prosecuted by the authorities for an act that they, but not the people, considered criminal. Starting out as victims of injustice meant that they were inspired by the need to correct at least one injustice that had happened to them. So, they would start from the personal injustice and go to their will to correct the collective injustice as they were active members of their community which they defended from the rulers who oppresed it. They created or belonged to collectives with relations of complete solidarity, equality, and identification, and adopted an alternative code of values based on these principles. They stole only from the rich and gave to the poor. They defended the weak and clashed with the strong. They killed only in defense or in revenge. And their actions were admired in their community, which helped and protected them when necessary. After all, they were their defenders, who had idealism and self-denial, and that was why they were usually invisible and invulnerable. They died only as a result of betrayal, although their own death was often disputed or not believed by their community. The people's defender could not be defeated because he responded to a social need or even a nostalgia for justice, for resistance against a social order that denied him, for a need to change things, even temporarily, even at a local level, even if he did not want or could not yet think of a social revolution, a universal protest against poverty and oppression, even if he did not challenge or compromise with the supreme power and simply changed its local exponents. It was enough for him to prove through his actions that justice is possible and that the poor did not have to be humble, helpless, and timid.

1   Robin Hood

Robin Hood is the ultimate example of such a myth. He wanted to fight the unjust and he too was a victim of injustice—the noble bandit who dealt with the representative of the law, the Sheriff of Nottingham, who pursued him on the orders of the king. The Sheriff committed widespread abuses of power, appropriating land, unjustly hunting the poor, and imposing exorbitant taxes on his subjects. Overall, stories featuring Robin Hood differed from season to season, as Robin himself changed character and experiences, depending on the values and ideals attributed to him each time. He started as an illegal avenger and ended up as a noble bandit. After all, Robin Hood had already been known as a criminal figure by the 1260s'. The first reference to an historical figure named Robin Hood comes from the work of Andrew of Wyntoun's Orygynale Chronicle, which was written in around 1420:

> Lytil Jhon and Robyne Hude
> Wayth-men ware commendyd gude
> In Yngil-wode and Barnysdale
> Thai oysyd all this tyme thare trawale.

The oldest surviving text on Robin Hood was written in around 1450 and is entitled *The Robin Hood and the Monk*. It contains many elements of the legend, from the Nottingham area to the feud between Robin and the Sheriff. The details added later are Robin Hood's romantic relationship with Maid Marian, a sixteenth-century addition, and the fact that Robin Hood was opposed to Prince John and collected the ransom for King Richard I's release in versions of the legend that appeared in the nineteenth and twentieth centuries (see Blamires, 1998; Coghlan, 2003; Deitweiler & Coleman, 2004; Dixon-Kennedy, 2006; Doel & Doel, 2000; Hahn, 2000; Knight, 1994, 2005; Phillips, 2003; Rutherford-Moore, 1999, 2002).

Corresponding "Robin Hoods" exist in myths throughout Europe, according to Hobsbawm (2000). In Russia, Scotland, Slovakia, Andalusia, Valencia, Catalonia, and elsewhere, there are stories of noble outlaws who protected the poor and clashed with local authorities, associated with collectives with equal ties, and hoped for a better world, as recorded in folk songs and stories. In the original form of the avenger who belonged to a collective and was stealing from the rich, folk tales have been respectively recorded about the Catalan bandits of the sixteenth and seventeenth centuries, the Cossacks in Russia, and the Haiduks in Ukraine, Hungary, and the Balkan Peninsula.

2   William Wallace and Rob Roy MacGregor

William Wallace, a Scottish nobleman and hero in the war against England during the First War Scottish Independence, was praised by poets and artists, especially the fifteenth-century troubadour Blind Harry, as an outlaw and an avenger, but also as a visionary for a better future for his community (Murray, 1996; Stevenson, 2004). Rob Roy MacGregor, also in Scotland, a popular hero and outlaw in the late seventeenth century, came from an illegitimate and violent family. Precisely because his family was notorious for its violence, the MacGregor family name had been banned by law since 1603. The law established the death penalty for anyone bearing that name. Rob Roy took part in various Scottish uprisings, but initially followed an "honest" life as an animal trader. This changed when he borrowed a large sum of money to increase the size of his herd, but due to the disappearance of the chief shepherd, to whom he had entrusted the money and his herd, he lost the money and the animals, and failed to fulfill his loan obligations. As a result, he was outlawed and his wife and children were evicted from their home, which was then burnt down. After a series of harsh winters, he began raiding the wealthy Lowlands properties to feed his clan. After his main creditor, James Graham, 1st Duke of Montrose, seized his fields, Rob Roy unleashed a private bloody vendetta against the Duke. Rob Roy plundered the Duke's land and the cattle breeders at that land. If he did not steal from them directly, he would ask them for money to protect them or not to steal from them. The wild area, with its forests, rocks, and ravines, as well as the sympathy shown to him by the poor, made his work almost harmless. Rob Roy repeatedly escaped prison, gaining a reputation similar to that of Robin Hood in England. Like Robin Hood, he was surrounded by a small group of supporters.

3   Rodrigo Diaz de Vivar or El Cid

Rodrigo Diaz de Vivar was a Castilian noble and military leader in medieval Spain (McNair, 2010). The Moors called him El Cid, which means "The Lord," and the Christians called him El-Kabeador, who was attributed to meaning the *Great Warrior* or the *One who stands out on the battlefield*. He was born in Vivar, a town near Burgos. After his death, he became the most honored national hero of Castile and the protagonist of the most important medieval Spanish epic poem, entitled "The Song of El Cid." He served as commander-in-chief of the Castilian army under King Sancho II of Castile, while he was exiled by the brother and successor of Alfonso VI. This exile was the trigger that spurred him into action and culminated in the conquest of the rich city of Valencia. The constant military triumphs against Christians and Muslims, as well as his habit of not governing according to the feudal customs of the time, made him beloved by the Spanish people and a role model for the knights of his homeland. After his death, his achievements, both real and imaginary, were sung by troubadours, creating a legend around his name. He is considered the national hero of Spain.

Avengers-heroes, outlaws but beloved in their community, who clashed with those in power, law enforcement, and the dominant value system, whether real or not, became myths and didactic oral and written stories, especially in the last centuries of the medieval era, when the conditions for the social change that was to come began to develop. These myths evolved, but their characteristics remained imprinted in these stories, characteristics that we find in the myths of previous centuries, such as the myths of King Arthur and the Knights of the Round Table. The position of power was acquired by a display of skills and is not given away (pulling the sword Excalibur from the stone), there was a collective with the main feature of equality (there was no head of the round table), and the main task was to correct the injustices done to the weak using means that were in opposition to the established order of things. When the heroic knights were unable to find a way forward, the one who gave the solution was the magician Merlin, the illegitimate son of a royal princess, with a demon father, who raised Arthur and helped the Knights of the Round Table in every adventure, using methods that the Christian religion did not condone.

4   Female Figures: Genevieve, Lady Godiva, Bluebeard's Wife, and Pope Joan

However, medieval Europe also had myths and didactic stories about women who aimed at and succeeded in correcting injustices (to the detriment of themselves or the people at large) or even claimed roles that did not suit their social status. Genevieve (also Genoveva or Genovefa) of Brabant is a central figure in a medieval legend about a chaste woman of the then Duchy of Brabant, a geographical area that now belongs to Belgium, Luxembourg, and Germany, who was falsely accused of adultery during her husband's absence (who was fighting the Arabs) and was expelled along with her son. When servants were called to carry out the order and kill her along with her young son, they refused and left her in the forest of the Ardennes, where she sought shelter in a cave to protect herself from the elements. Miraculously two days later, she saw a deer come and offer her milk to feed her son. She remained there for six years, so when Siegfried, her husband, was hunting in the area and following in the footsteps of the deer, he unexpectedly found Genevieve and his son. Lady Godiva (*Godgifu* in old English) was a late Anglo-Saxon noblewoman who is relatively well documented as the wife of Leofric, Earl of Mercia, took a stand against her feudal husband for the exorbitant taxes he imposed on his subordinates and reacted by riding naked in public until the unjust measures were taken back. Bluebeard's wife, in the French fairy tale, married to a rich and violent man who had a habit of killing his wives, avoided the fate of her predecessors and killed her husband, revealing his dark past. To reach such an act, she first went to explore a forbidden room, in which she immediately discovered that the room was full of blood and the murdered corpses of Bluebeard's ex-wives were hanging on hooks from the walls. Eventually, with the help of her family, she killed her murderous husband, inherited his property, which she used to pay for the marriages of her siblings, and finally remarried a man she loved. Pope Joan (*Ioannes Anglicus*, 855–857), a legend that has circulated widely since the thirteenth century, was a multi-talented and well-educated woman, who hid her true identity under men's clothes. Because of her abilities, she managed to ascend the ecclesiastical hierarchy and was eventually elected Pope. During her papacy, she fell in love with her steward, by whom she became pregnant. So, during a papal litany, while she was in the early stages of pregnancy, she gave, birth revealing her true sex.

5   Digenis Akritas

In Eastern medieval Europe, the tradition of disobedience and rebellion of the popular strata in rural and urban areas took the cultural dimension of folk and acritic songs and myths that would later lead to the epic poem of 'Digenis Akritas' in the ninth and tenth centuries. The inherent inability of the social systems of the Byzantine and Ottoman Empires to assimilate solid masses of population and the violent repulsion of the latter to the political or social fringes seems to obscure much more complex contradictions. Disobedient groups instead form a type of a society that point by point reversed the set of principles, values, and practices in which the institutions of the established society were established and functioned as organized networks between illegality and legality. However, often the points of coincidence with the ruling class were more than seemed to be the case at first glance.

The work with which the literature of modern Greek literature usually begins, as it was the first to be written in the colloquial language of the Byzantine Empire, Greek, the epic novel *Digenis Akritas*, is not preserved in its original version. The acritic songs were folk songs, most of which, in the tenth century, had as their main character the superhero Basil (Vassilios) Digenis Akritas ("two-blood border lord"); it has been speculated that, as the available evidence testifies, in the twelfth century an unknown scholar collected them and edited them to compose an extensive epic poetic work on a fictional character. Six later adaptations of the work have survived: of these, the two oldest and most studied are those of Grottaferrata (G) and Escorial (E), which are delivered in the respective manuscripts, the former in the monastery of the same name outside Rome, and the latter in the monastery of the same name in Madrid (Jeffreys, 1998). Both of these adaptations are written in iambic 15-syllable verse, but although they come from the common written archetype mentioned above, they have important differences: on the one hand, G is much more extensive, has been clearly worded, written at a higher linguistic level and has a more elaborated style, while presenting more obvious influences from the novels of Late Antiquity and incorporating different ideological elements (e.g., the ethos of the Byzantine aristocracy of the twelfth century); on the other hand, E is less than half the size of G, is characterized by an economy in style, a fast-paced narrative style, and liveliness in imagery. Digenis Akritas was a heroic knight of Byzantium who traced his family lineage to the leader of the Paulician movement. He displays all the characteristics of the illegal knights of the Western Middle Ages. He fought against the unjust, with his emblem that power creates law while treating the emperor as an equal. He believed that he had the right to give the emperor advice and to insist that it should be executed. Contrary to the prevailing view of his time, which propagated the notion that women were always cursed and the personification of Satan, and from her come the wicked, the *akrites* and Digenes himself sang love songs and considered women to be the personification of purity and virtue.

6   Demotic Songs: "Kleftic" Songs and Kleftarmatoloi

Demotic (folk) songs, "Kleftic" songs or kleft-songs (where "Kleft" means thief, and refers to the brave men who lived in the mountains during the Ottoman subjugation, fighting their oppressors), songs of outlaws continued in the following centuries of the Byzantine and Ottoman Empires as fiery praises the individual spirit of the mountaineering farmer who did not submit to the established order of things and stood up against the oppression of the powerful local ruler (toparch). The hero of these songs is a hero who has a special code of honor (targeting the rich and powerful and defending the weak) and endangers the local authorities with his actions because of their harsh tax collection, a practice often denounced as unfair. The "kleft," the thief of the East, not only does not live in a state of rupture with the rest of society, but, on the contrary, is a legitimate means of social regulation. After all, his power has its source in the existence of a vast network of real kinship ties. From the 15th centurey onwards, especially after the Ottoman subjugation of the Byzantine territories there was a further delevopment of the character of the "klefts"—thives and a creation of a new reality that was also glorified through myths and songs: The *Kleftarmatoloi* ("Klefts" [thieves] + "armatoloi" [Christian Greek irregular soldiers, or militia, commissioned by the Ottomans to enforce the Sultan's authority within an administrative district called an *Armatoliki*]). The term illustrates the one who steals and at the same time the one who pursues the thieves, someone who can steal on one occasion and police the situation on another. The term ultimately indicates a social and political strategy which was developed based on one's ability to successfully use violence and direct armed forces, sometimes looting and sometimes preventing the looting of one's fellow humans. The hero is now characterized by an antinomy, a self-defeating tautology: thief and guardian, subservient and disobedient, *ragias* (*raya* [Turkish from Arab]—enslaved) and armed.

The hero of the "Kleftic" ballads, demotic/folk songs was the one who, by stealing, undermined the security mechanisms in place in order to show the local community and the regional authority that he was capable of taking the position of guard himself. The same strategy also included the armed man (*armatolos*) who, after having been proven insufficient in the role of guard, resorted again to looting in order to weaken the one who replaced him, to strengthen himself through looting and to re-occupy the position of guard. However, in any case, the fundamental elements of his identity are not denied, which were also those that are praised in the folk songs: disobedience, freedom, and real integration into the community which he protected either as a thief ("kleft") from the evil ruler (Ottomans) or as an *armatolos* (armed man) from the evil thief. Things become even more relevant in the value model when we see in those stories about the armed man (*armatolo*) who, after having been proven insufficient in the role of guard, resorted to looting again in order to weaken the one who replaced him, tried to strengthen himself through looting and re-occupy the position of guardian. Those in power, for their part, appointed the most capable among them to the *armatolikia* in order to avoid the cost of prosecuting the "klefts." The *armatoliki* (singular of *armatolikia*), an enviable position and the intended end of the local armed forces, is at the same time a mechanism to integrate the disobedient and a field to confine rebellion and disobedience to the reproduction of the system. But the paradox and the interesting thing with the *kleftarmatoloi* and the corresponding "kleftic" songs is to legitimize not those who won the fight and were part of the contractual relationship between the conquerors (Ottomans) and the conquered (Greeks), but those who escaped persecution or whose persecution had been proven to be ineffective and uneconomical. The unconventional is praised and, in the end, this is what is rewarded, even in a symbiotic relationship, which would always be temporary.

7 Satirical Heroes

Heroes, knights, outlaws, and avengers who appeared in myths are not the only ones who opposed the value system and produced representations that conflicted with the established knowledge of right/justice, wrong/injustice, and legality/illegality. Equally important for the same purpose are the myths of satirical heroes that and in turn clashed with the dominant representations of the criminal phenomenon.[1] There are the anonymous satires with heroes (usually animals), such as *Synaxarion of the Honorable Donkey*, in which the donkey is unjustly accused of crimes it did not commit and is to be eaten by the wolf and the fox. But in the end the hard-working and ill-treated donkey outwits the wily wolf and the cunning fox, and manages to throw them into the sea.

---

[1] Available in Greek at http://georgakas.lit.auth.gr/dimodis/index.php?option=com_chronoforms& chronoform=showErgo&ergoID=56&Itemid=280.

In *Porikologos* (Πωρικολογος: lit. *Fruit Book*), in which all the parts are played by fruit, late Byzantium legal procedures and court ceremonial are satirized.

In the satire *The Childish Narrative of Four-Legged Animals*, the lion organizes an assembly of four-legged animals to describe the virtues and vices of each. Each one states its strengths and exposes the others' weaknesses. After the speeches are delivered, the battle commenced, and all the domesticated animals were pitched against the wild animals, and they defeated them. As it is often stated, power is in the many.

In the Western Middle Ages, there are fairy tales featuring Reynard, who is the main character in a literary circle of Dutch, English, French and German allegorical myths. Reynard is a cunning anthropomorphic red fox. His adventures usually involve him cheating other anthropomorphic animals to his advantage or trying to avoid retaliation from them as a result. His main enemy and victim throughout the circle is his uncle, the wolf Isengrim (or Ysengrim). The stories usually contain satire of the aristocracy and the clergy, making Reynard a character of a spatial hero who cunningly challenges established authority. More specifically, Reynard represents the medieval burghers, the lion represents the monarch, the bear represents the medieval landlords, the wolf Isengrim (or Ysengrim) represents the medieval knights, the donkey represents the clerical class, and small animals like the chicken, the hare, the snail, and others represent the populace.

8   Karagiozis or Karaghiozis (Turkish: *Karagöz*, "Dark Eye")

In the medieval Ottoman reality, another manifestation of popular culture developed as an externalization of an eternal popular soul that evolved over the years and persists to this day in modern Greece and Turkey. It is the shadow puppet theater and its hero, Karagiozis (or Karagöz in Turkish) who has starred in thousands of short comic stories by unknown authors (Myrsiades, 1988; Myrsiades & Myrsiades, 1992). Ottoman society, the immediate successor of the Byzantines, was a vast melting pot where an infinite variety of original products of an advanced cultural fusion came to light over the course of four centuries. Since his appearance, Karagiozis and the shadow puppet theater have experienced a significant spread in those urban centers with impoverished neighborhoods.

Karagiozis/Karagöz is the social type who most successfully embodies uncorrected agitation with a sparkling sarcastic spirit, an eternally cheerful person, a relentless mocker who parodies everyone and everything, even himself: a relentless and sincere liar, to the point of cynicism, naive but cunning at the same time, ignorant, stupid, and immoral, but also eloquent and generous, an object of contempt and the target of everyone's aggression. The harshness of Karagiozis' language, cynicism, and brutal manners are his first features. His other two main features are his incurable poverty and his unbridled call to theft. One of his chief characteristics is the minimal dedication he shows to current ethics, as recorded in the shadow-puppet theater stories. When Beis (local ruler) criticizes him, using the conventional expressions used by the rich for the poor that he is lazy but honest, Karagiozis accepts everything without objection, except the last adjective (honest), with which he strongly disagrees. Karagiozis ridicules the wishes that Beis gives him for his marriage and, he confuses marriage with a funeral. In another incident when he is invited to take something to a cafe to meet his future employer, he prepares to pick up all the furniture in the store along with the cash register and the box with the *lokums* (Turkish delight), thus showing ignorance of the good manners. The signs of the hero's popular origin and, in fact, of his marginal status are emphasized more in his external appearance. On the one hand, he is always barefoot and dressed in clothes with patches. On the other hand, the excessive length of his right hand consists of many joints and allows him to exercise his talents in both petty thefts and cuffs, emphasizing his illegal behavior and impulsive nature. His main opponent in all the stories of the shadow-puppet theater, apart from Beis, is Hadjiavatis, who is a caricature of the petty bourgeois classes and the elements that distinguish these classes—that is, work, order, stability of rhythms of life, deprivations, patience, and acceptance of the established order.

Hadjiavatis is a moralist and, gifted with a layer of a elaborated discourse that allows him to present himself as a privileged interlocutor of the upper classes, longs with all his heart to become a respectable person and to advance socially. That is why he tries to imitate the manners and language of the upper classes in order to look like someone who deserves their trust. And this is exactly what Karagiozis laughs at. Tricks and cunning, unexpected situations, puns, stage events, representation of the figure, physical and costume characteristics, postures, movement, joints, disguises and, especially, the language with misunderstandings of voice or grammar, distortion, tics, and puns, are some of the common ways to express a catalytic mochery, far beyond a simple social protest. Karagiozis is placed in the most radical version of questioning the system as a whole, as well as in its fundamental principles, social, cultural, and moral order, and its seemingly unshakable rationality. This disobedient, irreconcilable, and catalytic spirit of Karagiozis is activated through parody, exaggeration, or distortion words, objects, and situations, and is exercised against any element of the behavior, mentality, language, lifestyles, and values of the upper classes. A mockery of sophisticated language of the elected members of good society, of their knowledge, their refined taste and of their artistic sensibility. A mockery of the paternalistic and condescending attitude of the privileged who have invented the poor but honest man. Mocking the good manners that hide hypocrisy and cruelty of the rich boss towards the poor man who works for him. The comic findings are not the only elements through which the fundamental division between the common people and the upper class are projected. This bifurcation seems to be present in all the significant aspects of the spectacle, from the kinetic and the scenic to the symbolic in certain situations. The deeper meaning behind Karagiozis' repeated attempts to dig into the forbidden garden of the rich is to underline once again the impenetrable barrier that separates the world of waste from the wonderful world of wealth and education.

The significance of the stereotypical setting of the Karagiozis, which puts the hero's shack and the luxurious palace of the lord (that of the Vizier [i.e., the local Ottoman lord]) in direct contrast to each other is the visualization of the same barrier in the most categorical way. The violence (of Karagiozis against Hadjiavatis) against argumentation, savagery against the soft behavior, ignorance against the cultivated or falsely cultivated spirit, force against refined language, in a specific and liberating feeling that the popular public would feel, is the feeling of revenge that the lower culture gets towards the higher culture, the triumph of popular values that overestimate the physical strength against euphemisms of the rhetoric of the educated.

Karagiozis is a hero who, in every short story, commits violations and crimes according to the established code of values. But he is also the hero who raised dozens of children from medieval Anatolia to the present day.

References

Blamires, D. (1998). *Robin Hood: A hero for all times*. John Rylands University Library of Manchester.

Coghlan, R. (2003). *The Robin Hood companion*. Xiphos Books.

Deitweiler, L., & Coleman, D. (2004). *Robin Hood comprehension guide*. Veritas Pr Inc.

Dixon-Kennedy, M. (2006). *The Robin Hood handbook*. Sutton Publishing.

Doel, F., & Doel, G. (2000). *Robin Hood: Outlaw and greenwood myth*. Tempus Publishing.

Hahn, T. (2000). *Robin Hood in popular culture: Violence, transgression and justice*. D.S. Brewer.

Hobsbawm, E. (2000). *Bandits*. The New Press.

Jeffreys, E. (1998). *Digenis Akritis: The Grottaferrata and Escorial versions*. Cambridge University Press.

Knight, S. T. (1994). *Robin Hood: A complete study of the English outlaw*. Blackwell.

Knight, S. T. (2005). *Robin Hood: A mythic biography*. Four Courts Press.

McNair, A. J. (2010). El Cid, the impaler? Line 1254 of the poem of the Cid. *Essays in Medieval Studies, 26*, 45–68.

Murray, W. H. (1996). *Rob Roy MacGregor: His life and times*. Canongate Books Ltd.

Myrsiades, L. S. (1988). *Karagiozis heroic performance in Greek Shadow Theatre*. University Press of New England.

Myrsiades, L. S., & Myrsiades, K. (1992). *Karagiozis: Culture and comedy in Greek Puppet Theater*. University Press of Kentucky.

Phillips, H. (2003). *Robin Hood: Medieval and post-medieval*. Cornell University Press.

Rutherford-Moore, R. (1999). *The legend of Robin Hood*. Capall Bann Publishing.

Rutherford-Moore, R. (2002). *Robin Hood: On the outlaw trail*. Capall Bann Publishing.

Stevenson, D. (2004). *The hunt for Rob Roy: The man and the myths*. John Donald Publishers.

8

Literature

1. The history of societies should be based on an analysis of material structures. But many people regulate their behavior not only in relation to their real situation but also according to the image they have of it, which is never a reflection of reality. They try to subjugate it to patterns of behavior that are the fruits of a culture and that sometimes adapt to material realities that are sometimes better and sometimes worse during the course of history. An important role in these representations is played by the great works of literature of each era, which also address an important quantitative part of the literate population. It is probably true that criminologists have more to learn from the literary world than the reverse. The two disciplines are "two groups of thinkers, both looking at the same object but going their separate ways" (Sagarin, 1980, p. 75).

Art is the best weapon for thought, the best way to deconstruct simplistic schematic interpretations of reality. Without it, how could we move forward?

So, let's start our journey to indicative areas, authors, and works during the period under examination here and see the heroes imprinted on paper through the imprinted words and phrases (words and heroes

S. Georgoulas, *The Origins of Radical Criminology, Volume III*,
https://doi.org/10.1007/978-3-031-05925-4_9

timeless), elements that contribute to building an counter-paradigm of the dominant point of view of the era regarding crime and law. On this voyage, we will make four stops: England, Italy, Spain, and Southeastern Europe.

1   England: Chaucer and Shakespeare

In England, two of the most important creators who left their mark at different points in time of the eras examined in this volume, but whose works exceeded these times limits, are Chaucer and Shakespeare.

Geoffrey Chaucer (1343–1400), whose tomb is located in the pantheon of great tombs in "Poets' Corner" in Westminster Abbey, represents the great and revered tradition that refined medieval English. He wrote *The Canterbury Tales* in the spoken language in his days; he is considered to be the father of English literature and that he essentially developed the English iambic pentameter. The impact of his work was enormous on the English literature and beyond. In the 15th century, a school called "Chaucerians" was established, the members of which imitated his poetry.

The Canterbury Tales[1] are told by about 30 men and women who set out for a pilgrimage to Canterbury to visit the shrine of St. Thomas Becket at Canterbury Cathedral, aiming to win the prize of a free meal at the Tabard Inn at Southwark on their return. The distance between London and Canterbury is 85 km, a distance which, at the time, was significant, and the journey was long. So, in order to pass the time, the pilgrims told each other stories. Everyone was a representative type and together they formed a society in miniature. We have the Knight, the Friar, the Physician, the Merchant, and others, with the most representative of all, of course, the Pardoner, a unique, complex, and masterfully shaped character that has no equal in world literature. Chaucer mentions in his stories both John Wycliffe's uprising against the English

---

[1] Available at https://www.gutenberg.org/ebooks/2383.

Catholic Church and the Peasants' Revolt of 1381. The irony with which he treats the human as well as the Christian England of the time, which was in the midst of a deep crisis, ends in a vague and at the same time charming sadness. But the most fascinating thing about the whole book is not the stories themselves, but the way in which Chaucer highlights the narrators' personalities. Stories function as character projections. Whereas the narrative is linear (one story follows another), Chaucer creates levels that relate, on the one hand, the stories to each other and, on the other hand, to the narrators' personalities. Thus, one theme refers to the other, and each story looks like a preface to the next.

The role of the coordinator of the narratives with interventions, suggestions, remarks, or praise is taken over by the Host and owner of the inn. Chaucer planned to frame the five-day trek with four stories from each of the 30 or so narrators (two on the way and two on the way back) and to complete the work "in a circle" (with a meeting at the Tabard Inn, where the narrator of the best story would be offered dinner at the expense of the rest), but did not complete his plan.

Each of Chaucer's characters expresses different—sometimes very different—views of reality, creating an atmosphere of testing, empathy, and relativism. As Helen Cooper (1996) states, different genres give different readings of the world: the fabliau scarcely notices the operations of God, the saint's life focuses at the expense of physical reality, tracts and sermons insist on prudential or orthodox morality, and romances privilege human emotion. The sheer number of varying persons and stories renders *The Canterbury Tales* a set that is unable to arrive at any definite truth or reality.

Two characters, the Pardoner and the Summoner, whose roles were to apply the Church's secular power, are both portrayed as deeply corrupt, greedy, and abusive. On the one hand, pardoners in Chaucer's day were people from whom one bought Church "indulgences" for the forgiveness of sins and who were often guilty of abusing their office for their own gain. Chaucer's Pardoner openly admits the corruption of his practice while hawking his wares. Though the Pardoner preaches against greed, the irony of the character is based on his hypocritical actions. He admits extortion of the poor, pocketing of indulgences, and failure to abide by teachings against jealousy and avarice. He also admits quite openly that he tricks the guiltiest sinners into buying his spurious relics and does not really care what happens to the souls of those he has swindled. He is also deceptive in terms of how he carries out his job. Instead of selling genuine relics, the bones he carries belong to pigs, not departed saints. The cross he carries appears to be studded with precious stones that are, in fact, bits of common metal. Having completed his tale, the Pardoner appeals for gold and silver so that the pilgrims may receive pardons for their sins. The Host responds that he would sooner cut off the Pardoner's testicles than kiss his relics. On the other hand, summoners were Church officers who brought sinners to the church court for possible excommunication and other penalties. Corrupt summoners would write false citations and frighten people into bribing them in order to protect their interests. Chaucer's Summoner is portrayed as guilty of the very kinds of sins for which he is threatening to bring others to court and is hinted as having a corrupt relationship with the Pardoner. In "The Friar's Tale," one of the characters is a summoner who is shown to be working on the side of the Devil, not God. Both the Summoner and the Devil go to the house of a widow, where the Summoner fabricates a court summons so that the widow will have to bribe him to dismiss the case. He also demands she give him a new pan in payment for an old debt, falsely claiming he paid a fine to get her off a charge of adultery. The Monk and the Prioress, on the other hand, while not as corrupt as the Summoner or the Pardoner, fall far short of the ideal for their orders. Both are expensively dressed and show signs of lives of luxury and flirtatiousness, and a lack of spiritual depth. Equally corrupt is the judge who appears in "The Physician's Tale" as one who plots with a low fellow to abduct a beautiful young woman.

In *The Canterbury Tales*, the knighthood is also not so noble and ends in violence, as recorded in the story told by the Knight ("The Knight's Tale"), but also in the two stories narrated by Chaucer himself and "The Wife of Bath's Tale," where the knight is convicted of rape.

"The Man of Law's Tale" describes a story about the unjust guilt of a woman and her unjust punishment. In the preface to the story, the representative of the law states that he agrees to tell a story of his own like the rest of the guests because "the law that one person imposes on another person must also apply to himself, is correct. That's what we say."

Shakespeare may be the most studied writer of all times. His heroes and their dialogues are among the texts that have been referred to perhaps more than any other text in the history of world literature.[2]

Shakespeare "was the first philosopher of history" (Bloom, 2000, p. 29), he was the greatest of all contributors to the English language (Stewart, 2010)—or at least he "ranks high among true philosophers" (Craig, 2001, p. 12)—and along with Machiavelli, Montaigne, and Bacon, he "opened the way for … realistic ethics" (Heller, 2002, p. 18).

Shakespeare's work is part of an era characterized by important plays such as those written by Ben Jonson (1572–1637), who depicted scoundrels, eccentrics, and a whole gallery of morally deformed types of every shape and form, *who* in *Bartholomew Fair* ridicules the noble spendthrift, together with the predatory and hypocritical priest, the prototype of Tartuffe, and in *The Devil is an Ass* presents an interesting picture of the depravity and degeneracy of the court of King James I.

But Shakespeare surpasses all contemporaries of his time. He does not sermonize; he is never didactic. The moral aspects of each problem and each situation are revealed so forcefully that the reader is inescapably compelled to draw his or her own conclusions. Shakespeare elucidates the problems of the individual: his or her rights, his or her relations with the family, the state, and society, and the race question. He always stresses the social roots of every problem.

Criminologists have also focused on Shakespeare's connections with the science of criminology. Craig (2001) is interested in the way in which Shakespeare understands law, since law connects the dramatist with philosophy. Goll, in his early work *Criminal Types in Shakespeare* (1909), seems to have formed a direct nexus between Shakespeare's works and what is now included in the discipline of criminology. Shafer (1976) cites Homer and Shakespeare, among others, as some of the early precursors in the quest to understand criminality, and Pories (1995) examines in her dissertation, entitled "Fashioning the Face of

---

[2] All works available at http://shakespeare.mit.edu.

Poverty in Early Modern England," how poor people and criminals were portrayed in the sixteenth and early seventeenth centuries by "legislation," "debates in parliament," "sermons," "literature," and "canonical studies", relying in part on Shakespeare's *Henry* plays and *The Taming of the Shrew*. Cohen (1993) studied the legitimization of violence in *Henry IV*. The purpose of Cohen's study was to look at violence that was made lawful because it was carried out by "the court of the rich and powerful." Cohen argued that the violence in *Henry IV* was intended to "glorify physical violence as a necessary force of morality" (1993, p. 30). Hal's killing of Hotspur was a "socially useful idea of the possibility of violence being good—moral, legitimate, and, even sacred" (1993, pp. 30–31). Cohen's analysis suggests that because of the "sacred historical tradition," the violence in *Henry IV* was necessary. Therefore, the motive for the murder of Hotspur was "legalized and made to supply a social need" (1993, p. 31): to end violence and restore authority. Bates (2003) uses Shakespeare to discuss criminal rehabilitation, Bernthal (1992) discusses how Shakespeare is staging justice, and Cormack et al. (2013) begin a conversation between Shakespeare and the law.

Curran (2012), Spinrad (1992), and Stoll (1912) discuss the criminal types in Shakespeare, while on the same subject, Time (1999) explores how Shakespeare used the themes of law and justice in his plays, and how his writings present theatrical scenarios that are of direct relevance to historical as well as contemporary criminological thinking. In her book, she wonders how Shakespeare's theatrical scenarios concerning criminality and crime causation appear to anticipate or foreshadow the criminological theory that has appeared in the subsequent professional literature hundreds of years later, and how Shakespearean plays offer explanation and analogies for various models of social control. She concludes that Shakespeare's writings were not based on imaginary themes; rather, they reflected social activities and problems of the time. The rulers' response was inadequate, and the judicial system handed down severe penalties even for minor offenses. Not everyone suffered from the dwindling economy: rich merchants, lawyers, entertainers, and bankers, among others, prospered, while others suffered.

Wilson (2014) addresses the dynamic and mutually beneficial relationship between Shakespeare studies and criminology—how Shakespeare depicted crime and justice, how criminologists have used Shakespeare's drama, how criminology surfaces in modern Shakespearean adaptations, and how his works remain a valuable resource for criminology at both a theoretical level (helping criminology scholars build theories) and a pedagogical level (helping criminal justice professionals develop skills of analytical and ethical reasoning). He states that Shakespeare was one of England's first criminologists: the practice of developing abstract theories of why crime happens—precisely what Shakespearean tragedy does—*Why do some people cause harm to others?* He also adds that, as we use criminology to unpack Shakespeare, we can also use Shakespeare to build better criminological theory.

However, something is missing from the aforementioned analyses. Against those who seek to promote Shakespeare's narrative as an apolitical and quaint advocate of "Merrie England," devoid of any radical or subversive messages, we should be alert to the dissident potential of a uniquely gifted voice that lived on the cusp of the transformation that catapulted early modern England from the feudal to the capitalist epoch, as Marx was. In fact, to illustrate the greed of the Rhineland rich and the claim to make the wood thief into a serf, Marx turns to a celebrated scene from *The Merchant of Venice* in which the moneylender, Shylock, is confronted by Portia, one of his debtors:

> Shylock. Most learned judge — A sentence! come, prepare!
> Portia. Tarry a little; there is something else. This bond cloth give thee here no jot of blood; The words expressly are "a pound of flesh": Take then thy bond, take thou thy pound of flesh. (Act IV, Scene 1)

We have, however, reached a point where the forest owner, in exchange for his piece of wood, receives what was once a human being.

Marx would return to *The Merchant of Venice* to encapsulate the depravity of the system in his later work. In *Capital*, published in 1867, he uses the words of Shylock to sum up the mentality of English factory owners who mercilessly exploited child labor without any respite, forcing them to work up to 12 h a day:

> My deeds upon my head! I crave the law,
> The penalty and forfeit of my bond. (Act IV, Scene 1)

Marx, according to Ledwith (2016), assimilates the complexity of the character by also using him in *Capital* as the voice of the oppressed, as well as the oppressor. Shylock depicted a representative of the least productive and most rapacious section of the bourgeoisie. At the same time, the trial scene in *The Merchant of Venice* reveals how easily one can become a criminal based on the decisions of those in power.

Marx describes the destructive effect of the new work process on workers' well-being, then quotes Shylock's words to those the Venetian regards as his tormentors:

> No, go ahead and take my life. Don't pardon that. You take my house away when you take the money I need for upkeep. You take my life when you take away my means of making a living.

Marx recognized that one of the keys to Shakespeare's genius was the playwright's appreciation of the complexity of human behavior and ability to subtly question the motivation of those in power. According to Smirnov (1936), in his historical plays (such as the three parts of *Henry VI*, *Richard II*, *Richard III*, *King John*, the two parts of *Henry IV*, and *Henry V*), Shakespeare fully revealed his political philosophy, his attitude toward royal power and his understanding of the historical process. The eponymous character in *Timon of Athens'* exposes the corrupting influence of money in his celebrated monologue (IV, 3). In *Coriolanus*, there is a total absence of positive characters drawn from the privileged classes, and in *Love's Labour's Lost*, Biron (the most positive character of the play) rejects the aristocratic way of life. The powerful feudal nobles depicted by Shakespeare—the Percys, the Glendowers, and the Mortimers—are arrogant and refractory. *Henry V* is a concrete political depiction of bad kings. *Richard III* at first committed murder to fulfill his quest for power, and even after he became king, his criminal ploys became more extreme as he engaged in a series of senseless killings. Falstaff (who makes his first appearance in *Henry IV,* is mentioned in *Henry V,* and is resurrected in *The Merry Wives of Windsor*) is a parody of the degenerate feudal nobility, being the embodiment of all their vices—boastfulness, swashbuckling, drunkenness, libertinism, the feudal lord for whom money became "the power of all powers." *Titus Andronicus* opens with the title character returning from war and ritually slaughtering the eldest son of his enemy's empress. The title character in *Macbeth* who, with the support and encouragement of his wife, becomes power hungry, is a killer. *Julius Caesar* (written at a time when absolutism in England was beginning to show clear signs of deterioration) is an ambitious egoist who attains power through clever political maneuvering, while Brutus is a hero, the defender of liberty, whose sole aim is to free the people from the yoke of a tyrant. *King Lear* is absorbed in the illusion of kingship even more than the half-mad Richard II. Later, Lear's delusions are dispelled. He undergoes great suffering. He begins to sense the monstrous injustice of the feudal-aristocratic system, the system which he had unthinkingly upheld:

> Through tatter'd clothes small vices do appear;
> Robes and furr'd gowns hide all. Plate sin with gold,
> And the strong lance of justice hurtless breaks;
> Arm it in rags, a pigmy's straw doth pierce it. (IV, 6)

Here and elsewhere, Lear merely repeats that which his jester, who symbolizes the wisdom and expresses the moral of the play, expounds in his bitterly sarcastic song:

> When nobles are their tailors' tutors;
> No heretics burn'd, but wenches' suitors;
> When every case in law is right; No squire in debt, nor no poor knight;
> When slanders do not live in tongues;
> Nor cutpurses come not to throngs;
> When usurers tell their gold the field;

And bawds and whores do churches build;—
Then shall the realm of Albion
Come to great confusion:
Then comes the time, who lives to see't,
That going shall be us'd with feet. (III, 2)

However, Shakespeare also described in his plays how the forces of change are slowly but surely preparing to sweep all elites aside. The social background in Shakespeare is not a mere detail of the plot. The social aspect of the love theme in *Romeo and Juliet* is obvious. Smirnov (1936) states that here it becomes the struggle of the new man of the Renaissance against the feudal order. This struggle takes the form of a demand for freedom in love an opposition to antiquated moral traditions. The struggle of the lovers against their social environment is the struggle of bourgeois humanism against feudalism, the Renaissance against the Middle Ages, with the help of Friar Lawrence, a churchman in name only, but in fact both a scholar and a philosopher, a stranger to all ecclesiastical bigotry, a true pantheist.

The old world and its law and order must die because it is rotten. The answer to Hamlet's question of what is rotten in Denmark is the whole world. His revenge is not an act of personal justice. He is horrified by the rampant hypocrisy and debauchery of the entire court, the corrupt agents of the King, Rosencrantz and Guildenstern, the empty-headed and obsequious Osric, the shrewd but foolish Polonius, even his beloved Ophelia. In his monologue "to be or not to be," he reaches the highest point of skepticism possible at that time. Hamlet's reasoning—that "your worm is your only real emperor for diet," that "your fat icing and your lean beggar is but variable service, two dishes, but to one table" (IV, 3), and that Alexander of Macedonia "returned into dust; the dust is earth; of earth we make loam; and why of that loam whereto he was converted might they not stop a beer-barrel?" (V, 1)—destroys the idea of feudal monarchy and the entire feudal dogma of class hierarchy in general. "Then are our beggars' bodies, and our monarchs and outstretched heroes the beggars' shadows," says Hamlet to Rosencrantz and Guildenstern (II, 2). "The toe of the peasant comes so near the heel of the courtier, he galls his kibe," he says to the grave-digger (V, 1), hinting at agrarian revolt.

Shakespeare was an integral part of his *epoch*, the era of the Renaissance in England, the era of the revolutionist humanism. He did not permit resignation and apathy to enter the soul of man; to him, struggle was the whole meaning and content of life—a struggle against the authority of divine right and in favor of the authority of responsibility, expressing the collective will of the people and their collective welfare, and against metaphysical interpretations and in favor of a scientific attitude toward the world, life, and reality, against the degenerate nobility and the narrow-minded legal system and dominant interpretations of the criminal phenomenon of the time, whose severity in the extermination of vice engendered new vices. In *The Tempest*, we witness the real dangers involved in mocking and demonizing the criminal, even one as offensive as a rapist, if we just let a criminal justice system run its course (Wilson, 2014). This is also the case (albeit more detailed) in *Measure for Measure*, where we can all clearly see the abuses of power that can occur when individual law enforcement agents receive both a mandate to crack down on social disorder and the authority to decide for themselves what counts as disorder and how to combat it. Angelo, the deputy Duke, has the power to sit in judgment of others; he is technically a judge. The fact that Angelo is dedicated to his job and has good intentions to follow the strict letter of the law is indisputable: "It is the law, not I, condemn your brother; were he my kinsman, brother, or my son, it should be thus with him: He must die tomorrow" (II.2.105–108). He even refused to consider facts that mitigate against Claudio's offense even after a solemn plea from Escalus, his deputy. Isabella protests against the literal interpretation of the law and pleads for mercy:

> Well, believe this,
> No ceremony that to great ones 'longs,
> Not the king's crown nor the deputed sword,
> The marshal's truncheon nor the lodge's robe,
> Become them with one half so good a grace
> As mercy does. (II, 2)

Angelo succumbs to temptation and solicits lewdness; ironically, all his outspokenness about the deterrent effect of capital punishment does not in any way deter him from engaging in a similar offense. He is not deterred because he believes that he will not be caught, as he is deputy to the Duke. When Isabella threatens to expose his sexual gestures, he replies:

Who will believe thee, Isabel? My unsoil'd name, the austereness of my life, my vouch against you, and my place i' the state will so your accusation overweigh that you shall stifle in your own report, and smell of calumny' (II.4.182–87).

The law enforcement of the time, entrusted with public trust and power, had been proven to be unethical. But then the Duke Vicentio comes and reverses the penalties. He is the authority of responsibility, who deplores his ignorance of the life of his subjects, criticizes himself, realizes his responsibilities, and seeks better ways of governing the people (I, 1, 4). He also speaks on the integrity of an official of the law:

He who the sword of heaven will bear should be as holy as severe; Pattern in himself to know, Grace to stand, and virtue go; More nor less to other paying, Than by self-offences weighing. Shame to him whose cruel striking Kills for faults of his own liking! Twice treble shame on Angelo. To weed my vice and let his grow! O, what may man within him hide, Though angel on the outward side! (III.2.287–298)

2   Italy: Dante Alighieri and Giovanni Boccaccio

In Italy, the works of Dante Alighieri and Giovanni Boccaccio dominated and highlighted the coming of a new era: the Renaissance. Dante Alighieri (1265–1321) was one of the most important Italian poets. He is considered the first major creator in Italian poetry and his famous work, *The Divine Comedy* (*Commedia*),[3] is considered to this day to be one of the most important works of world literature and an additional important contribution to the formation of the Italian language. Dante

---

[3] Available at https://www.gutenberg.org/ebooks/1001.

was involved in the political events of his time, such as movements in favor of granting freedoms to the common people; however, he paid, a very high price for this involvement, as he was exiled from the city of Florence until the end of his life. Dante originally named his most important work *Commedia*, but it was renamed *The Divine Comedy* when Boccaccio referred to it by that name (that is, *La Divina Comedia*) because of its subject matter and lofty style. The theme of the work is the author's imaginary journey to the realm of the dead, guided by the epic poet Virgil and Beatrice (his childhood love). The idea of a journey to Hades and Paradise had precedents in Antiquity, both in Homer with Ulysses (in *The Odyssey*) and in Virgil with Aeneas (in *The Aeneid*). The work is divided into three parts: *Hell (Inferno)*, *Purgatory (Purgatorio)* and *Paradise (Paradiso)*. Each part includes 33 odes and an introduction. In *Hell (Inferno)*, which is described as having a conical shape, Dante scolds all his criminals and political opponents by showing them being tortured in horrible ways. In *Purgatory (Purgatorio)*, he describes how, according to medieval conceptions, the human soul is cleansed of its sins before it enters Paradise, where all virtuous people are accepted. Finally, in *Paradise (Paradiso)*, he describes his encounter with saints and great thinkers.

The duration of Dante's journey in the work is estimated to be seven days. This calculation is based on relevant references within the writing itself. More specifically, we can distinguish the following stages: staying in *Hell (Inferno)*, lasting one night and one day, going through *Purgatory (Purgatorio)*, lasting one day and one night, ascending *Purgatory (Purgatorio)* for three days and three nights, staying in the earthly *Paradise (Paradiso)* for one day (or more), and staying in *Paradise (Paradiso)* the rest of the time. After crossing the Acheron River with Charon, Virgil leads Dante to *Hell (Inferno)* in succession through the nine cycles of sin, which include the following:

- *Circle 1*: *unbaptized babies and virtuous pagans*, whose punishment is that they are unable to reach Paradise (Canto 4).
- *Circle 2*: *kissers* are punished by being doomed to swirl in a constant windstorm, unable to touch another human presence (Canto 5).
- *Circle 3*: the souls of the *greedy* are devoured by Cerberus (Canto 6).

- *Circle 4*: the *covetous* and *avaricious* are doomed to carry heavy weights on their chests (Canto 7).
- *Circle 5*: the *vindictive* hit each other in muddy swamps (Canto 8).
- *Circle 6*: *heretics* are trapped in fiery tombs (Cantos 10–11).
- *Circle 7*: this includes the violent, who are divided into three groups. The first includes those who are *violent toward other people* and are punished by being put in a swamp of boiling blood. The second group includes those who are *violent toward themselves* and are transformed into trees or chased by wild dogs. Finally, in the third group, there are those who are *violent against God and nature*, and are isolated in a desert of burning sand where a fiery rain is falling (Cantos 12–18).
- *Circle 8*: here, *swindlers* are punished in ten different abysses. More specifically, *seducers* are punished by flogging, *flatterers* are immersed in impurities, *simoniacs* are hung upside down in pits and fires by their feet, *magicians* or *false prophets* (with their heads placed upside down so that they can only see their back), *corrupt politicians* (trapped bubbling tar), *hypocrites*, *thieves* are chased by and then transformed into snakes, *deliberately bad counselors* are trapped in flames, *heretics* are devoured by demons, and *counterfeiters* are punished by being afflicted with diseases (Cantos 19–30).
- *Circle 9*: here, *traitors* are punished by being trapped up to the neck in a frozen lake. In particular, the following groups are placed in in four different areas: *traitors of relatives* (Caina), *traitors of the homeland* (Antinora), *traitors of friends* (Ptolemy), and *traitors of their benefactors* (Judea) (Cantos 32–34). At the deepest point of Hades, in the center of the Earth, the two wanderers observe the giant Lucifer who eternally tyrannizes Brutus and Cassius (traitors against Julius Caesar), but also Judas (traitor against Christ).

In the second part of *The Divine Comedy*, Dante and Virgil are transported to the southern hemisphere of the Earth in front of its highest mountain, *Purgatory (Purgatorio)*. The first nine Cantos (songs) of *Purgatory* describe its structure, which consists of seven circles, symbolizing the seven deadly sins. In each cycle, sinners struggle to be purified after being subjected to a certain punishment:

- *Circle 1*: *selfishness*, constantly carrying a weight around their neck (Cantos 10–12).
- *Circle 2*: *envy*, having eyes sewn with thread (Cantos 13–15).
- *Circle 3*: *anger*, trapped in dense smoke (Cantos 15–17).
- *Circle 4*: *laziness/sloth*, running non-stop (Cantos 18–19).
- *Circle 5*: *avarice*, lying with their heads on the ground (Cantos 19–22).
- *Circle 6*: *greed*, punished with hunger and thirst (Cantos 22–24).
- *Circle 7*: *lust*, burning in flames (Cantos 25–27).

In *Purgatory (Purgatorio)*, sinners repent for a period of time until they are purified and are finally allowed to climb to the top of the mountain, where Eden, the earthly Paradise, is located. Virgil, as a pagan, has no right to enter *Paradise (Paradiso)*, and Beatrice now becomes Dante's guide. *Paradise (Paradiso)* consists of nine concentric spheres (heavens). These spheres revolve around the stationary Earth and the greater their radius, the faster their rotation. The human souls reside in the realm that belongs to them, thus setting a hierarchical order even in *Paradise (Paradiso)*. The nine spheres and the corresponding souls that are hosted are as follows:

- *Sphere 1*: the Moon, for *those who did not keep their promises* (Cantos 2–5).
- *Sphere 2*: Hermes/Mercury, for *those who did good out of ambition* (Cantos 5–7).
- *Sphere 3*: Aphrodite/Venus, for *those who did good out of love* (Cantos 8–9).
- *Sphere 4*: the Sun, for *the wise* (Cantos 10–14).
- *Sphere 5*: Mars, for *those who defended religion* (Cantos 14–18).
- *Sphere 6*: Jupiter, for *the righteous* (Cantos 18–20).
- *Sphere 7*: Saturn, for *visionaries* (Cantos 21–22).
- *Sphere 8*: the stars, for *the blessed* (Cantos 22–27).
- *Sphere 9*: *angels that move around God* (Cantos 27–29).

It is understandable that the whole of *The Divine Comedy* deals with the issues of crime and punishment, and good and bad. However, it is important to note that even *Hell (Inferno)* has degrees and in the highest rank before the traitors in the Circle 8 and under the general term "swindlers" are included those types of people who exercised power in the medieval era and defined the dominant definition of law and the practices of dealing with injustice.

In Canto 19, Dante delivers a denunciation of *simoniacal corruption* of the medieval Church and forcefully expresses his condemnation of those who committed simony (or the sale of ecclesiastic favors and offices):

> Rapacious ones, who take the things of God, / that ought to be the brides of Righteousness, / and make them fornicate for gold and silver! / The time has come to let the trumpet sound / for you.

The *sinners* are placed upside-down in round, tube-like holes within the rock, with flames burning the soles of their feet. The heat of the fire is proportionate to their guilt.

In Canto 21, Dante mentions the *barrators*, the corrupt politicians, who made money through trafficking in public offices (the political analogy of the *simoniacs*). These people are immersed in a lake of boiling pitch, which represents the sticky fingers and dark secrets of their corrupt deals. In Canto 22, Dante mentions Friar Gomita (a corrupt friar in Gallura who was eventually hanged for accepting bribes in order to let prisoners escape, and Michel Zanche, a corrupt vicar). In Canto 23, Dante and Aeneas find hypocrites listlessly walking around a narrow track for eternity, weighed down by leaden robes. The robes are brilliantly gilded on the outside and are shaped like a monk's habit—the hypocrite's "outward appearance shines brightly and passes for holiness, but under that show lies the terrible weight of his deceit."

On the other hand, *Paradise (Paradiso)* again has degrees in the higher realms—above the wise and the defenders of religion are the righteous and the visionaries. And here in Canto 22, Dante criticizes the official church, a criticism that extends when he reaches the highest stage, the 9th circle, in which he begins a dialogue with Beatrice, who proceeds to give a forceful criticism of the preachers of the day (Canto 29):

Christ did not say to his first company:
"Go, and preach idle stories to the world";
but he gave them the teaching that is truth,
and truth alone was sounded when they spoke;
and thus, to battle to enkindle faith,
the Gospels served them as both shield and lance.
But now men go to preach with jests and jeers,
and just as long as they can raise a laugh,
the cowl puffs up, and nothing more is asked.
But such a bird nests in that cowl, that if
the people saw it, they would recognize
as lies the pardons in which they confide.

Giovanni Boccaccio (1313–1375), together with Dante and Francesco Petrarca, is part of the so-called "Three Crowns" of Italian literature, an important Renaissance humanist and one of the most important figures in European literature in the fourteenth century. He is also connected to the Byzantine humanism as a student of Barlaam of Calabria, with whom he studied Greek language and who encouraged him to translate works by Homer, Euripides, and Aristotle.

Boccaccio's most notable work is *The Decameron*,[4] a collection of tales which had an important influence on authors such as Chaucer (*The Canterbury Tales*) and Shakespeare (whose play *All's Well That Ends Well* was based on Boccacccio's Tale III from *The Decameron*). The book is structured as a framing device containing 100 tales told by a group of seven young women and three young men who find shelter in a secluded villa just outside Florence in order to escape the Black Death. The various tales of love in *The Decameron* provide, in fact, a document of life at the time. Recurring plots of the stories include mocking the lust and greed of the clergy, and tensions in Italian society between the new wealthy commercial class and noble families.

Throughout *The Decameron*, commercial and urban values are treasured, while the traditional rural feudal and monastery values are not. In fact, the Roman Catholic Church, priests, and religious belief become

---

[4] Available at https://www.gutenberg.org/files/23700/23700-h/23700-h.htm.

the satirical source of comedy throughout the work. Clergymen are immoral, while feudalists are violent and vicious. Some examples are as follows. In the first tale of the first day, Master Ciappelletto, the worst of men in his lifetime, was reputed a saint and was called Saint Ciappelletto after his death. In the second tale, Abraham the Jew becomes a Christian when he sees the depravity of the clergy. In the fourth tale, a monk, having fallen into a sin deserving of very serious punishment, quitted himself of the penalty. The sixth tale of the same day also mentions the perverse hypocrisy of religious orders. In the first tale of the second day, Martellino pretends to be paralyzed and makes it appear as if he has been cured by being placed upon the body of St. Arrigo. The immorality of the clergy is mentioned in the eighth and the tenth tales of the third day. In the first tale of the fourth day, the Prince of Salerno and father of Ghismonda slays his daughter's lover, Guiscardo, and sends her his heart in a golden cup, while in the second tale of the same day, Friar Alberto deceives a woman into believing that the Angel Gabriel is in love with her. Friar Alberto tells her that Gabriel can enter his body in order to sleep with her. In the third tale, two murderers escape death by bribing the guards, and Dioneo narrates the tenth tale of the sixth day, which mocks the worship of relics.

4. Miguel de Cervantes Saavedra (1547–1616) was a Spanish writer who is widely regarded as the greatest writer in the Spanish language. His work belongs to the "Golden Age" of Spain, during which there was an exceptional flourishing in the arts. His most famous novel, *Don Quixote*,[5] is one of the classic works of world literature and has been translated into more than 60 languages (it is the 8th most-translated book in the world after *The Bible*). It was the first novel to be published in two parts in 1605 and in 1615. It describes the adventures of the protagonist Alonso Quijano, a simple farmer who, having read many books on chivalry, believes he is a knight and assumes the name Don Quixote. The books do not specify the exact location of his residence, but he tells us that he lives with his niece and his housekeeper. He embarks on his travels and adventures alone, with his skinny horse

---

[5] Available at https://www.gutenberg.org/files/996/996-h/996-h.htm.

named Rosinande wearing an old metal suit of arm he has found. During his adventures, he is injured and taken back to his home, where he is cared for by his niece and his housekeeper. He is told that the costume disappeared by magic. A short time later, he finds Sancho Panza, a neighbor, and convinces Sancho to follow him in exchange for giving him a share of land in an island. Don Quixote is in love with a young neighbor, who he calls Dulcinea and tries to save her because he has convinced himself that he is under the influence of magic. Of course, Dulcinea knows nothing of all this and never appears in any of the books. Don Quixote's journeys with his faithful companion often do not end well. They usually become objects of ridicule and laughter, especially, his comrade Sancho Panza. Toward the end of the second book, we see that Don Quixote somehow finds his logic and returns with his friend and fellow traveler back to their home.

It could be said that on January 16, 1605 (the publication date of the first volume) the death certificate of the feudal society was issued. The astonishing irony of aristocratic values, the genesis of vulgar capitalist materialism, the references to religious fundamentalism (which was strong at the time), and the dream of another society ("the golden age has no mine and yours") make *Don Quixote* a work of unsurpassed social criticism centuries before philosophers and politicians realized this. The hero of the novel is described as a man who is easily given to anger. Already in his original stories, a code of values and symbols is recorded, a code different from the dominant one of the time.

Don Quixote calls the prostitutes he meets "ladies"; he "frees" a slave named Andres who is tied to a tree and beaten by his master, and makes his master swear to treat the slave fairly. He attacks traders from Toledo who "insult" the imaginary Dulcinea. When he returns home after his first journey, the priest burns some of his books and seals up the room which contained the library.

After that, Don Quixote decides to go on his next trip with a companion, Sancho who is a just poor and simple farmer. Their famous adventures begin, starting with Don Quixote's attack on windmills that he believes to be ferocious giants. The phrase "tilting at windmills," which describes an act of attacking imaginary enemies (or an act of extreme idealism), derives from that iconic scene in the book.

The two heroes next encounter two Benedictine friars traveling on the road ahead of a lady in a carriage. Don Quixote takes the friars to be enchanters who hold the lady captive and knocks a friar from his horse. In the next chapter Sancho and Don Quixote fall in with a group of goat herders. Don Quixote tells Sancho and the goat herders about the Golden Age of man, in which property does not exist and men live in peace.

In the following adventures, the heroes free a group of galley slaves. For that reason, Don Quixote is now a criminal and an officer of the Santa Hermandad issues a warrant for his arrest. Don Quixote is locked in a cage, but frees himself again to continue his adventures until he retires to his bed suffering from a mortal illness and eventually dies.

But let us see in more detail how Cervantes describes in the words of Don Quixote this Golden Age and its values in Chapter 11 of the first book,[6] during the meeting with the shepherds, describing in essence an anti-hegemonic model of social organization and justice:

> Round the skins six of the men belonging to the fold seated themselves, having first with rough politeness pressed Don Quixote to take a seat upon a trough which they placed for him upside down. Don Quixote seated himself, and Sancho remained standing to serve the cup, which was made of horn. Seeing him standing, his master said to him:
>
> That thou mayest see, Sancho, the good that knight-errantry contains in itself, and how those who fill any office in it are on the high road to be speedily honoured and esteemed by the world, I desire that thou seat thyself here at my side and in the company of these worthy people, and that thou be one with me who am thy master and natural lord, and that thou eat from my plate and drink from whatever I drink from; for the same may be said of knight-errantry as of love, that it levels all.

When Don Quixote had quite appeased his appetite, he took up a handful of the acorns, and contemplating them attentively delivered himself somewhat in this fashion:

---

[6] http://www.gutenberg.org/files/996/996-0.txt.

Happy the age, happy the time, to which the ancients gave the name of golden, not because in that fortunate age the gold so coveted in this our iron one was gained without toil, but because they that lived in it knew not the two words "mine" and "thine"! In that blessed age all things were in common; to win the daily food no labour was required of any save to stretch forth his hand and gather it from the sturdy oaks that stood generously inviting him with their sweet ripe fruit. The clear streams and running brooks yielded their savoury limpid waters in noble abundance. The busy and sagacious bees fixed their republic in the clefts of the rocks and hollows of the trees, offering without usance the plenteous produce of their fragrant toil to every hand. The mighty cork trees, unenforced save of their own courtesy, shed the broad light bark that served at first to roof the houses supported by rude stakes, a protection against the inclemency of heaven alone. Then all was peace, all friendship, all concord; as yet the dull share of the crooked plough had not dared to rend and pierce the tender bowels of our first mother that without compulsion yielded from every portion of her broad fertile bosom all that could satisfy, sustain, and delight the children that then possessed her. Then was it that the innocent and fair young shepherdess roamed from vale to vale and hill to hill, with flowing locks, and no more garments than were needful modestly to cover what modesty seeks and ever sought to hide. Nor were their ornaments like those in use to-day, set off by Tyrian purple, and silk tortured in endless fashions, but the wreathed leaves of the green dock and ivy, wherewith they went as bravely and becomingly decked as our Court dames with all the rare and far-fetched artifices that idle curiosity has taught them. Then the love-thoughts of the heart clothed themselves simply and naturally as the heart conceived them, nor sought to commend themselves by forced and rambling verbiage. Fraud, deceit, or malice had then not yet mingled with truth and sincerity. Justice held her ground, undisturbed and unassailed by the efforts of favour and of interest, that now so much impair, pervert, and beset her. Arbitrary law had not yet established itself in the mind of the judge, for then there was no cause to judge and no one to be judged. Maidens and modesty, as I have said, wandered at will alone and unattended, without fear of insult from lawlessness or libertine assault, and if they were undone it was of their own will and pleasure. But now in this hateful age of ours not one is safe, not though some new labyrinth like that of Crete conceal and surround her; even there the pestilence of gallantry will make its way to them through chinks or on the air by the zeal of its accursed importunity, and, despite of all seclusion, lead them to ruin. In defence of these, as time advanced and wickedness increased, the order of knights-errant was instituted, to defend maidens, to protect widows and to succour the orphans and the needy. To this order I belong, brother goatherds, to whom I return thanks for the hospitality and kindly welcome ye offer me and my squire; for though by natural law all living are bound to show favour to knights-errant, yet, seeing that without knowing this obligation ye have welcomed and feasted me, it is right that with all the good-will in my power I should thank you for yours."

5. The 12th century saw a particularly important development for the Byzantine Empire, in parallel to that seen in the West, as detailed above[7]: the first written literary works in the vernacular, a popular language that imitated or recorded the dialect of Constantinople, which, because it was used only in literature during this early period, it has been proposed is called "popular/demotic poetic common." The first work is the epic novel about *Digenis Akritas*, which we analyzed in Chapter 6, a continuation of the Akritic, folk songs, most of which, during the tenth century, had the superhero Vassilios Digenis Akritas as their central character and, for which we speculate, as the available evidence testifies, that in the twelfth century an unknown scholar collected and edited them in order to compose an extensive epic poetic work of a fictional character.

The first surviving forms of popular literature also include four poems known as the "Ptochoprodromic poems" or *Ptochoprodromos*, which have satirical elements and comic entertainment characteristics, and belong to the broader type of begging or pleading poetry—that is, the poetry written by court scholars in order to ask the emperor or senior officials for financial or other forms of support.

Another popular work from this century is *The Verses of the Scholar Michael Glykas* (1159), which is also an indicator of the colloquial

---

[7] All works available in Greek at http://georgakas.lit.auth.gr/dimodis/index.php?option=com_chronoforms&chronoform=showErga&c=2&t=%CE%94%CE%B9%CE%BA%CE%B1%CE%B9%CE%BF%CF%83%CF%8D%CE%BD%CE%B7&tag=20&Itemid=280.

language in Byzantine Empire. In his relatively short work (581 15-syllable iambic verse), the poet, theologian, and secretary of the imperial court addresses Emperor Manuel (Comnenus), to whom the last two *Ptochodomic writings* were addressed, and asks him to release him from prison, where he was unjustly incarcerated, as he himself claimed. In fact, he says about his experience that nothing is worse than prison.

Unlike the previous text, which survived in the form of a single manuscript, the next known popular work, the so-called *Spaneas*, was preserved in 19 manuscripts and a printed edition from the 16th century, a sign of its popularity for many centuries. One of the titles which has come down to us is *An admonishing teaching of Alexios Komnenos (Alexius Comnenus)*, the so-called *Spaneas*. This title attributes the work to the son of Emperor John II Komnenos, who addresses advice to one of his nephews, an identification that has not been universally accepted. But the work that achieved an unrivaled circulation and number of adaptations from the 11th to the 19th centuries, as evidenced by the 80 manuscripts in which it survives in some form, is *Stefanitis and Ichnilatis*, a narrative text that teaches through a complex system of animal narratives the way in which the good ruler must deal with moral and political problems. In one of the excerpts from the text, it states that the bad guy can also be a well-known person: "It is good that one leaves the cunning people and the wicked, even if they are kins/relatives and acquaintances."

Along with the above, there are a multitude of literary works of the time which do not hesitate to question a dominant value system, as well as the issue of law and the delimitation of the criminal phenomenon.

In *The History of Belisarius* (a moral novel in verse from the 14th century), the plot concerns Belisarius, the legendary general of Justinian, who falls victim to the envy of the aristocracy because of his brilliant achievements and the love shown to him by the people. This is made clear to the reader in the first nine verses of the text:

> What a miraculous paradox, what a great calamity
> and sorrow unsurched, grief and bitterness!
> On the day of the Romans and their welfare
> of the King Justinian, great emperor,

and there was envy of the Romans too much
and, in spite of all things from the beginning, envy does not
disappear,
neither in kings, lords, rich and penniless;
countries and castles were knocked down by people's tongues—
and they lost their day from too much envy

In the work *An excellent erotic and strange Narration of Florios of the blissful and daughter Platziaflora*, which belongs to the category of erotic-knightly novels in verse of the Palaiologan period (between the end of the 14th and the beginning of the 15th centuries), the King, Florios' father, with the help of the head of the servants, plots against his daughter, Platziaflora, that she allegedly tried to poison him, and sentences her to death. Florios is informed of the incident, arrives in disguise, and challenges the housekeeper to a duel in order to save Platziaflora.

Opsarologos (lit. *Fish Book*), a short prose text with eloquent content, written around the end of the 14th century or the beginning of the 15th century, describes a fish trial and parodies the court process, as well as the language of the Byzantine court and its stereotypical expressions. Although it only survives in the form of a single manuscript, its translations into other languages show that it was a very popular text. At the final end of the trial, the King-judge Kitos (a whale) unjustly condemns the poor and small fish Tziro (a mackerel) for conspiracy, who also curses Tziros:

The King Kitos [Whale], having heard and become angry
A big pair of scissors was brought, and he cut Tziros [Mackerel]'
beard and
Tziros raised his voice loudly and, weeping, he said;
Cursed you, Sea Beam, and cursed be your genus. And took
his beard went and showed it to his brother
Tricheon. And he, after he has seen it, he cried bitterly and painfully and
said; Alas, what has happened to Tziros [Mackerel], my brother.
Then the king cursed Tziros [Mackerel] and said; From
The mouth of a poor person don't escape, Tziros [Mackerel], your
price should be,

What is called folin [small coin], and from kicks and dirty don't
escape, Tziros [Mackerel], Tziros [Mackerel]!
And immediately all the fish shout out once; For
many years, despot!

The literary production in the demotic Greek language continued
even after the subjugation of the Byzantine Empire by the Ottomans
and other territories of the East by the rising forces of Western medieval
states. More specifically in Venetian-occupied medieval Crete, a flourishing of fiction was recorded, the main representatives of which were
George Chortatsis or Chortatzis and Vitsentzos Kornaros.

In *Erofili*, a tragedy by Georgios Chortatsis written in the late 16th
century, which takes place in pre-Christian Egypt, the secret marriage
of the Princess Erofili with a general serving her father ignites the rage
of the latter and results in the deaths of the three main characters. In
verses 333–370, the ghost of the King's brother makes his appearance
on stage. This "shadow" tells the public how he and his children were
killed by the current king, with whom they co-ruled, and how he took
his wife, with whom he had the only child of Erophili. So, now that
the audience is listening to the arrogant monologue of King Filogonos'
arrogant monologue followed, but now the audience knows his sinful-
behavior. When Filogonos retires, his brother's ghost will ask the gods
for his quick punishment. In the immediately following verses, the
dance of the girls condemns the man's greed for wealth and glory as
coming from Hades, the world of evil. The following excerpt contains
the first eight verses of the chorus, which focus on the power of avarice
and the mania for power to separate people and not let two lovers live
happily:

The insatiability of wealth, the hunger of glory,
of the accursed precision,
how many dead bodies did you have left
how many unjust wars have arisen,
how many hairs do you have
heard in the globe all day long!
In Hades let your name be willed

and out on earth let your misfortune not go out to chasten
human mind no longer.
For, as I say, a demon had sent
To come to the world,
And after people he can poison you.
You are hating regret, and are holding
Justice exiled far away,
and you consider neither just nor beautiful.
The heavens are sealed for you
And here in the world below people
Cannot be resting;
with so many brothers and sisters fighting [against each other]
and friends to renounce their friendships
and the children hate their lord [father].
The gifts of lust are ruined
often with you, that's why so many
sighs are heard by two who are in love.

The tragedy ends with an important scene of justice being done by
the people (the chorus), who kill the King. After Erofili's suicide, the
young woman with the dance girls appears on the stage and finds Erofili
covered in blood with a knife in her hand. When the young woman fin-
ishes her obituary, the King appears, unrepentant even when faced with
the sight of his dead daughter. The girls of the chorus, in order to give
justice, rush at him and kill him.

Erotokritos is a romantic epic poem by Vitsentzos Kornaros written
in the early 17th century, structured into five parts, and consisting of
about 10,000 verses. This is the most popular, and to this day, story of
Princess Aretousa who fell in love with the son of her father's councelor.
They both endured four years of unhapinness (he was on exile and she
was in prison), until the king accepted their love.

Already in the first pages of the poem, it is understood that justice is
being done by the King with absolute arbitrariness:

Rigas [The King] is right in whatever he defines
And as he wants, and as it seems to him, he makes his own
judgment.

In his parliament it is our good and our bad,
And in his hand he holds our lives and death.

The Poet who intervenes (with his own discourse) in the text between the dialogues of the protagonists informs us about the conditions that prevailed in the prisons of the time:

In the worst of the prison, in the darkest
Where like mud and clay, we made it and it comes in
And flickering fists to see outside
With an ounce of bread and volumes of water, until he dies.

However, no threat or repression frightens the protagonist Aretousa, who responds to the pressure of her father the King with the following words:

In this prison.... and if it is too dark, put me aside,
But no prison, no irons, no a hundred deaths,
Will take me to the palace as a bride.

References

Bates, L. R. (2003). The uses of Shakespeare in criminal rehabilitation: Testing the limits of 'Universality.' In L. Davis (Ed.), *Shakespeare matters: History, teaching, performance* (pp. 151–164). University of Delaware Press.

Bernthal, C. A. (1992). Staging justice: James I and the trial scenes of *Measure for Measure. Studies in English Literature, 32*, 247–269.

Bloom, A. (2000). *Shakespeare on love and friendship*. University of Chicago Press.

Cohen, D. (1993). *Shakespeare's culture of violence*. St. Martin's Press.

Cooper, H. (1996). *The Canterbury Tales: Oxford guides to Chaucer* (2nd ed.). Oxford University Press.

Cormack, B., Nussbaum, M., & Strier, R. (Eds.). (2013). *Shakespeare and the law: A conversation among disciplines and professions*. University of Chicago Press.

Craig, L. H. (2001). *Of philosophers and kings: Political philosophy in Shakespeare's Macbeth and King Lear*. University of Toronto Press.

Curran, K. (2012). Feeling criminal in *Macbeth*. *Criticism, 54*(3), 391–401.

Goll, A. (1909). *Criminal types in Shakespeare* (C. Weekes, Trans.). Haskell House.

Heller, A. (2002). *The time is out of Joint: Shakespeare as philosopher of history*. Rowman & Littlefield.

Ledwith, S. (2016). *Marx's Shakespeare*. Available at https://www.counterfire.org/articles/analysis/18300-marx-s-shakespeare

Pories, K. G. (1995). *Fashioning the face of poverty in early modern England (Criminals, Idle Poor)*. Ph.D. dissertation, University of North Carolina, Chapel Hill.

Sagarin, E. (1980). In search of criminology through fiction. *Deviant Behavior, 2*(1), 73–92.

Shafer, R. (1976). *Introduction to a lecture series titled Shakespeare and history: Interdisciplinary perspectives*. Indiana University Press.

Smirnov, A. A. (1936). *Shakespeare: A Marxist interpretation*. The Critics Group. Available at https://www.marxists.org/subject/art/lit_crit/works/shakes.htm

Spinrad, P. S. (1992). Dogberry hero: Shakespeare's comic constables in their communal context. *Studies in Philology, 89*, 163–169.

Stewart, S. (2010). *Shakespeare and philosophy*. Routledge.

Stoll, E. E. (1912). Criminals in Shakespeare and in science. *Modern Philology, 10*, 65–80.

Time, V. M. (1999). *Shakespeare's criminals: Criminology, fiction, and drama*. Greenwood Press.

Wilson, J. R. (2014). Shakespeare and criminology. *Crime, Media, Culture, 10*(2), 97–114.

9

A Dialogue with Historical Criminology

This book is a sequel to two previous volumes and is a part of a whole, of a common goal, and from a common motivation. As I wrote in the first volume (Georgoulas, 2018), what has motivated me to make this long journey into the past is this: like any written text, its author is the product of his or her time. I live in Greece, in a country where policies are implemented and their victims are the people of the country; rights that have been won as a result of decades of struggles have just been lost and democracy has disappeared. At the same time, in this situation where transnational/state/corporate crimes are normal, criminological (and not only) thought, apart from a few exceptions, is absent, and when it declares its presence, it simultaneously declares its faith in the TINA (There Is No Alternative) theory. Bleak darkness has fallen and the worst thing is that at present, there is a new evil coming, that most people are beginning to get used to this situation, to legitimize it; it has becoming their habitus, their second nature. We ought to react with actions and words. And regarding the latter, we have to keep the flame of hope lit, in the only way we know how, with the tools and concepts we have learned. We have to support critical thinking in the field of crime study, outlining even if only dimly a better future. But

S. Georgoulas, *The Origins of Radical Criminology, Volume III*,
https://doi.org/10.1007/978-3-031-05925-4_10

how do we keep the field open to follow the alternative? By weeding out the seeds that have started rooting from the TINA theory's omnipotence, showing how another path was taken in the past. History is essential to an understanding of the modern era. It is indeed amazing if one thinks that in social systems that regarded the majority of people as beings without human substance, where excessive political powers came to dominate, and where the whole of the population suffered very low living standards and a lack of education, a radical train of thought was born and continued to live.

Modern radical criminology would benefit from following the journey we have taken here. Braudel (1993) wrote that there is no civilization nowadays that can be truly understood if the paths it took, the old values it believed in, and the experiences it lived are not known. Every civilization is a past that is still alive. Consequently, the history of a civilization is the search among the old coordinates of all those elements that are still effective today, all those elements thanks to which the past comes and intersects with the present. If we are to understand the discipline's relation to institutional practices and concerns, if we are to understand some of the key terms and concepts that structure the discourse, then we will have to ask genealogical questions about the constitution of the science and examine the historical processes that led to the emergence of this disciplinary specialism (Garland, 2002).

Michel Foucault (2002) proposed a specific way of looking at the areas and ways of producing knowledge as well as of the produced truth and scientific objectivity as the results of the fundamental interdependent practices of knowledge-power and their historical transformation. Every interpretative endeavor is mediated by power relations, whereas each theory does not constitute clear knowledge, but a practice of discourse. Historical practice is replaced with the archaeology of knowledge. More specifically, Foucault studied the processes and rules out of and by which the "discourses" or "discursive formations" historically emerged and formed, especially in the human sciences. "Exclusion procedures," principles of prohibition, division, and rejection, define what the legitimate object of thinking is and what it is not, and thus participate in delineating and constructing objects of thought themselves, determining when, where, how, and why it is permissible (or not) to speak, and delimiting areas of discourse beyond the limits of legitimacy. Relationships that are developed, both inside and outside of "discursive formations," are relations of power. Knowledge production practices themselves are most of the time carried out within a defined framework of discourse formations and within specific political, economic, and institutional truth production regimes. Therefore, from the outset, they constitute controlled and "disciplined" practices. The very world of the production of scientific knowledge is a world of power governed by historically shaped boundaries, divisions, rules, bans, hierarchies, and controls. Knowledge can never be returned to a subject that is free in relation to power, as power can never be separated from the forces of knowledge that activate it.

All three volumes are entitled *The Origins of Radical Criminology*. With the word "origins," we would denote the "principle" which precedes the process of creating the object of radical criminology, but at the same time is part of it, as it constitutes all the necessary and capable historical conditions for the appearance of this discipline. And this implies that through the radical criminological analysis of the written evidence of slave-owning society and feudalism, we can reveal an internal systematic interrelationship between laws and categories of this form of social theory. This (pre)history of radical criminology is not a revealing field of action of chance and voluntary arbitrariness, but is rather the past, the present, and the prospects of development that constitute a single process of causality. When modern scientists of the criminal phenomenon give up the investigation of these social causalities and reject the historical causality, they are organically connected to the social attitude of those who consider the current socio-economic status as insurmountable. On the contrary, the scientific diagnosis of social causality must be linked to the critical attitude toward the existing status quo and its forms of awareness. So, the "principle" itself ought to be—and is under certain conditions—part of the process of radical criminology.

We have to bear in mind that radical criminology does not please the political and administrative elite, and for that there is a cost. It does not reproduce the established knowledge—the hegemonic, the ephemeral, the present. Radical criminology is scientifically consistent and honest when it challenges the dominant scientific examples, conceptual categories, and methods of research, and does not follow that what is "fashionable." When it recognizes the great "enemies" attacks and deconstructs them: such is the extreme positivism, the determinism, the reification, the supposed "neutrality" of science, and the refusal of politics in science. It claims a new social structure that can be characterized by opponents as romantic, utopian, and politically irresponsible, but history has shown that it is not only desirable but also a conclusive necessity. It is a science with theory and research that ought to become the driving force of history, to be clear to redraft the scientific and political agenda for the benefit of the popular needs, to be a guide for the revolutionary act.

It is this admittedly not-easy-to-digest radical criminological analysis in the Marxist oeuvre. It is the moral degradation of the lumpen proletariat, but it is also a primitive rebellion; it is the main mechanism to criminalize, as described in the article on the wood of the Rhine; it is its utility for the capitalist production, and all this together in the light of the fact that the capitalist system itself is both criminogenic and criminal. Such a multi-layered analysis cannot be understood by the consciousness of two-dimensional—that is, flat—scholars who can only think in terms of cause and effect. The above perspectives have been recorded in different scientific "discourses" of the same author. They are part of a whole and are not just pieces that can independently guide current and future studies. And this is the key to an additional dimension of the scientific work that follows this "anti-positivistic" perspective: the complementarity and dialectical co-formation of the whole, as part of a dynamic process. In this dialectical part of the whole, the interpretive is included.

The phenomenon brings meaning that frames it—meaning for the subject itself, but also meaning that converses with the meaning of the whole, when this whole is determined by corresponding images for the past, the present, and the future. Ideas and prejudices are closely linked to its perception and interpretation, and are its requirements. Thus, more broadly, the representations of the phenomenon, the abstract extension of the existing situation, as Marx had said in the Introduction to the Philosophy of Law, should be recorded and subjected to the rigors of scientific criticism. But scientific criticism itself exercised by the scientist of the criminal phenomenon does not take place on a *tabula rasa*, but within the context of an already semantically formed (and/or under construction) social reality. So, criticism must be, in another dimension, self-criticism, a critique of criticism, a scientific reflection. And, at the same time, the process through which a dialogue process must take place – it is the dialectical relationship - with the main feature of dynamic evolution and, therefore, the opposition to the static, the finite, the ephemeral. A precondition for this is the exercise of infinite suspicion as an integral part of researchers' work in relation to the criminal phenomenon. Consequently, when some people exercise control to the point of scientific skepticism that a scholar must exercise, it is because they either consciously perform a function of conservatism and reproduce the status quo, or unconsciously because at their mental level the scholar is not "visible"—he or she "does not exist," just as the three-dimensional being is not visible for a two-dimensional one.

At the same time, understandings of meanings in all the aforementioned dimensions should have a dialectical discussion with institutions, structures and social forces that seemingly have exceeded the framework of meaning and have acquired an entity character with specific material consequences, effects, limitations, exclusions and all this with emphasis on their dynamic dimension. In this case, we must include "discourses" that have become "contracts," which are considered prerequisites for us to be able to exist and operate in the present. For example, criminology (as well as politics) tends to turn into a discussion of a "technical character," and this has direct material consequences for "anti-positivistic" scholars of the criminal phenomenon, from their inability to make publications (reproduction of their work) to their inability to do primary studies from the beginning due to the fact that there are no resources, until their losing their job due to controls and established procedures (e.g. flexible and precarious work) in the specific labor market. Classes continue to exist in relation to the means of production, different material interests continue to exist, conflict continues to exist between them, and "consensus" is produced only as an ideological mechanism and as an attempt to deceive, and seeks to lead to a constructed meaning that is in contrast to the existing materially experienced reality so that the former prevails over the latter. This "lie" must be deconstructed, and this is a very important part of the work of an anti-positivist criminologists. This is exactly where our "real" and "final" work is included. If people really understood the system in which we live, if they became aware of who they really are and not who they think (either by coercion or by "consent") they are, then they would not accept the system and would demand radical social change.

Within this context, the covert and overt procedures of criminalization and decriminalization, penalization and depenalization, problematization and deproblematization, etc. by official and unofficial bodies/agencies, should be highlighted, imprinted, and critically deconstructed; they should be linked to material dimensions and corresponding interests, and this whole process should be communicated to wider populations. At the same time, this whole dimension must be "seen" through its dynamic rather than its static perspective. An evolving society has within it the seeds of its own destruction and therefore it must be thoroughly ascertained that the above processes are produced as an imposition not only from the top down but dialectically. Then, there is room for an "applied" "anti-positivist" the criminological act as a step toward social change, which should reach the root of the issue and will not remain meteoric.

The social act aiming at radical change is a multifaceted and multidimensional struggle. It is a struggle through and against material conditions of existence and structured and meaningful frameworks of domination, power, hegemony. It is a struggle within and against the systems of creating and reproducing knowledge and specialized knowledge of the same "scientific space," the process of producing "our truth," which must be deconstructed and highlighted exactly what it is: playful production systems of "discourses" that satisfy specific material interests falsely meaningful as such. Let us understand that knowledge is not anindependent means of production, and nor it is entirely deterministically determined. Our own very "Logos"[1] is discipline and control,

---

[1] *Logos* is a polysemous ancient Greek word denoting "word," "speech," "discourse" "account," "reason," and "proportion," depending on the context. Ancient Greek philosophers, such as Heraclitus, the sophists, and Aristotle, used the term in different ways. On the one hand, Heraclitus used *logos* to denote "a principle of order and knowledge" (whose "reasoning" is the thread knitting order and knowledge); on the other hand, the sophists used *logos* to mean "discourse". Finally, Aristotle referred to *logos* primarily in two different ways: (1) as "reasoned discourse"; and (2) as "the argument," a term that is used primarily in rhetoric and claims that *logos* is one of the three modes of persuasion, together with *ethos* and *pathos*.

and, at the same time, there are undisciplined producers who are threatened, restricted, and excluded, but who have the opportunity to produce against the dominant scientific "habitus," when they dare to take a stand. And this very possibility is the hope, it is a heart that continues to beat, it is an unfinished process that should not be limited even by ourselves, so it should go hand in hand with self-criticism, reflection, and deconstruction of any authority, even if it is our own image in the mirror.

Apart from the above, all three volumes attempt to present a logic of history for criminological thinking and to open up a dialogue. It is unfortunately understandable that the objective appearance of modern production relations has led many modern criminologists to think that they are captive to managerial criminology as an eternal and unchanging scientific truth—and the only possible one. Consequently, the scientists of the criminal phenomenon operate almost exclusively only as interpreters and apologists of the status quo of things. This market scientific consciousness leads them to present the interpretations of the criminal phenomenon using tools such as the incoherence, fragmentation, and disintegration of a system. But the written evidence presented in all three volumes shows another way of analysis: Even in a socio-economic system seemingly as absolute and strict, material conditions have been created for the society's transition to another way of production and another form of social consciousness. Our history has shown that no empire has survived forever. Perspective is change and critical thinking about the criminal phenomenon is one of the "apostles" of this change. If we truly want to discuss (modern and future) radical criminological thinking, we could gain much from taking a journey to the genealogy of it, to discuss unity within difference, unity through multiplicity, and internal interconnectedness of contradictory processes by using sources such as: the works attributed to Homer, Hesiod's works, militant lyric poetry and rhetoric, ancient Greek theater, ancient philosophy, the principles of utopias, literature, the New Testament, medieval and Byzantine philosophy, myths and fairytales, Thomas More, Shakespeare, and Cervantes in relation to modern radical criminological thought—and all this in a functional unity with the present that is related to the awe-inspiring rival of modern managerial criminology and the future.

In the first volume we discovered that in the Homeric epics, conflict is something given in the relationships of people and gods, and the final dominant power decides on the rules. Not everyone has the same price and value. However, retaliation as a judicial mechanism is already a characteristic of that era. There is a process of justice that involves the participation of a wider public. Hesiod presents king-judges as hawks who have no respect for the law and who are paid to make judgments in the buyer's best interest. Lyric poetry has an immediate political goal. In the conflict between the rising city (demos) and the lost aristocracy, it takes a position (whether on one side or the other, depending on the poet). At the same time, some of the lyric poetry highlights the instability and variability of human things, the vulnerability of the individual's existence, and calls him to resist and fight, to stand upright and defend himself. With the dramatic plays written by Aeschylus, the ideals of the new radical democracy are brought to the forefront, and with them the roots of a radical concept of evil and good, crime and justice are clearly depicted. Aeschylus focuses on personal conflicts, on issues of power and its abuse, and commends political news. According to Marx, Aeschylus is the finest saint and witness of philosophical chronology. Pre-Socratic philosophy is a weapon of struggle within the tradition of materialism and dialectics, as a revolutionary discourse that cannot be included in postmodern and metaphysical worldviews, precisely because it was born in a particular historical period. The world is composed by the opposite, is worn out and reborn through constant war, according to Anaximander. Heraclitus stresses that the change of the world is the only constant and a constant feature of its course, as it occurs due to ongoing conflict. War is common and justice is dispute, and everything happens through dispute and necessity. Whatever is good for one can be bad for another; objective reality is governed by laws that have no morality an absolute notion of justice does not exist. Archelaus explains that law is not "in nature," but is only the dominant view, while Democritus makes a real radical rupture in philosophy: humans have the ability to change good into evil and harm into benefit; this is an active part of social reality, and it can and must change the whole distorted situation described by previous philosophers. The sophists argued for moral and philosophical relativism, and at the same time proclaimed citizens' equality and freedom; they also claimed that law should respect human dignity, something was in direct opposition to the aristocratic status quo. We ought to challenge those in power, as well as morality and religion; we should respect democratic principles, the opinions of others, and peace. We should be against the technocratic perception of politics and should highlight the importance of people, the poor, direct democracy, and those institutions that support it. Power and authority have no right to monopolize truth, and we have a duty to resist social discrimination based on people's wealth and origins.

The second volume (Georgoulas, 2021) covered eight centuries that followed the archaic period in ancient Greece (Classical period, Hellenistic period and Greco-Roman period), with concepts such as "citizen," "equality of political rights" (*isonomia*), "equal right of speech" (*isigoria*), "equality of power" (*isokratia*). Sophocles' heroine Antigone fought against despotic power as expressed by Creon and preached that there is an unwritten law that allows us to violate authoritarian laws. Hellenistic philosophy attempted to respond to people's agonizing questions, such as the precariousness of their existence, and the Cynics broke totally with the world of social conventions by rejecting it as being in opposition to human nature. The Stoics began as a radical philosophical movement established by Zeno, who claimed that philosophy should serve practical purposes—that is, to seek to moralize society. Zeno and Chrysippus preached that all people should live under the same laws as siblings, emphasizing that natural law is greater than statute law. Epicurus stated that "senses" are the only criteria of truth by fighting not only against subjective sensationalism but also against any one-sided explanation. The liberating power of the Epicurean philosophy is conspicuous not only in the battle against necessity but also against chance. According to Epicurus, within nature, whatever is done is a result of natural causes and everything is done following the sequence of cause and effect. Hence, there is no fate or word or providence and no purposeful destination. Skepticism had the main purpose of preserving freedom against any kind of doctrine. To this end

Skeptics stated that juxtaposed arguments or different views on a matter are equivalent (*isostheneis*). There is neither good nor shameful, just nor unjust, said Pyrrho, the founder of this philosophical movement, while Arcesilaus, another important proponent of the Sceptics, claimed that one has to put everything in question so to free oneself from prejudices, develop critical thinking, and even challenge oneself. He put this into practice in Rome in 155 BC when he delivered a long speech on justice, and the following day he attacked his own speech with another speech that took the opposite view, and he criticized the justice he had previously exalted. A utopian novel *Islands of the Sun* written by Iambulus, which who was very widespread in the East, inspired a revolution, the Pergamon Revolt, since it managed to combine the most essential elements of all utopias into a profoundly revolutionary synthesis: the rule of statute law, the law that goes against physical order and enshrines social inequality and mischief. Conversely, there can be a society without crime, a society of equality, purity, and bliss simply because there is no individual property. In the Greco-Roman period, there were still voices of resistance, voices that continued to strive to build an "anti-hegemonic" paradigm on law and crime. Aesop's fables, a folk reading and educational material for children of the time, with speaking animals as protagonists, criticize the powerful, the gods, the rich, and the wealthy who associate with the wicked, the King who – when he intervenes he does it for his own of interest. Lucian (of Samosata), in a tongue-in-cheek style, scorned the gods and referred to judges (who received money in order to prosecute in favor or against) as tyrants who attached importance to penalties because they could rule only by coercion. Lucian calls for equality for all slaves, free, poor, and rich. The neo-skeptic philosophers Aenesidimus and Sextus Empiricus oppose causality and absoluteness of the terms good and evil, just and unjust. Above all, Lucretius (Titus Lucretius Carus) in his work *De rerum natura* opposed all forms of idealism by using atheism and Epicurus' materialistic philosophy as his weapons. This ancient Roman materialist sought to link philosophy with the vital problems in contemporary Roman society. He wanted to rid his contemporaries of reactionary traditions that were obscuring their consciences and, more particularly, of religious conservatism that was distinguished by its strict dogmatism, its crude prejudices, and its deep hostility to scientific knowledge. Last but not least, there were the early Christian movement, a social movement that had a specific moral policy, which was not a closed or homogeneous system initially but in constant dialogue with corresponding philosophical movements of the time. The early Christians neglected their political duty by refusing to serve in the military or even in the civil service, while at the same time developing a community of alternative solidarity and offers to outcasts, and proletarian middle classes at a time when earthly life was increasingly losing its value and there was no welfare state. At the same time, in the early texts of the new religion, it was easy to find elements of subversive political and social philosophy such as: "it is easier for a camel to go through the eye of a needle than for a rich man to enter the kingdom of God," the persecution of the merchants from the Temple, who were called "robbers," rules such as communion of goods and severe punishments for those who disobeyed to it, "the great evil" that is the accumulation of wealth and the question of law and functioning of the courts of the time. The new religion's radicalism is epitomised in a passage from the Letter to the Romans, where it is written: "where there is no law, there is no violation." The present volume continues this journey and uncovers and discusses aspects of medieval philosophy, Byzantine thought, medieval utopias, myths and tales, the humanist movement, and the great works of literature of the Middle Ages.

How can the above specific logic of history communicate with the logic of similar published papers and books in the field of historical criminology? Thompson (1978) has argued that the historical logic is a distinct logic that is appropriate to the historian's materials. It cannot usefully be brought within the same criteria as those of physics. The immediate object of historical knowledge is composed of facts or evidence which are certainly real. Historical knowledge is by its nature provisional and incomplete, selective and limited, but not therefore untrue. Historical evidence has the necessary properties. Concepts can only acquire a meaning from a particular position in the present, a position of value in search of its own genealogy. Such genealogies exist within the evidence. Within this framework, Bosworth (2001) demonstrates that the ways in which a criminologist interprets his or her data reveal the researcher's ethical stance toward his or her subject and the allegiances he or she creates with them. These problems of interpretation, evidence, and emotion transcend time in culture and are built into the research goals of the discipline of criminology itself; Lawrence (2012) adds that historical criminology is (or should be) an area of collaboration.

However, most of the work published is this field is by historians and not criminologists bringing their own interpretations to the discussion. According to Xavier Rousseaux (1997), even though many specialists in the social sciences still consider crime to be a marginal or temporary subject of research, there is published work credited to a number of different "fathers": institutional and legal history, economic and social history, anthropological and cultural history, and political history. All this work has different sources and methods (judicial archives, quantitative, and qualitative) and different focuses. Others are focusing on patterns of crime (violence, theft, political and religious), while others are focusing on criminals or patterns of repression. There are also histories of the cultural representations of crime, representations of repression, representations of procedure, and representations of law, justice, and regulation. All of the above follow a criminal (but not criminological) reading of social history according to the civilizing of social relations (influenced by the work of Norbert Elias), the modernization of administration, the formation of the state, or finally the constitution of social identities.

According to Spierenburg (2017), writing the global history of all crime and punishment surely has to be a collective enterprise that stretches over more than one generation of scholars. Such collective enterprises have made significant contributions to the field, such as the German Workshop "Historische Kriminalitätsforschung in der Vormoderne" (Blauert & Schwerhoff, 1998), influenced by the methodological and theoretical discussions of historical anthropology and micro-history (but not criminology), and the journal *Crime, History & Societies*. According to the editorial committee of the journal (Editorial Committee, 1997), behind the question of crime lies a set of problems shared by today's societies: the socially accepted definition of order and disorder, the legitimacy of the structures and the means employed to maintain order, the capacity of society to take in new groups, and what precisely people expect of the justice system. From this perspective, the study of societies whose relation to crime is very different from that of our own contemporary Western societies, such as ancient, medieval and early modern or non-European societies, fosters a reassessment of present-day relationships between crime, regulation, and society. In the 1960s, social historians "chanced upon" judicial and police archives and found in them a means of accessing voices not heard in history. They privileged the study of constants and variants in criminal behaviors. However, researchers rapidly came to see the very notion of "crime" as anachronistic and fuzzy, and "criminological" positivism as too narrow. Inspired by the more critical approach of sociologists specializing in deviance, other researchers shifted their attention to the agencies responsible for controlling crime and focused on the complex functions of the legal institutions and their place in societies struggling with the problem of violence. Even more recently, historians have included crime in the social history of legal developments and the processes of political domination. As a result, tracing the history of crime has become tracing the history of disorders and order, one of the essential sites in which, as far as the monopolistic control of violence is concerned, the evolution of modern society is played out. The growing number of works on penal institutions, the justice system, penalties, policing, and crime is thus bound up with the conjoined interest on the part of historians and legal historians in the methods of the social sciences and of sociologists, anthropologists, political scientists, and jurists in a diachronic approach. These reciprocal interests testify to the importance of exchange between disciplines in terms of advancing knowledge.

Relevant collective enterprises are rare within the criminological spectrum. Becker and Wetzell edited a collected volume of essays in 2006, which grew out of a conference on criminology that took place in 1998. This volume consists of a range of themes and approaches related to 19th-century criminological thinking, and the underlying theme was the relationship between criminological thinking of the late 19th and early 20th centuries, and the infamous programs of eugenics undertaken by the Third Reich; it was stated that during that time, criminology was not yet a recognized academic discipline, so theorists and practitioners came from many different backgrounds, having nothing in common other than claims to possessing special insight into and knowledge of the nature of criminals and how best to deal with them. The European Group for the study of deviance and social control has set up a working group on the historical aspects of crime and social control (which I have the honor to coordinate), which has participated in all annual meetings of the Group since 2017.

Concerning the period from the end of Antiquity to the beginning of the modern era (the early 17th century, the timeline covered in the present volume), only historians have published relevant works. Johnson and Monkkonen (1996) published an edited volume on the civilization of crime since the Middle Ages, Emsley (2011) has described the pattern of crime using official figures in 20th-century England, McMahon (2008) has written on crime, law, and popular culture in Europe, and Dunn (2013) has used legal records to excellent effect in terms of shedding light on the sexual and marital mores of medieval England. Bettoni (2008) has tried to better understand the discipline of miscarriages of justice in the 16th and 17th centuries, and Griffiths (2008) has extensively analyzed the administrative jurisdiction and processes of London's first house of correction. Vitiello (2016) has focused on an interesting case study: the city and the territories of Reggio Emilia in the Visconti era (the second half of the fourteenth century, following the Black Death). Through an almost complete run of trial records dating from 1373 to 1408, she has focused on the role of "fama," a crucial aspect to our understanding of proofs, the use of judicial torture, and the determination of guilt or innocence, based on differences of status such as class, wealth, gender, and lineage. In a similar vein, Boes (2013) has brought together new and existing research she has conducted into criminal justice in the late 16th and 17th centuries in the Frankfurt am Main archival sources, concluding that wealth and social status had selective influence on the penal structure, Jews were systematically treated more harshly than non-Jewish citizens, and women were subjected to partiality as they were more readily subjected to torture than men, their testimonies were more easily ignored, and they were generally treated with less leniency when punished. Spierenburg (2006) has examined the attitudes of Protestant moralists and Reformed synods toward interpersonal violence in the Dutch Republic from the 1580s to the early 18th century, concluding that Protestants saw violence as an integral part of a sinful lifestyle. The Reformed Church condemned the traditional procedure of reconciliation after a homicide and the Church contributed to the full criminalization of homicide. Lavarda (2007) has examined the case of the bandit and hero Count Ludovico da Porto, who symbolizes the power struggle among Vicenza's main noble families; his experience and the confiscation of his property exemplify Venetian action to control the turbulent mainland state, proving the long-term efficacy of the exceptional measures taken by the authorities. Gaskill (2000) has used an interesting methodological agenda in his work on three aspects of serious crime: witchcraft, counterfeiting coinage, and homicide. In all three areas, he has been anxious to distance himself from studies of early modern crime based on statistical analyses, instead being concerned with mentalities, seeing how crime provides insights into mentalities, how people of all social ranks perceived themselves, their social environment, and their universe, and how those perceptions in turn helped to shape popular beliefs and practices. He has combined evidence from court archives with that provided by literary sources, broadsides, ballads, newssheets, diaries and letters, and such normative sources as statutes, proclamations, and sermons.

However, and despite all the above, the main issue, as Churchill (2017) put it in his definition of "historical criminology," remains. We need a clearer recognition of historical criminology as a discrete intellectual enterprise. "Historical criminology" immediately speaks to engagement between two established disciplines or fields—history and criminology—which may range from cross-disciplinary dialogue to interdisciplinary fusion. However, its primary scholarly domain would appear to be criminology: this suggests historical works of criminology rather than a work of history as such—the work of criminology done in an historical mode. Churchill states that "historical criminology" seems to demand accompanying quotation marks, as if to hold it together; the phrase is not an uncontentious reference to an existing endeavor, but rather an assertion, in spite of appearances, that there is such a thing at all. His definition makes it possible to draw contrasts with "criminal justice history" and "criminological history." In the first case, criminal justice history is the work of history concerned with crime and criminal justice as topics; in the second, one might define criminological history as the work of history informed by criminological concepts, theories, or methods. By contrast, historical criminology is not the work of history as such, but an historical work of criminology. The most urgent question, then, is what it means to study criminology "in an historical mode." Historical criminology should exhibit how "the historical" is central to the core categories, concepts, and theories of criminology in general. He adds that we need to elaborate upon ways in which scholars might engage further with concepts of historical time, and thus exhibit the historical character of matters of criminological concern. Historical criminology might be advanced through more sustained attention to how traces of the past—in material and memorial forms, both within particular institutions and amongst the population at large—persist in the present, and the role these traces play in contemporary crime and justice. We need to explore the role of popular memory in shaping public attitudes toward crime and justice, and especially how diverse pasts are mobilized by different social groups.

I truly hope that the present volume and the two preceding volumes will be useful in terms of opening up this necessary dialogue.

References

Becker, P., & Wetzell, R. F. (2006). *Criminals and their scientists: The history of criminology in international perspective.* Cambridge University Press.

Bettoni, A. (2008). Res judicata and null and void judgment in the Italian and German doctrine of sixteenth- and seventeenth-century criminal law: Certain interpretative profiles. *Crime, History & Societies, 12*(1), 1–34.

Blauert, A., & Schwerhoff, G. (1998). Crime and history: The German workshop 'Historische Kriminalitätsforschung in der Vormoderne'/'Early modern crime and criminal justice history.' *Crime, History & Societies, 2*(1), 137–140.

Boes, M. R. (2013). *Crime and punishment in early modern Germany: Courts and adjudicatory practices in Frankfurt am Main, 1562–1696.* Ashgate.

Bosworth, M. (2001). The past as a foreign country? Some methodological implications of doing historical criminology. *British Journal of Criminology, 41*(3), 431–442.

Braudel, F. (1993). *Grammaire des civilisations.* Flammarion.

Churchill, D. (2017). Towards historical criminology. *Crime, History & Societies, 21*(2), 379–386.

Dunn, C. (2013). *Stolen women in medieval England: Rape, abduction and adultery, 1100–1500.* Cambridge University Press.

Editorial Committee. (1997). Editorial English version. *Crime, History & Societies, 1*(1), 7–8.

Emsley, C. (2011). *Crime and society in twentieth century England.* Longman.

Foucault, M. (2002). *The archaeology of knowledge* (A. M. Sheridan Smith, Trans.). Routledge.

Garland, D. (2002). Of crimes and criminals: The development of criminology in Britain. In M. Maguire, R. Morgan, & R. Reiner (Eds.), *The Oxford handbook of criminology* (pp. 7–50). Oxford University Press.

Gaskill, M. (2000). *Crime and mentalities in early modern England.* Cambridge University Press.

Georgoulas, S. (2018). *The origins of radical criminology: From Homer to Pre-Socratic philosophy.* Palgrave Macmillan.

Georgoulas, S. (2021). *The origins of radical criminology, vol II: From classical Greece to early Christianity.* Palgrave Macmillan.

Griffiths, P. (2008). *Lost Londons: Change, crime and control in the capital city (1550–1660).* Cambridge University Press.

Johnson, E. A., & Monkkonen, E. H. (Eds.). (1996). *The civilization of crime: Violence in town and country since the Middle Ages.* University of Illinois Press.

Lavarda, S. (2007). Banditry and social identity in the Republic of Venice: Ludovico da Porto, his family and his property (1567–1640). *Crime, History & Societies, 11*(1), 1–29.

Lawrence, P. (2012). History, criminology and the 'use' of the past. *Theoretical Criminology, 16*(3), 313–328.

McMahon, R. (2008). *Crime, law and popular culture in Europe, 1500–1900.* Willan Publishing.

Rousseaux, X. (1997). Crime, justice and society in medieval and early modern times: Thirty years of crime and criminal justice history. A tribute to Herman Diederiks (K. Dwyer, Trans.). *Crime, History & Societies, 1*(1), 87-118.

Spierenburg, P. (2006). Protestant attitudes to violence: The early Dutch Republic. *Crime, History & Societies, 10*(2), 1–27.

Spierenburg, P. (2017). Writing a global history of crime and punishment: The great challenge. *Crime, History & Societies, 21*(2), 31–39.

Thompson, E. P. (1978). *The poverty of theory and other essays*. Merlin Press.

Vitiello, J. C. (2016). *Public justice and the criminal trial in late medieval Italy: Reggio Emilia in the Visconti age*. Brill.

Index